AIRLINE PILOT

AIRLINE PILOT

Future Aviation Professionals of America
with
David Massey

ARCO
New York   London   Toronto   Sydney   Tokyo   Singapore

A R C O

Simon & Schuster, Inc.
15 Columbus Circle
New York, NY 10023

DISTRIBUTED BY PRENTICE HALL TRADE SALES

Designed by Future Aviation Professionals of America
Manufactured in the United States of America

1 2 3 4 5 6 7 8 9 10

Library of Congress Cataloging-in-Publication Data

Airline pilot / Future Aviation Professionals of America with David
  Massey.
        p. cm.
    ISBN 0-13-115015-4
    1. Aeronautics, Commercial—Vocational guidance. 2. Jet
transport—Piloting—Vocational guidance. I. Massey, David.
II. FAPA (Association)
TL561.A39 1990
629. 132'52' 023—dc20   90-31011
                                                        CIP

CONTENTS

Introduction

The primary purpose of this book is to assist you in maximizing your potential for employment in the airline industry and to provide you with a fast and efficient path to your career-goal job. In addition, representative paths to other aviation careers are explored.

We will assume that your career goal is to find employment as a professional pilot with either a major or regional airline, corporate flight department or helicopter operator. The following chapters discuss what determines and affects your competitiveness and how to manage a job search. They deal with the airline, commuter and corporate jobs themselves and answer some frequently asked questions about pursuing an aviation career. Since most of the better jobs are with the airlines, the bulk of discussion deals with the airline industry. The authors believe this information, plus the data on the various charts, will make you more knowledgeable and successful as you pursue your goal.

Chapter 1
THE LANDSCAPE

The rise of civil aviation has not occurred in a vacuum. It has coincided with the development of (among other things):

- Better and faster aircraft.

- More efficient service delivery systems.

- Government regulation and deregulation.

- A consumer-oriented economy and a public to do the air travelling and shipping that keeps the airlines growing.

- The digital revolution.

- And a pilot force to fly the planes.

Modern airliners are inherently faster than competing modes of transportation, and the airlines have been ingenious in finding ways to enhance this natural advantage and make sudden service a reality. Of current long-distance delivery systems, only the telephone, the telegraph, and other electronic media (e.g., radio, TV, facsimile transmission) are faster. And like these other methods of delivery, the airlines keep getting speedier, in part by capitalizing on technological advancements.

The last several years in aviation have witnessed the airlines' pioneering of both computerized real-time transaction processing and the hub-and-spoke system of service delivery; not merely by coincidence, they also have witnessed unprecedented growth of the U.S. airline industry. While other sectors of civil aviation have grown less rapidly than the airlines, the overall result of aviation growth has been an extraordinary market for flying skills and mounting pressure on various strata of aviation either to yield up their quota of pilots for major airline flying or to provide constantly enhanced pay and benefits for their aviators in order to keep them.

Flying is a booming occupation. It also is one of the few occupations, short of professional sports, that can make "a mere employee" rich.

Traditionally, by virtue of the demands of piloting, an accident of history, and the activities of the Air Line Pilots Association (ALPA), the major airline pilot has enjoyed a privileged position among American workers — a "professional" role akin, in public image, to the roles of doctor and lawyer and compensated on a grand scale. For example, in a recent year the average pay for a pilot of a major airline was about $81,500 a year. The average starting pay was around $24,000; the average for flight engineers, $42,000; the copilot average, $65,000; and the average captain's pay, $107,000. At retirement, a captain then typically was earning about $130,000 annually, with the maximum being around $165,000. Annual retirement compensation was about half of the final pay. In addition, retirement could include a lump sum that might go anywhere from $350,000 to $1.1 million.

Not too shabby.

By what route did major airline pilots arrive at so lucrative a rung on the American ladder of success?

The airline industry grew initially from the government-operated air mail service. Flying for the air mail was a glamorized occupation, and pilots were hailed in the press of the day as superior mortals. Airline pilots inherited this early idolization.

Under the grinding pressures of the Great Depression, when cost-cutting "captains of industry" exerted unrelenting pressure on the pilot corps for lower wages, professional airline flying undoubtedly would have lost its lustre if not for the successful efforts of ALPA, under the leadership of its first president, Dave Behncke, to get the pilot's job protected under federal legislation. A second substantial victory for ALPA was the negotiation, in the 1960s, of a revised basis for pay in the new jet aircraft that were becoming the industry standard. Jet pay rules greatly increased pilot pay.

Deregulation of the U.S. airline industry in 1978, expected by many to devalue the pilot's job, proved another boon to pilot pay. After initial attempts by the airlines to lower pilot pay via "B scales," pay rose under the pressure of industry expansion: Growth of the airlines created a demand for competent pilots that threatened to outstrip the supply.

Today, with airline and general aviation growth continuing, the overall picture for well-prepared, experienced pilots is very good, to wit:

- The oil industry, TV news, law enforcement, and agriculture provide fine jobs for helicopter pilots.

- Corporate flying is the job of choice for many airplane pilots (both jet and non-jet).

- Fixed-base operators (FBOs) offer charter flying jobs, as well as (in some cases) first-rate "feeder" operations for major and national air cargo airlines.

- Commuter and regional passenger carriers yield another network of job opportunities in both origin-and-destination (O&D) service and "feeder" flying into the hub airports of major and national airlines.

- And the majors and nationals themselves form the upper echelon of pilot job markets.

Moreover, the major and national airlines draw on the pilot pools of all the other markets. On rare occasions, such major carriers as American, United, Northwest, Eastern and Continental have hired helicopter pilots to fly their jet aircraft; corporate flying has traditionally sent a small percentage of its pilots up to the major and national airlines, as have the FBOs; and the regional/commuter airlines, especially those providing "feed" to large hubs, have become the primary civilian training ground for pilots who are hired by the majors and nationals. In fact, by the late 1980s the regional/commuter airlines had begun to outstrip the military forces as a source of major and national airline pilots.

Basic Industry Structure

A few of the terms in the last several paragraphs bear explaining, not merely for intelligibility, but because the explanations are bound up with the overall picture of a bustling industry offering wonderful job opportunities for those with the inclination and ability to make flying a career.

Fixed-base operators (FBOs) are found at every civilian airport of any size at all, including not only major airports but hundreds of small general aviation airports scattered all over the United States.Their primary function is to serve general aviation with technical services (aircraft maintenance, repairs, flying lessons, etc.); another function, often lucrative, is to serve airlines with such services as fueling and ground technical support; yet another is charter flying; and a recent development for some of them is "feed" flying for large cargo airlines, such as Federal Express, Airborne, Flying Tigers and DLT.

The word "feed" means bringing "traffic" (whether cargo or passengers) to the hub airport of a large airline. One of the biggest changes brought about by deregulation of the airline industry in 1978 was the spectacular growth of the hub-and-spoke system. The large airlines discovered that their most efficient service delivery system was a hub airport at which they could receive passenger and cargo feed from smaller carriers while delivering passengers, baggage and cargo to points all over the United States and to many points in other countries. On the other end of a jet flight, a regional turboprop airline can become the destination carrier, delivering the passenger to a small town from a hub airport. The hub-and-spoke system, once it became aligned with code-sharing and ownership of regionals by majors, extended the profitable reach of major airlines and at the same time increased their per-passenger profit by keeping passengers within their systems from beginning to end of a journey.

Code-sharing is a joint marketing arrangement between a major and a regional airline under which the feed airline shares the major carrier's two-letter designator and is identified in the public eye as part of the major's service delivery system. In the 1980s, several major airline companies, among them USAir, AMR (parent of American) and Texas Air (parent of Continental), acquired a number of regional carriers to provide feed traffic to their major airlines.

For passenger airlines, a "hub" airport originally was an airport at a major city like Atlanta, Chicago or Dallas but, with the spread of the hub system, came to include airports at lesser cities, e.g., Charlotte, N.C.; Dayton, Ohio; Memphis, Tenn. The idea of the hub is that it acts as a clearing point for traffic coming from and going to dozens of smaller towns in the region served by the hub airport. The system of feeding cargo and

WestAir Holding Inc. Hub and Route Systems

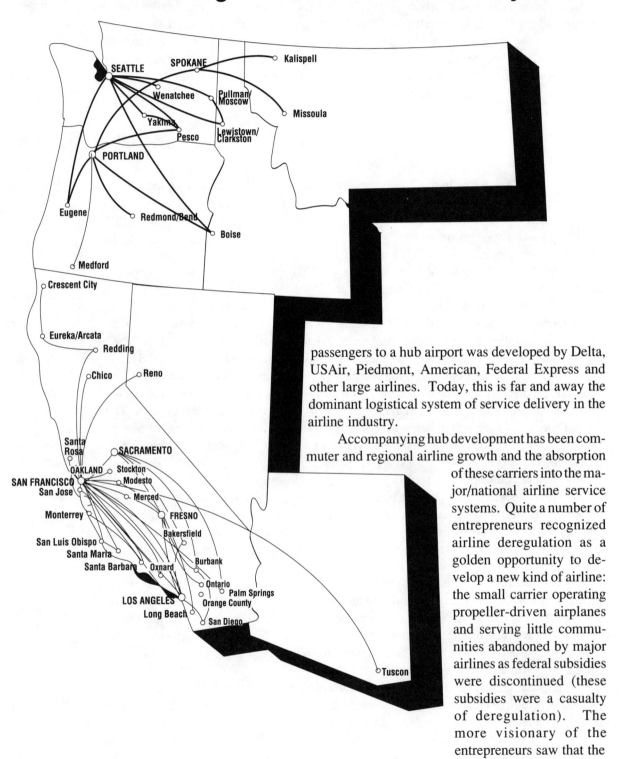

passengers to a hub airport was developed by Delta, USAir, Piedmont, American, Federal Express and other large airlines. Today, this is far and away the dominant logistical system of service delivery in the airline industry.

Accompanying hub development has been commuter and regional airline growth and the absorption of these carriers into the major/national airline service systems. Quite a number of entrepreneurs recognized airline deregulation as a golden opportunity to develop a new kind of airline: the small carrier operating propeller-driven airplanes and serving little communities abandoned by major airlines as federal subsidies were discontinued (these subsidies were a casualty of deregulation). The more visionary of the entrepreneurs saw that the

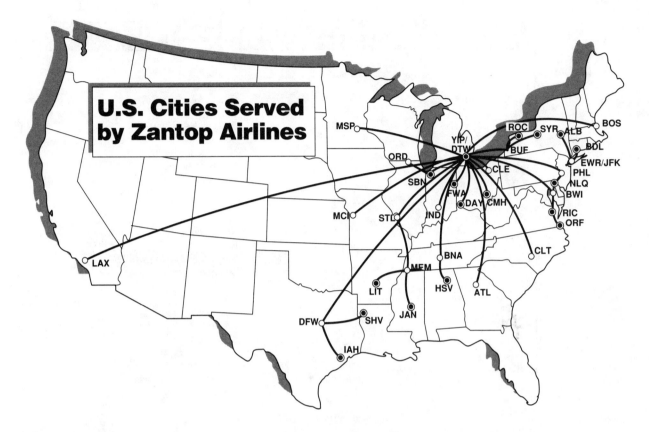

most dynamic area of growth for these small airlines would be the feeder service. Atlantic Southeast Airlines (ASA) in Atlanta, for example, was set up from the start (1979) entirely as a feeder for Delta Air Lines. From the time of its creation from Sunbird, a small commuter, CCAIR in Charlotte was set up entirely as a feeder for Piedmont. And so on. (There were numerous commuter airlines set up for origin-and-destination service, not feed, but ultimately the vast majority of regional/commuter airlines were forced either to adopt the feeder strategy or die.)

The various types of airlines can be confusing without some definitions. According to the U.S. Department of Transportation:

- A major airline is one with more than $1 billion in annual revenue.

- A national airline is one with revenue from $100 million to $1 billion.

- A turbojet airline is a jet carrier with less than $100 million in revenue.

- And a regional airline is one (generally) flying turboprop or other propeller-driven aircraft and having less than $100 million in revenue. Some regionals do fly turbojet aircraft as well as turboprop.

- Special note: Some airline industry people feel a distinction should be made between very small origin-and-destination (O&D) carriers and similar airlines that have grown to substantial size by carrying feed traffic to a major or national airline at a hub airport. According to this distinction, the small O&D

Major/Regional Relationships

Major	Network	Regionals
American	American Eagle	Chaparral Command Executive Air Charter Metroflight Nashville Eagle, Inc. Simmons Airlines Wings West
Braniff	Braniff Express	Air Midwest
Continental	Continental Express	Bar Harbor Britt Rocky Mountain Airways Southern Jersey
Delta	Delta Connection	ASA Business Express Comair Skywest
Eastern	Eastern Express	Bar Harbor Eastern Metro Express Southern Jersey
Midway	Midway Connection	Iowa Airways Midway Commuter
Northwest	Northwest Airlink	Northwest Airlink (formerly Big Sky) Mesaba Express Airlines I/Northwest Airlink Precision
Pan Am		Pan Am Express Resort Commuter
TWA		Air Midwest Metro Airlines Northeast Pocono Airlines Trans World Express
United	United Express	Air Wisconsin Aspen NPA Presidential WestAir Airlines
USAir	USAir Express	Allegheny Commuter Airlines, Inc. Chautauqua Crown Henson/USAir Express Pennsylvania USAir Express/CCAir USAir Express/Jetstream

carrier would be called a "commuter airline"; the feed carrier, which almost invariably is able to outgrow an O&D rival, would be called a "regional airline."

The two types of propeller-driven aircraft in use by regional airlines are turboprop aircraft, i.e., planes with jet-type engines that drive propellers instead of sending a jet of hot air out through an opening; and reciprocal, or piston-engine, propeller planes. In the 1970s, the majority of aircraft in commuter airline fleets were piston-engine planes. By the mid-1980s, the vast majority of aircraft in these fleets were turboprops. The fleet makeup has continued to evolve with the introduction of small jet airliners by aircraft makers Canadair and Embraer. (See Glossary for a full definition of "turboprop" and "turbojet.")

Some industry listings do not exclude the $100 million-plus turboprop carriers from the group of turboprop airlines — or another way to say this is that the annual revenue figure makes no difference in some listings, e.g., those of Future Aviation Professionals of America: to FAPA, a turboprop carrier is a turboprop carrier, period.

Most of the distinctions are rather arbitrary. All of the major airlines began as small propeller-driven carriers. In 1978, the year of deregulation, Piedmont Airlines, a major airline by the time it was acquired in 1987 by USAir, was still functioning as a regional 'puddle-hopper' airline with a lot of propeller-driven aircraft. Some of the national airlines are all-jet carriers, while others fly both turbojet and turboprop airplanes. Some of the carriers characterized as turbojet actually have more turboprop aircraft than jet aircraft. Several of the national airlines have just recently graduated from the ranks of the turboprop carriers, and their function in the national air transportation system remains exactly what it was before they grew to the magical size, in terms of annual revenue, that allowed them to change the way they refer to themselves. On top of all that, the turbo-jet is on the manufacturers' table of offerings to the major airlines in a new form, the pusher-type propeller-driven airplane.

A better way to characterize the airlines might be in terms of their function. Seen in this light, a 'major' airline would be a quite large one that maintains a national and international flying schedule and manages to compete against the double fistful of other big U.S. airlines that likewise fly domestic and international schedules.

By 1989, the remaining major passenger airlines under DOT's definition were American, Continental, Delta, Northwest, Pan Am, TWA, United, and USAir/Piedmont. Closing in on major status was America West. Also having more than $1 billion in annual revenues and thereby classified as major airlines were such cargo carriers as Federal Express and Flying Tigers.

The group of feed-oriented "national" airlines in 1989 included (among others) ASA, Express Airlines I (with corporate headquarters in Atlanta), Air Wisconsin (head-quartered at Appleton, Wis.), Simmons Airlines (Chicago), Bar Harbor Airways (Bar Harbor, Maine), Comair (Cincinnati, Ohio), Metro Airlines (Dallas), and WestAir (Fresno, Calif.). Of these, Air Wisconsin and WestAir were flying the British Aerospace BAe 146 jet airliner as well as smaller, typically short-haul turboprop aircraft. The rest were flying all-turboprop fleets.

Examples of national airlines flying only jet equipment were Alaska, Southwest, Braniff and Midway. Some of these were operating their own hubs (e.g., Midway at Chicago's old Midway Airport); then again, Southwest maintained primarily an O&D, or origin-to-destination, route strategy.

The national airlines are a real hodgepodge of types of carrier, ranging in 1989 from an airline like Braniff that had been around a long time and simply had fallen out of the race for a nationwide market, to a deregulation-era niche carrier like Midway, to a strapping big regional like Air Wisconsin, to express carriers like DHL and Airborne Express. In 1989, there were around 25 of these airlines in the United States, but with the numbers and relationships constantly changing.

The turbojet airlines are another mixed bag. They include a number of airlines (e.g., Presidential Airways) that in function are regional feeder airlines, as well as some that are O&D passenger carriers, and others that carry only cargo.

In terms of function, the best distinction among the various smaller airlines is this: Does the airline act as a feeder for a major or national carrier at one or more hub airports, or does it fly its own system, either of O&D passenger flights or of hub-oriented cargo and/ or small-package flights? A cargo airline like Ypsilanti, Mich.-based Zantop has a nationwide route structure "cleared" through a single hub of its own making. Air Wisconsin flies BAe 146s in support of United Airlines.

The Job Market and the Pilot Pool

Some pilots are content to remain with a corporation, a helicopter operation, or a non-major airline; others are unable to advance; and many use the less competitive jobs as steps to a seat with a major airline.

The late 1980s brought more pilot hiring by the large carriers than ever before in U.S. commercial aviation history. The now-adult "baby boomers" swelled the ranks of Americans who travelled by air while deregulation of the airline industry sparked lower ticket prices and growth of the hub system. The hub-and-spoke system further contributed to the creation of traffic by stimulating economic growth in hub cities and by bringing access to national and international markets to backwater communities.

The growth in trade has added to fleet sizes, destinations, frequencies and, of course, the number of pilots needed to fly the planes. As mentioned, the demand for people capable of flying planes has driven pay up in all kinds of piloting jobs.

There is a good life waiting for anybody with the ability, health, fitness and desire to be a professional pilot. At any given time, however, a large proportion of the total pilot pool simply does not qualify for the better flying jobs, such as a seat with a major airline.

Your task, if you choose a professional flying career or already are embarked on one, is to make sure you qualify for the best job to which you aspire. For many of you, that will be a job flying for a major airline.

In any event, you will find that the jet age has come to participate fully in the digital age as well as in the overall economic life of the nation; the planes you will fly are studded with computer-age avionics and systems devices. Given the complexity of a pilot's job and the heftiness of pilot paychecks at many airlines, the status of the professional aviator is likely to remain a lofty one for many years to come.

Chapter 2
PILOT DEMOGRAPHICS

The pilot is able to live a gratifying life. Buoyed by substantial monetary rewards and a tinge of the glamour of piloting's early years, today's professional pilots project a conservative, family-oriented, prosperous image and lifestyle. The most financially successful, with a few exceptions (e.g., some TV pilot-journalists buck the trend by making huge salaries), are the national and major airline pilots. In their off time, which is extensive, these pilots are able to enjoy a wide range of leisure activities; they also may run their own businesses, manage their investments, or work with others in a sideline vocation.

According to ALPA, the average annual household income of a pilot flying for a major or national airline in 1988 was $92,200, with more than 22 percent of pilots earning between $80,000 and $99,999. Of retired pilots surveyed, the average household income was $64,100. With the average age of professional flight crew members being 35 to 44, airline transport pilots continued to be in the prime age group that buys homes, automobiles, second homes and all the accessories that (from a material standpoint) constitute the good life.

A unique benefit of the airline pilot position is the flexibility offered in the work schedule. Working airline pilots fly an average of 80 hours in 15 days each month, are in uniform at the airport about 160 hours, and are away from home 240-320 hours. This leaves them with a lot of time to pursue other interests. In the ALPA study, about 39 percent of all pilots had second incomes producing an additional $10,000 to $19,999, with the average second income being around $19,000. Among all airline pilots, 28 percent worked for themselves in their second jobs; 12 percent worked for others.

Pilot investments are more extensive than those of most middle-class Americans. The average portfolio value for airline pilots in 1988 was $163,200. Thirty-five percent had portfolios valued at $200,000; investments ranged from stocks and bonds to money market funds.

As might be expected, pilots as a group love to be on the go. They frequently avail themselves of their companies' often liberal travel benefits. Interline agreements are an employee benefit offered by most air carriers. Pilots and other employees can travel on airlines other than their own at a 50 to 90 percent reduced rate and in some cases even free (jump seat). They also can fly free on their own airline. Many pilots take advantage of this privilege and travel frequently using their passes.

Like most Americans, however, they use the automobile as their primary form of transportation: More than 99.9 percent of the pilot households surveyed owned more than one car. Other forms of transportation popular among professional aviators are recreational powerboats/sailboats and private aircraft (28 percent owned one or the other or both in 1988).

Being in good health is important to the airline pilot since health plays such a major role throughout an aviation career. Eighty-six percent of pilots in 1988 were performing some form of exercise daily in order to stay in good physical condition. The most popular form of exercise is jogging; the most popular sport and leisure activity, boating.

How many professional pilots are there? According to a 1986 Aircraft Owners & Pilots Association (AOPA) survey, there were 709,118 rated pilots in the United States. Of that number, 147,798 had commercial licenses (the mark of a professional); 87,186 with commercial licenses also had the airline transport pilot (ATP) license. More than 262,380 pilots were instrument rated (as opposed to type rated; see Chapter 10 for details on ratings).

The survey reported 43,082 rated woman pilots. Of that group, 4,176 had the commercial license, and 1,334 had the ATP. You will find quite a few women flying for the regional airlines; as these pilots advance their careers, the number of women flying for major and national airlines will increase, too.

Numbers in all categories have risen considerably since the AOPA study. The reason is that career opportunities in piloting are beckoning.

In recent years, all financially sound major airlines have been hiring or recalling pilots. When the major airlines are in a hiring mode, a domino effect occurs throughout the industry. Major airline pilots come from the ranks of military, corporate or commuter pilots. As these pilots leave smaller carriers or corporate employers to go fly for the major airlines, vacancies are created; then the smaller operations have to hire pilots to replace the ones who have left.

In December 1987, Embry-Riddle Aeronautical University predicted that "the projected growth of the air transportation industry, coupled with the increased retirement rate of senior airline pilots, will generate a continuing high demand for qualified pilots for the foreseeable future." According to Embry-Riddle, a conservative estimate of demand would be 6,000 pilots per year at least through 1998.

Atlanta-based Future Aviation Professionals of America (FAPA), a career counseling firm for pilots, has issued a slightly more conservative estimate: 52,000 to 62,000 pilots over the next 10 years (through 1998), with 32,000 in large jets and 20,000 to 30,000 at mainly non-jet regional airlines.

Predictions of pilot corps growth are based on both known scheduled retirements and known and likely expansion plans among the airlines. Expansion of airlines will be affected by ups and downs in the national economy as well as by the health of individual carriers. In turn, expanded or contracted pilot need at airlines and other aviation companies will affect piloting career opportunities. As might be expected, aviation company slot qualification requirements vary with pilot supply and demand. In times of oversupply, companies can demand a much higher qualification level than during pilot shortages, when requirements are not as stringent. Not all types of companies may experience pilot shortages at the same time. The airline industry is dynamic and cyclical, expanding or receding with great sensitivity to the economy and to the profits of each company. Airlines often go for years without hiring any new pilots, then suddenly need thousands of pilots in a matter of months. In the other direction, a pilot may be furloughed (laid off temporarily) if business and economic conditions require. While not the most stable of industries for newcomers, the airline industry is somewhat predictable. Anticipated hiring cycles, which often vary among airlines, may be followed by maintaining a membership with FAPA (the career counseling firm for pilots), reading aviation trade journals, and talking with airline crews.

The trick is to be aware of and utilize these forecast hiring cycles. You will want to concentrate on long-term preparations during a no-hiring period, then pursue job openings relentlessly before and during a hiring surge.

As noted, the "baby boom," with its ensuing concentration of young adults, underlay rapid airline expansion in the 1980s. That boom was followed by the "baby bust," a period of low birth rate. Actual airline expansion plans may be tempered by the knowledge that at some point in time, the air travel market will be weakened as the baby boom population is replaced in the overall economy by the much smaller baby bust group. Airline managements could factor demographic predictions into their plans to keep from overexpanding. This can be accomplished (in part) through lease rather than purchase of aircraft and through hiring practices; the recent trend, at some large airlines, of hiring many older pilots could prove to be a felicitous way of reducing the pilot force through retirements instead of furloughs when leaner times come.

The world community also has to be factored into any demographic predictions that might affect U.S. air travel in the future. It is not hard to foresee relaxed immigration should the United States face serious labor shortages growing out of the baby bust period. The overall impact on transportation industries when the effects of the baby boom wane may wind up being less than could be predicted from studies of current U.S. population trends in isolation.

In any event, predictions of a steady, strong market for airline pilots through the year 2010 are based on sound demographic and retirement projections and on a prognosis for an essentially healthy, expanding economy over most of that time span.

In a nutshell: If you want to be a pilot, you have your sights set on a field that should continue to expand for the foreseeable future.

Chapter 3
QUALIFYING FOR THE JOB

You've decided you want to go ahead and pursue an airline or other aviation career. How do you proceed? What qualifications do you need to meet? How should you go about meeting qualifications and acquiring the necessary experience for the kind of job you are seeking?

FAPA has done qualifications studies of FAPA-member pilots who are hired by major airlines. Since about 50 percent of pilots hired by the major airlines are FAPA members, the results of these studies will withstand scrutiny.

In one study, FAPA sought to determine the actual qualifications of pilots being hired by the major, national, turbojet and regional air carriers. The categories surveyed ranged from flight ratings and certificates, flight experience, and aviation background to education and physical data. The comprehensive chart on page 14 of this book shows details of that survey.

Generally, most airlines look for qualified applicants between the ages of 21 and 50 (this varies among companies) in top physical condition and good health, with a college education and flying background. A person must be an experienced licensed pilot before he or she can be considered for an airline pilot's position. Most people who become major or national airline pilots will first do either military, corporate or regional airline flying. Once hired, the pilot is trained by the airline to fly its aircraft, as either a co-pilot or a flight engineer. Specific qualifications vary among airlines and are heavily influenced by the supply of pilots as measured against the number of jobs available. When the airlines were rapidly expanding in the mid-1960s, new-pilot needs were overwhelming, and some people were hired as soon as they met the bare minimum requirements: a commercial pilot's license and about 200 hours of flying time. In recent years, requirements have been much higher since there has been a supply of experienced pilots in the right age range. Current hiring trends reveal an emphasis on a well-rounded education, suitable temperament for the job, and specific personality traits, as well as the ability to fly.

The average qualifications of major/national airline new-hires:

- Height in proportion to weight.

- Vision correctable to 20/20, but not worse than 20/200. Eighty percent of pilots in 1988 had 20/20 uncorrected. Depending on the airline, from 10 to 30 percent of pilots had less than 20/20 uncorrected vision.

1989 Jan. - Jun. New-Hire Pilot Qualifications

	Major	National	Jet	Regional
Survey criteria:				
Total pilots hired	3171	916	608	2233
% pilots surveyed	29.2	19.1	16.4	19.9
# pilots surveyed	927	175	100	445
% FAPA member	52.1	N/A	53.0	38.9
Flight ratings and certificates (%):				
Total with ATP	80.8	88.0	81.0	51.7
Total with FE or FEw	88.7	59.4	46.0	42.9
ATP and FE	17.6	18.9	17.0	3.1
ATP and FEw	53.7	33.7	19.0	24.2
ATPw and FE	0.4	0	0	0.4
ATP only	9.5	35.4	45.0	24.5
FE only	2.8	4.6	5.0	2.2
ATPw and FEw	7.7	1.1	1.0	6.5
ATPw only	0	0.6	2.0	8.1
FEw only	6.5	1.1	4.0	6.5
Comm. and Inst. only	1.8	4.6	7.0	24.5
Multi	84.9	83.4	93.0	92.8
CFI/CFII	33.9	53.1	58.0	74.4
Type rating	29.7	43.4	17.0	10.6
A & P	5.4	12.0	11.0	6.3
Flight experience:				
Flight time range	650-17500	1300-16400	650-23000	400-11000
Total hours (avg.)	3910.9	6657.8	4165.2	2644
Jet hours (avg.)	2003.1	1908.7	1212.5	169.4
Turboprop hours (avg.)	1068.2	2077.2	1036.0	474.2
Rotor hours (avg.)	140.7	167.7	177.8	201.5
% jet time	77.4	67.9	55.9	26.5
% turboprop time	68.2	82.9	80.0	70.9
% neither jet nor turboprop	1.7	0.6	7.5	25.1
% rotor	10.6	12.4	9.2	13.8
% pilots with less than 2000 hours	14.5	1.7	21.0	36.2
Aviation background (%):				
General aviation	45.3	59.4	75.0	80.9
Corporate	17.8	37.1	40.0	32.6
Regional/commuter	28.8	48.0	54.0	32.8
Flight instructor	59.5	49.1	60.0	70.6
Previous civilian	35.5	58.3	63.0	82.4
Previous military	39.9	15.4	15.0	4.3
Military and Civilian	24.6	26.3	22.0	13.3
Branch of military (%):				
Air Force	67.3	74.0	62.2	39.8
Navy	21.2	8.2	24.3	20.5
Army	3.3	15.1	8.1	26.9
Marines	6.4	0	5.4	9.0
Coast Guard	1.8	2.7	0	3.8
Education (%):				
Master's degree	20.7	9.1	9.0	3.8
Four years college	71.7	45.1	63.0	61.1
Two/three years college	5.7	34.9	17.0	18.2
Less than two years of college	1.9	10.9	11.0	16.9
Physical data:				
Age range	22:2-53:2	23:6-56:3	21:7-56:2	20:7-57:1
Age (avg.)	34:2	36:9	34:4	30:3
% over 40 years of age	22.0	42.3	28.0	9.0
Height range	62"-78"	62"-78"	64"-76"	61"-80"
Weight range	105-230	108-265	115-220	100-247
% female	6.8	2.9	3.0	4.0
% less than 20/20 vision	21.9	30.9	29.0	24.3
Lowest visual acuity	20/100	20/200	20/200	20/400

- Minimum height, 5'2" for men and women at most airlines.
- High school graduate or better. Eighty percent had a four-year degree in 1988; 98 percent had two years or more of college.
- Twenty-one years or older; average 32.9 years old.   Airlines are hiring older pilots than formerly. Fifteen percent of those hired in 1988 were over age 40.
- ATP rating (84 percent of pilots had it) and FE written (91 percent).
- Flight time in proportion to age:
  - 21 years — 1,200 hours
  - 31 years — 3,000 hours
  - 41 years — 5,000 hours
  - 51 years — 8,000 hours
- Less than 64 percent with military background.

There are three main areas of qualifications to be met if an applicant wishes to be competitive today.

1. *Flying experience.* The airlines like to hire people who have as much flying experience as possible, especially pilot-in-command, multi-engine, turboprop and jet. Since it is quite expensive to rent or buy an airplane just to build up flying hours, most people look for work as a pilot, starting out in small airplanes. A commercial flying background is more impressive than recreational when you are trying to convince an airline to hire you. Depending on the preparatory job or jobs you get, in a full-time civilian flying occupation you may accumulate up to 800 or 1,000 flight hours per year (average 300 to 600 hours). The average new-hire airline pilot of the late 1980s had approximately 3,000 hours of flying experience and over 1,200 hours of turboprop or jet time, but at many airlines these figures were on the decline. Some majors had reduced total flying hours required of candidates to as low as 1,200, although the pilot who is hired with so few hours is the rare exception.

2. *Pilot licenses and ratings.* The usual minimum licensing requirement is a commercial pilot certificate with instrument and multi-engine ratings. The Air Transport Pilot (ATP) rating and FE written certificates are the most important qualifications you can obtain if you are seeking major/national airline employment. With regional carriers, the ATP is the important rating (62 percent hired in 1988 had the ATP). With the major/national airlines, the FE written exam may carry equal weight with the ATP (90.6 percent hired in 1980 had the flight engineer rating or written). Your preference as to carrier type will help determine which ratings to pursue, but consulting the "New-Hire Qualifications" survey chart on page 16 will yield a quick overview of what the carriers actually prefer when they hire pilots. The full ATP certificate and Flight Engineer (FE) written exam are a "must" with most major carriers.

   If you cannot afford or do not have time to pursue these ratings or written exams, you should at least consider getting the written portions completed. As for the "full" ratings, the FE will have to be in a large turbojet aircraft, such as

1989 Major Airline January-November New Hire Pilot Qualifications

	American	Continental	Delta	Eastern	Federal Express
Survey Criteria:					
Total Pilots Hired	686	?	534	1131	86
#Pilots Surveyed	181	13	229	20	34
(% total pilots hired)	26.4	?	42.9	1.8	39.5
% FAPA member	58.0	23.1	64.6	45.0	41.2
Flight Ratings & Certificates (%):					
Total with ATP	77.3	69.2	70.3	90.0	97.1
Total with FE or FEw	93.9	69.2	99.6	80.0	76.5
ATP and FE	9.9	7.7	4.8	20.0	5.9
ATP and FEw	61.9	30.8	65.1	50.0	67.7
ATPw and FE	0.0	7.7	0.4	0.0	0.0
ATP only	5.5	30.7	0.4	20.0	23.5
FE only	2.2	0.0	0.4	5.0	0.0
ATPw and FEw	7.7	7.7	15.7	5.0	2.9
ATPw only	0.0	0.0	0.0	0.0	0.0
FEw only	12.2	15.4	13.1	0.0	0.0
Comm & Inst only	0.6	0.0	0.0	0.0	0.0
Multi	74.6	84.6	78.6	85.0	94.1
CFI/CFII	23.2	30.8	6.6	70.0	32.4
Type rating	34.8	46.2	17.0	35.0	32.4
A&P	5.0	0.0	0.9	30.0	2.9
Flight Experience:					
Flight time range	1,300-15,000	2,100-15,000	1,243-7,000	1,500-17,000	1,520-7,500
Total Hours (average)	3,223	4,322	2,498	5,488	3,423
Jet Hours (average)	1,862	1,469	1,858	1,415	1,064
Turboprop Hours (average)	918	1,492	543	839	1,394
Rotor Hours (average)	251	34	44	350	0
% jet time	84.3	66.7	90.6	55.0	63.6
% turboprop time	59.7	76.9	43.1	80.0	79.4
% neither jet/turboprop	0.7	0.0	0.5	15.0	3.0
% rotor	13.3	16.7	5.2	5.0	3.1
# pilots with < 2000 hours (%)	16.6	0.0	26.2	10.0	23.5
Aviation Background:					
General Aviation	26.5	30.8	41.9	70.0	26.5
Corporate	8.8	7.7	1.3	60.0	5.9
Regional/Commuter	14.9	53.8	0.9	50.0	35.3
Flight Instructor	46.4	53.8	75.1	60.0	26.5
Previous Civilian	16.0	23.1	1.7	90.0	38.2
Previous Military	61.9	46.1	57.3	0.0	47.1
Military and Civilian	22.1	30.8	41.0	10.0	14.7
Branch of Military:					
Air Force	72.4	60.0	72.1	0.0	47.6
Navy	15.8	20.0	16.4	0.0	47.6
Army	5.9	20.0	0.4	50.0	0.0
Marine	4.6	0.0	9.3	50.0	4.8
Coast Guard	1.3	0.0	1.8	0.0	0.0
Education:					
Masters degree	27.1	38.5	28.8	0.0	5.9
Four years college	67.9	46.1	70.8	40.0	88.2
Two/three years college	2.8	15.4	0.4	35.0	5.9
< two years of college	2.2	0.0	0.0	25.0	0.0
Physical Data:					
Age Range	22.8-46.9	28.7-45.4	27.2-43.6	27.2-53.2	25.0-43.1
Age (average)	33.4	37.4	32.6	39.7	31.5
Height range (inches)	65-77	66-75	66-76	62-74	65-78
Weight range (lbs.)	110-216	115-240	120-230	150-225	145-200
% female	1.7	7.7	0.4	0.0	2.9
% < 20/20 vision	14.4	15.4	0.0	20.0	8.8
Lowest visual acuity	20/60	20/70	20/20	20/40	20/30
% over 40 years of age	17.1	38.5	7.9	60.0	5.9

1989 Major Airline January-November New Hire Pilot Qualifications

Northwest	Pan Am	TWA	United	USAir	All Majors
590	500	417	982	624	5,550
348	240	135	356	310	1,866
59.0	48.0	32.4	36.3	49.7	33.6
56.3	59.2	54.8	36.8	49.4	52.1
76.7	77.9	81.5	82.0	91.3	80.3
96.3	90.8	88.9	80.6	92.3	90.9
18.4	15.4	14.1	37.2	18.1	18.4
54.9	55.8	59.3	29.5	65.9	53.3
0.9	0.8	0.0	1.4	0.3	0.7
3.4	6.7	8.1	156.4	7.4	7.7
2.6	1.7	2.2	5.6	1.9	2.6
10.6	10.0	5.2	1.7	4.2	7.6
0.0	0.0	0.0	0.0	0.0	0.0
8.9	7.1	8.1	5.3	1.9	7.5
0.3	2.5	3.0	3.9	0.3	1.4
79.9	87.5	85.9	85.4	72.9	80.7
18.7	30.0	51.1	57.3	41.3	33.2
31.0	38.3	24.4	34.3	36.8	31.9
1.7	2.1	8.1	7.3	6.5	4.6
1,200-13,700	950-11,500	820-10,500	650-25,000	2,000-15,000	650-25,000
3,794	3,773	3,502	5,162	4,122	3,880
2,350	1,634	1,126	2,632	1,526	1,939
978	1,168	1,155	1,382	1,418	1,125
86	188	115	120	78	118
89.3	81.7	64.0	72.5	64.7	78.0
61.6	73.8	80.5	77.2	82.4	69.5
0.3	0.5	2.4	5.2	0.7	1.8
9.0	15.4	13.5	11.1	7.1	10.1
14.7	17.1	13.3	8.4	0.0	13.0
32.2	41.2	48.9	66.0	40.3	43.1
6.9	18.8	25.2	29.5	25.5	16.8
12.6	27.9	48.1	43.8	45.8	28.3
63.2	49.6	60.7	66.3	54.5	59.3
13.5	29.2	57.1	59.9	55.8	34.4
58.6	45.0	29.6	20.2	30.3	42.2
27.9	25.8	13.3	19.9	13.9	23.4
72.0	57.5	69.0	76.2	72.2	69.9
20.3	26.5	22.4	9.8	19.7	19.2
1.7	2.4	5.2	5.6	2.2	2.9
4.7	12.4	1.7	7.7	4.4	6.7
1.3	1.2	1.7	0.7	1.5	1.3
31.0	22.9	20.0	16.6	16.1	22.5
68.4	74.2	60.0	68.3	73.6	69.6
0.6	1.2	10.4	12.6	9.0	5.8
0.0	1.7	9.6	2.5	1.3	2.1
24.2-48.6	24.2-47.2	22.1-49.4	22.2-52.0	23.1-47.2	22.1-53.2
35.9	34.6	32.8	35.3	32.5	34.2
59-78	64-77	62-76	62-78	64-77	59-78
113-225	109-230	118-235	105-220	117-245	105-240
2.0	4.6	6.7	19.9	3.9	6.2
23.6	20.4	26.7	31.5	24.8	21.0
20/80	20/100	20/100	20/70	20/70	20/100
31.3	28.8	25.2	30.6	15.2	23.4

a B-727 or a DC-8; however, the ATP can be obtained in any multi-engine aircraft (a light twin is fine). There is no doubt that having a type rating or a full FE ticket will enhance your qualifications. However, these ratings are very expensive and should be obtained, if at all, at the appropriate experience level and only after you have received your ATP license and completed the FE written exam.

3. *Education.* A majority of recently hired airline pilots have a four-year college degree, and most of the rest have some college education. Although a number of aspiring pilots concentrate their studies in aviation, aerospace or other technical fields, the airlines do not specify a particular degree or major. You should consider a four-year degree as a "must have" qualification when making your career plans.

Making a Plan, Checking It Twice

You may still ask, "How do I make these plans?" After all, the question was raised: How should a pilot go about meeting qualifications and acquiring the necessary experience for the kind of job being sought? Is there a reasonable way of working toward the desired career position?

For the pilot aspiring to an airline seat, good planning will entail laying out a well-defined career path, either military or civilian, and sticking to it. Under current conditions, the quickest path to a major or other large jet airline is most likely the civilian, or a combination of military and civilian.

In the past, military pilots with multi-engine jet and/or heavy aircraft experience had a strong advantage over civilian pilots, who had difficulty building up their multi-engine and jet qualifications.

Between 1983 and 1986, there were more civilian pilots than military pilots hired by the majors. In 1987, military pilots took the lead again, with 66 percent of pilots being hired by the majors coming from this group. This was primarily due to older pilots' being hired. In 1988, 85 percent of the pilots over age 40 at date of hire were ex-military. The overall trend is toward an increase to about 50 to 60 percent in the percentage of civilian pilots hired by the majors and the bigger national airlines.

One fact needs stressing right off the top: No amount of planning can get you to your career choice flying position if you fail to keep your logbook correctly. Your logbook(s) must be kept faithfully and accurately, so stay current with each and every flight. Your pilot's log will accompany you throughout your career. In it, you will record each flight you make, the type of aircraft, tail number, date, point of takeoff and landing, duration of flight, flight conditions, and training received. All of your logbooks are legal documents that will be inspected thoroughly by prospective employers and the FAA to verify your flight training and experience.

Several companies provide logbooks. Jeppesen Sanderson has a logbook designed to hold up to 10 years' worth of data. Published as a complement to Jeppesen Sanderson's airway manual binders, the logbook has 256 pages of 24-pound ledger paper; the scheme of the book is incremental six-month pages that allow pilots to turn with ease to

1989 Jan-Jun New Hire Pilot Qualifications: Pilots 40 Years or Older

	Major	National	Jet	Regional
Survey criteria:				
Total pilots hired	3171	916	608	2233
% pilots surveyed	10.2	10.2	8.9	3.0
# pilots surveyed	324	93	54	66
% FAPA member	56.2	6.8	59.3	50.0
Flight ratings and certificates (%):				
Total with ATP	83.0	91.4	75.9	74.2
Total with FE or FEw	92.6	52.7	70.4	48.5
ATP and FE	23.5	21.5	29.6	7.6
ATP and FEw	53.7	26.9	22.2	30.3
ATPw and FE	1.5	0	0	0
ATP only	5.9	43.0	24.1	36.4
FE only	2.5	2.2	14.8	3.0
ATPw and FEw	8.3	0	3.7	4.5
ATPw only	0	0	3.7	3.0
FEw only	3.1	2.2	0	3.0
Comm. and Inst. only	1.5	4.3	1.9	12.1
Multi	83.6	83.9	88.9	93.9
CFI/CFII	22.5	41.9	33.3	53.0
Type rating	34.9	52.7	35.2	27.3
A & P	4.3	7.5	5.6	3.0
Flight experience:				
Flight time range	1,088-17,500	2,200-16,400	1,650-23,000	950-11,000
Total hours (avg.)	5,646	9,073	6,775	4,772
Jet hours (avg.)	4,037	3,135	2,513	987
Turboprop hours (avg.)	1,180	2,618	1,304	896
Rotor hours (avg.)	235	340	195	680
% jet time	94.9	82.6	75.0	60.0
% turboprop time	64.4	85.9	80.8	70.7
% neither jet nor turboprop	0.7	1.2	3.9	11.3
% rotor	14.8	22.5	14.9	25.5
% pilots with less than 2000 hours	.3	0	3.7	6.1
Aviation background (%):				
General aviation	34.3	52.7	53.7	66.7
Corporate	16.0	39.8	24.1	31.8
Regional/commuter	15.7	32.3	35.2	24.2
Flight instructor	58.3	45.2	42.6	51.5
Civilian only	14.5	36.6	38.9	40.9
Military only	54.6	26.9	37.0	18.2
Military and Civilian	30.9	36.6	24.1	40.9
Branch of military (%):				
Air Force	75.1	66.1	60.6	56.4
Navy	13.7	11.9	30.3	20.5
Army	3.6	16.6	6.1	15.4
Marines	5.8	1.7	3.0	5.1
Coast Guard	1.8	3.4	0	2.6
Education (%):				
Master's degree	49.1	17.2	22.2	19.7
Four years college	45.4	47.3	57.4	51.5
Two/three years college	4.3	24.7	13.0	13.6
Less than two years of college	1.2	10.8	7.4	15.2
Physical data:				
Age range	40-53.2	40-56.3	40-61.5	40-57.1
Age (avg.)	43.5	44.8	45.1	45.6
Height range	59"-78"	62"-77"	64"-80"	66"-76"
Weight range	115-235	108-269	115-265	148-230
% female	2.8	1.1	1.9	3.0
% less than 20/20 vision	37.0	34.4	50.0	40.9
Lowest visual acuity	20/100	20/200	20/100	20/200

DATE 19_87_	AIRCRAFT TYPE	AIRCRAFT IDENT	ROUTE OF FLIGHT FROM	TO	NR INST. APP.	REMARKS AND ENDORSEMENTS	NR LDG	SINGLE-ENGINE LAND		MULTI-ENGINE LAND	
10/8	PA-28-140	4690R	U42- PVC- PVU-U42		0	BOB DARKADY SAFETY PILOT	3	2	6		
10/20	C-150	9397U	U42-PVU-U42-LCL		7	3 ILS 13 PVU, VORA PVU, HOOD OVER TURNS, STEEP BANK, TIMED TURNS 200	3	4	6		
11/3	C-150	9397U	U42-U14-U42		0	PATTN A&B STOP NEPHI SAFETY PILOT TO BOB DARKADY	2	3	0		
11/5	PA-28-140	4690R	U42-DTA-PVU-U42		3	DELTA VOR 34, PVU ILS 13, PVU VOR2A BOB DARKADY SAFETY PILOT	2	4	0		
08/03 3AUG	C-172	8895V	PVU	LCL	—	BFR, App, dg stall, Vg stall, slot/gd Touchdoes for currency	3		8	PILOT	
8/3	C-152	67853	PVU	LCL	—	NIGHT CURRENCY 4 FULL STOP LANDINGS TO RWY 13 PVU	4		8		
8/7	C-172	9918Q	PVU-LIS-PVU			KIDS TO VEGAS	2	7	0		
10/05	C-152	67853	PVU → LIS			TO HENDERSON, WALL CLOUD ½mi at Milford	1	3	7		
10/07	C-152	67853	LIS	LCL		DAVID & TONI NIGHT RIDES BOULDER CITY & LASVEGAS LIGHTS	2	1	2		
10/08	C-152	67853	LIS→PVU			BRING CONNIE BACK HOME CLEAN SMOOTH SAILING	1	3	6		
10/11	C172	106ES	PVU	Lcl	1	VOR A Prov Att 600 Instr Flying Referral ATC Clearances Hugh Bangerter CFI 5728A4 7781 7/80	1	1	2		
10/13	C-172	9918Q	PVU	Lcl	2	ILS Prov Holding Patterns Clearances Hugh Bangerter CFI 5728A4 7781 7/84	1	1	3		
10/25	C172RG	6345V	PVU	Lcl	1	Complex Low Prop Steep Spd Hugh Bangerter CFI 5728A4 7781 10/80	4	1	2		

I certify that the entries in this log are true,

John A. Pilot

PILOT'S SIGNATURE

TOTALS THIS PAGE	35	0
AMT. FORWARDED	171	0
TOTALS TO DATE	206	0

AND CLASS		CONDITIONS OF FLIGHT				TYPE OF PILOTING TIME				
COMPLEX	2IC	NIGHT	ACTUAL INSTRUMENT	SIMULATED INSTRUMENT (HOOD)	FLIGHT SIMULATOR	CROSS COUNTRY	AS FLIGHT INSTRUCTOR	DUAL RECEIVED	PILOT IN COMMAND (INCL. SOLO)	TOTAL DURATION OF FLIGHT
				2 4		2 6			2 6	2 6
				3 5					4 6	4 6
	30					30			3 0	30
				2 6		4 0			4 0	4 0
								8	8	8
		8							8	8
						7 0			7 0	70
						3 7			3 7	3 7
		1 2							1 2	1 2
		1 5				3 6			3 6	3 6
				1 0				1 2		1 2
				1 1				1 3		1 3
2				8				1 2		1 2
1 2	30	3 5		11 4		2 3 9		4 5	31 3	350
00	90	1 1 2		19 3		102 3		45 3	126 0	171 0
1 2	120	14 7		30 7		126 2		49 8	157 3	206 0

AT. # 267480840 HAS SATISFACTORILY PASSED THE BIANNUAL FLIGHT REVIEW FOR PRIVATE PILOT *a.j.oll* 886905 79 CFI 7/99

information from specific time periods. Logbooks of this type, if well kept, can come in handy when a prospective employer decides to grill you about your flying record. (See pages 20-21 for examples of logbook entries.)

There are several speedy routes to a major or national airline seat. If you would like to obtain an aviation-related degree, there are over 30 colleges and universities that offer aviation bachelor degrees and more than 80 schools that offer a two-year associate degree. Some of the colleges include flight training as part of the degree program; others do not. Much will depend on your preference of airline to make a career with, but if you plan right, you can reach your career goal in the minimum time.

In fact, in the late 1980s, a few of the major carriers became so intent on protecting themselves against any pilot shortage and on providing stability at the regional airlines which fed passengers to them that they took initiatives to provide career tracks. Some of these tracks begin with enrollment at a university that has a good aviation school, funnel students through regionals, and culminate with a successful candidate's hiring by the major carrier from an affiliated or owned commuter. Note the word 'successful.' Nobody involved with an *ab initio* program is guaranteeing anybody a job.

Ab initio means "from the beginning." Not all the track systems start there; some begin later in the pilot's career — after the pilot has acquired the ratings and experience to be hired by a regional carrier.

Some of the major airlines went even further, actually giving a seniority number as soon as a pilot took a seat with one of the major's feed carriers. If you are on such a program and are accepted later at the affiliated major, the seniority number carries over to your career with the major airline. The first major airlines to establish such track systems were Pan Am and Continental.

That seniority number is a great carrot. All airlines base promotions and pay increases on a seniority system. Such a system is keyed to date of hire and governs an entire career. Pay, trips, vacations, time off, etc., are determined through a bidding system that lets the most senior pilots choose first; then the junior pilots get what is left. You will find seniority governing your career even at those companies without labor unions. Consequently, you need to reach your career-goal airline as soon as possible. You cannot advance your position within the company by your individual accomplishments; only seniority counts.

Schooling is far more important than many pilots realize. So are ratings and other factors. Too many pilots overstress the importance of total time as they compete for jobs. Usually, once a pilot has between 2,000 and 3,000 hours, his or her competitiveness is not greatly increased by adding flight time. The most important factors then become additional ratings, inside contacts, education, the kind of equipment flown, and the time spent in the job search.

The other thing to remember about flight time is the value of the right kind of flying experience. The best experience background you can have is to fly equipment comparable to that flown by the airline at which you are applying, and over a wide route structure. While it is not essential, experience carrying passengers is preferred by the passenger airlines. The closer your background is to the actual airline operation, the better your chances of being hired.

For the military pilot, this could mean flying C-141s, C-9s and other modern jet aircraft. Large turboprops, such as the C-130, also would be good choices.

For the civilian pilot, the best choice would be to land a job with a good commuter airline flying sophisticated turbine equipment or a corporate job flying jet equipment.

Remember, evaluation is always comparative because you are going up against a lot of other applicants.

More will be included on most of the preceding topics in later chapters.

Landing a Range of Jobs

Little has been said so far about how pilots commence their aviation careers. Many pilots start out their professional aviation careers as flight instructors at airports close to their homes. (This, of course, requires commercial and flight instructor ratings, as well as a medical certificate.) They also may fly sightseeing trips, haul skydivers, tow gliders or banners, fly pipeline patrol, crop dust, ferry aircraft, contract themselves to various aircraft owners, volunteer for humanitarian flight agencies (e.g., Angel Plane, Flight for Life), fly charters or freight, fly corporate, fly for a commuter. They can scan the Trade-A-Plane publication for job opportunities during visits to a local FBO, check newspapers for possible job listings, check with county or state agencies for flying jobs (police, fire, traffic control).

Sources for information about who is hiring include *Aviation Week & Space Technology*, *The Wall Street Journal*, local newspapers, Janice Barden's Corporate Aviation Agency (for those seeking corporate jobs), FAPA's *Career Pilot Job Report*, and FAPA's *Career Pilot Magazine*. *Air Transport World* has long been a standard among monthly commercial aviation publications, while a more recent rival is *Airline Executive*; *Commuter Air Magazine* was adopted in 1988 by the Regional Airline Association as a monthly forum; and *Business/Commercial Aviation* has the advantages of experienced staff and coverage of both corporate and airline flying (particularly of the smaller airlines). All of these magazines can prove valuable in keeping a pilot informed about who is expanding, who is cutting back, and who is more likely to be hiring. They also add to a pilot's store of information about particular airlines and other companies.

A valuable source of information for corporate jobs is the pilot grapevine.

Why are all of these sources of information important? Easy: Because they can help you gain the flying experience needed for your ultimate piloting career destination.

Chapter 4
WHERE WILL AIRLINE FLYING JOBS COME FROM?

Approximately 46,259 pilots worked for major airlines in 1989. FAPA's predictions for future airline hiring are based on the following assumptions: an average of six crews per aircraft, two-man flight crews for twin-engine aircraft, three-man crews for three-engine aircraft, and a retirement age of 60.

The major and national airlines have represented more than 75 percent of all jet airline hiring since 1987. They will continue to grow and replace retiring pilots in increasing numbers. FAPA predicts that this airline group will account for the majority of new jobs in large jets through about 2005 A.D.

Most established major airlines will have a significant number of pilot retirements over the next several years. FAPA anticipates that the majors will have to replace 1,540

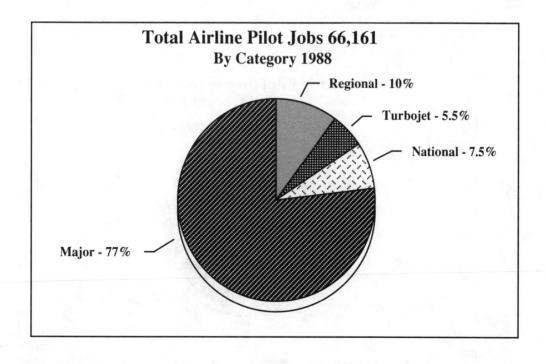

Total Airline Pilot Jobs 66,161
By Category 1988

Regional - 10%

Turbojet - 5.5%

National - 7.5%

Major - 77%

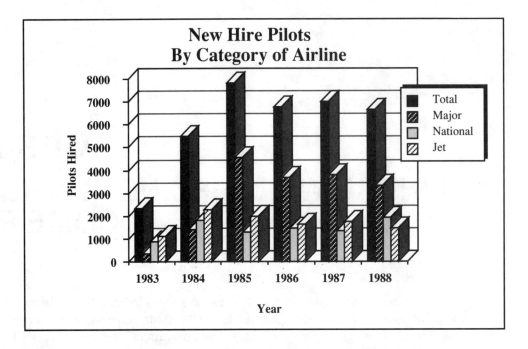

New Hire Pilots
By Category of Airline

to 1,823 pilots per year due to attrition alone. If any of the variables change, the projection for new-hires will change; for example, if the retirement age is increased to 65, then the number of projected new-hires would decrease to a probable range of 1,143 to 1,427 pilots per year. Remember, however, that these figures do not reflect expansion. When considering future demand for pilots, FAPA includes a modest five percent growth rate. At this level, companies operating large jets would need to hire about 3,200 pilots per year in order to fill their cockpits.

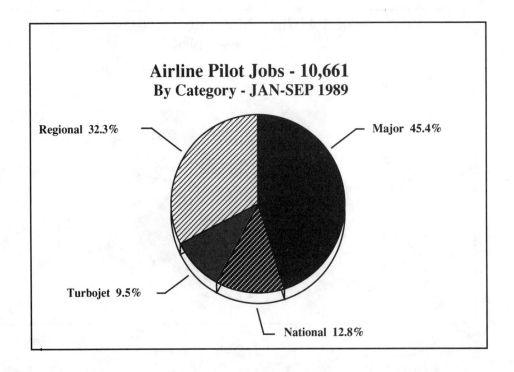

Airline Pilot Jobs - 10,661
By Category - JAN-SEP 1989

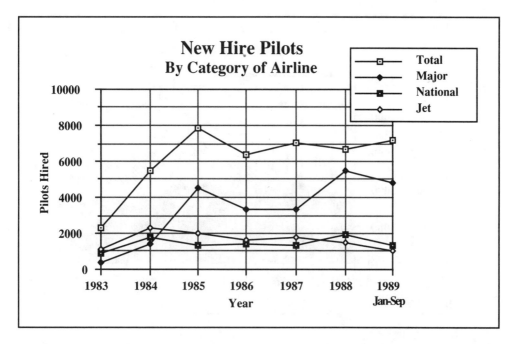

The formula for pilot demand is based on two factors: the amount of equipment in service and the general public's desire to travel. Aircraft orders directly affect the capacity of the airlines; that is, the more airplanes in the fleet, the more passengers in the airline's traffic report. Further, you must not consider only the passenger transport industry; aircraft orders within the cargo transport industry are a factor as well. It was projected in 1988 that within the passenger airline industry, capacity would increase 66 percent from 1989 to 2001. In the cargo transport industry, the capacity was projected to increase

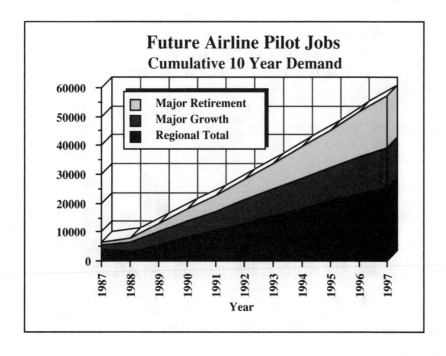

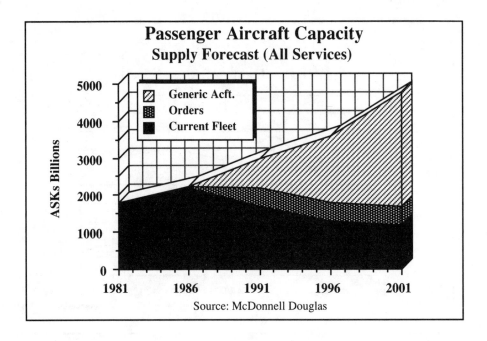

100 percent over the same time span. In order to handle this rate of growth among the passenger and cargo transport industries, FAPA calculated, the airlines would have to increase their pilot ranks by 75 percent over the 10-year period.

More than ever, the traveling public has strongly influenced the need for airlines to buy more planes. There are two groups that the airlines have to accommodate: business travelers and recreational travelers.

The trend in business during the period of healthy economic growth in the 1980s was toward much more frequent travel than in earlier "boom times." The airlines themselves

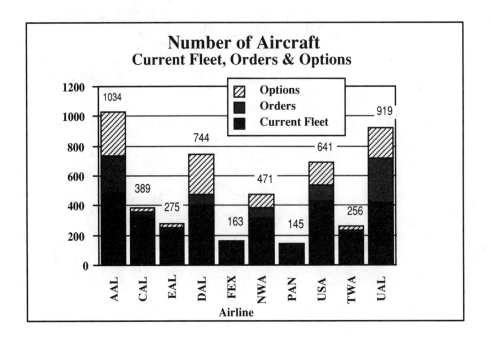

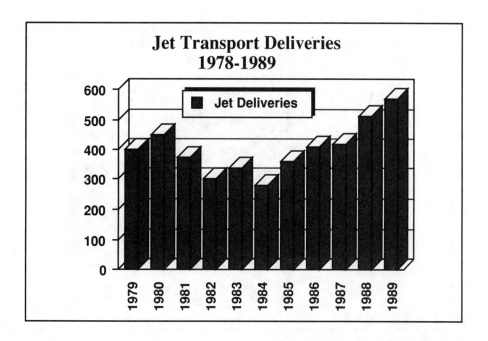

contributed to this trend by developing the hub-and-spoke system of service delivery. The effects of this system are much more far-reaching than is generally recognized. The hub-and-spoke system provided frequent, reliable air service to a great many communities that previously had been dependent on one or two subsidized stops a day by major or national carriers, which often took passengers hundreds of miles (and five to eight hours) out of their way to get them to their destinations. But the revolution in service did not stop there. The volume of passengers delivered to the hubs by feed carriers permitted the major and national airlines to initiate service between a large number of city-pairs which otherwise

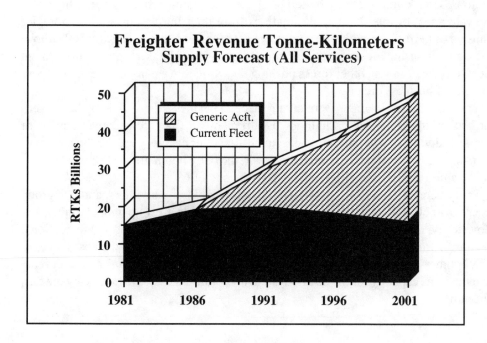

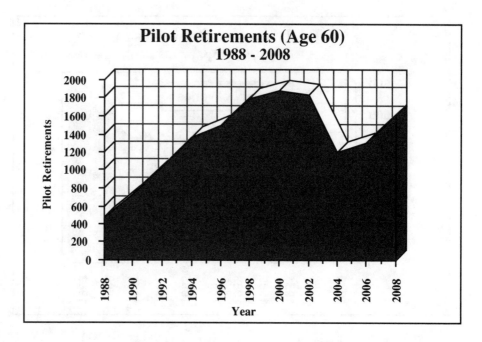

Pilot Retirements (Age 60)
1988 - 2008

could never have had dedicated routes. The reason they could not receive dedicated service under the old system of mainly origin-and-destination routes was that one or both of the cities in question would have been unable to supply enough passengers to make flights profitable for the airlines. The hub-and-spoke system augments the supply of passengers from each of the paired cities, thus providing enough traffic to make these city pairings feasible.

The vastly increased air service to most parts of the United States was only one portion of a complex of forces creating a global business community that now reaches even into U.S. backwaters and ex-hinterlands. Another contribution by the airlines was their development of international destinations from their hub systems. Technologies growing out of the digital revolution have accounted for a very large measure of the move toward a global business community. Profound changes in banking and in investment practices have been among other forces pushing the world into a pan-continental network of interrelated business arenas.

While all of these changes were taking place in business, the U.S. baby boom generation was enlarging the base of individuals sufficiently affluent to become frequent air travellers. Individuals who fall into the frequent-traveller category are for the most part between the ages of 40 and 60. In time, however, the baby boom group probably will increase the amount of air travel by retirees past the age of 60.

Thirty percent of the current population consists of baby boomers, and this group represents over 50 percent of the flying public. These people grew up with air travel, and they love to fly. This group is heavily represented in both the business and recreational travel groups. In the late 1980s, the first baby boomer turned 40. Over the next 13 years, the baby boomers are expected to bring more frequent flyers into the prime air travel years and to require the capacity for the airline system in the United States to double by the turn of the century.

Some have predicted that only large airlines (and their feeders) would be able to compete and grow in the deregulated environment. These experts have predicted a decrease in the number of major airlines to five or six large profitable companies, increasing the stability of the industry and the pay and benefits offered to pilots.

However, the airline industry has continued to surprise the pundits: It was a surprise to many when Midway Airlines survived and flourished in the late 1980s; it was a surprise to many when Kimberly-Clark Corp. founded a jet airline, Midwest Express, in 1984, and nurtured it into an outstanding success story; it was a surprise to many when Fresno, Calif.-based WestAir grew in only two years from a tiny, struggling commuter to a jet carrier of national airline size (by DOT definition). The industry demonstrates a resilience that often confounds those who try to say what it is going to do next.

Quite a number of industry observers were stunned by the spectacular success of such hubs as Republic Airlines at Memphis and Detroit (Republic later was absorbed by Northwest); Piedmont (since absorbed by USAir) at Charlotte and Dayton; and Delta at Cincinnati. And just as some pundits were declaring the nation "hubbed out," airlines began scoring coups with "mini-hubs."

The biggest surprise of all may have come from America West, which at the turn of the decade to the 1990s was poised to become a major airline with annual revenues in excess of $1 billion. In part, Phoenix-based America West accomplished its rise from shaky new-entrant carrier to a billion-dollar airline by virtue of a wholly-integrated commuter operation, using Boeing/de Havilland Canada Dash 8 turboprops to complement its Boeing 737-200s and -300s and 757-200s.

Because the industry keeps finding ways to exploit deregulation, no one can say definitively that an airline of modest proportions today will not be a giant of tomorrow, just as America West in six years rose from its three-airplane beginning to a developing David among major airline Goliaths. (This is not bad news, but good; it means the ongoing creation of jobs for pilots with jet airline flying ambitions.)

The airline industry is cyclical and is directly related to the nation's economy. When the economy is strong, airline passenger traffic increases. Then the airlines must increase their flights, purchase new aircraft, and hire new pilots to fly those aircraft. Timing is very important in competing for airline jobs. When the economy slows down, the airlines frequently cut back flights and furlough those crew members with the least seniority. Although such times are depressing, they offer excellent opportunities for you to improve your qualifications and make contacts with the people who do the hiring. When a significant amount of hiring is going on, airline personnel departments are saturated with phone calls and letters. The same goes for the chief pilot's office. It is almost impossible to get through. During times when the airlines are not hiring, it may be easier to talk with someone who could make the difference when hiring resumes.

One factor that affects pilot demand is the attrition of senior airline captains as they reach age 60. Airlines have never been faced with massive pilot retirement, but now they find that the flight crews who were hired during the post-Korean war era are retiring. The retirement factor will increase flight crew demand and have a considerable impact on pilot hiring in the coming years unless the retirement age were to be raised above age 60 by the FAA. Such change would temporarily alleviate the problem for the number of years that the retirement age is raised; however, the problem then would begin anew. [A Pilot

Retirement Chart (page 33) is included showing approximately how many pilots would be needed for the replacement of retiring pilots.]

Possible negative factors affecting pilot demand (which could cancel out the positive effects of attrition) are increasing fuel costs, rising labor costs, a rising rate of inflation, a decrease in passenger traffic, and the replacement of outmoded equipment with more cost-efficient aircraft flown by fewer crew members.

Since all these factors are variables, accurately predicting pilot demand is very difficult. Demand is great enough, however, that many airlines, among them major and national airlines, have new-hire pilots flying copilot in the first year instead of remaining flight engineers for a long time while waiting for promotion. Under recent market conditions, your chances of retiring as a captain are excellent if you are less than 50 years old when hired by a large carrier.

FAPA estimates that reaching captain should take less than 10 years at most established major or national airlines. At many regional/commuter airlines and cargo carriers, it will take far less.

Major Airline Pilot Retirements 1988-2052

	American	Continental	Delta	Fed Ex	Northwest	Pan Am*	TWA	United	USAir	Total	Cumulative Industry Total	5 yr. Incremental Industry Total
Approx. # Pilots On seniority list	7,200	4,500	6,400	2,011	4,500	2,200	3,164	7,000	5,226	42,201		
1988	51	2	32	15	28	19	96	165	18	426	426	
1989	61	7	46	17	23	15	75	181	34	459	885	
1990	110	18	65	23	46	35	92	219	25	633	1,518	
1991	133	18	53	21	57	30	78	234	45	669	2,187	
1992	188	22	79	31	87	72	74	267	62	882	3,069	
Past 5 Years %	8.0%	1.6%	5.2%	6.5%	6.1%	12.9%	13.0%	15.9%	4.1%	8.2%		
1993	208	25	83	27	90	68	122	272	90	985	4,054	
1994	237	43	125	23	77	95	167	350	95	1,212	5,266	
1995	205	59	177	24	83	102	187	312	78	1,227	6,493	
1996	218	53	237	30	109	116	189	303	115	1,370	7,863	
1997	220	76	258	18	118	130	189	324	98	1,431	9,294	6,225
5 yr. incremental %	16.1%	6.2%	16.6%	7.5%	12.1%	38.7%	26.7%	23.3%	10.7%	16.6%		
10 yr. cumulative %	24.1%	7.8%	21.8%	14.0%	18.2%	51.6%	39.7%	39.1%	14.8%		24.8%	
1998	250	101	294	32	174	114	264	273	136	1,638	10,932	
1999	224	108	290	33	203	112	268	344	145	1,727	12,659	
2000	165	104	290	43	246	100	256	382	149	1,735	14,394	
2001	112	112	308	42	224	75	208	295	163	1,539	15,933	
2002	149	126	368	59	160	42	188	285	143	1,520	17,453	8,159
5 yr. incremental %	13.3%	13.4%	29.3%	12.8%	25.5%	33.5%	37.1%	23.5%	16.6%	21.8%		
15 yr. cumulative %	37.4%	21.2%	51.2%	26.8%	43.7%	85.1%	76.8%	62.7%	31.4%		46.6%	
2003	121	149	240	72	146	28	133	217	159	1,265	18,718	
2004	155	117	219	66	106	13	71	167	103	1,017	19,735	
2005	155	169	182	98	104	6	52	190	122	1,078	20,813	
2006	185	238	148	101	94	16	42	154	185	1,163	21,976	
2007	206	300	188	90	175	33	57	182	231	1,462	23,438	5,985
5 yr. incremental %	12.2%	23.6%	18.5%	26.1%	15.8%	7.3%	11.1%	13.6%	18.0%	16.0%		
20 yr. cumulative %	49.6%	44.8%	69.6%	52.8%	59.5%	92.4%	87.9%	76.2%	49.4%		62.6%	
2008	390	236	240	96	158	35	50	157	155	1,517	24,955	
2009	422	220	225	84	171	23	49	155	196	1,545	26,500	
2010	343	206	212	89	140	18	39	219	172	1,438	27,938	
2011	251	202	213	72	151	12	35	88	216	1,240	29,176	
2012	204	206	157	86	146	7	28	108	209	1,151	30,329	6,891
5 yr. incremental %	23.8%	26.0%	19.8%	26.1%	19.4%	7.2%	6.3%	10.8%	21.3%	18.4%		
25 yr. cumulative %	73.4%	70.8%	89.4%	78.9%	78.9%	99.5%	94.2%	87.1%	70.7%		81.0%	
2013	217	160	110	76	162	2	26	103	223	1,079	31,408	
2014	236	121	102	66	175	1	25	111	218	1,055	32,463	
2015	247	131	105	53	149	1	24	92	185	987	33,450	
2016	262	163	92	55	130	1	14	125	157	999	34,449	
2017	238	134	85	41	99	0	21	99	133	850	35,299	4,970
5 yr. incremental %	17.7%	17.2%	9.3%	17.8%	18.1%	0.4%	3.4%	7.9%	20.6%	13.3%		
30 yr. cumulative %	91.1%	88.0%	98.0%	96.7%	97.0%	99.9%	97.7%	94.9%	91.3%		94.3%	
2018	178	110	26	22	46	0	16	104	143	645	35,944	
2019	136	83	20	13	36	0	16	76	92	472	36,416	
2025	122	93	7	9	25	1	14	57	82	410	36,826	
2021	94	74	8	5	9	0	17	65	43	315	37,141	
2022	47	53	3	5	3	0	7	27	20	165	37,306	2,007
5 yr. incremental %	8.5%	10.0%	1.2%	3.3%	3.0%	0.1%	2.2%	4.9%	8.5%	5.4%		
35 yr. cumulative %	99.7%	98.0%	100.0%	100.0%	100.0%	100.0%	99.8%	99.9%	99.9%		99.7%	
2023	18	50	1	0	0	0	5	6	3	83	37,389	
2024	4	27	0	0	0	0	0	3	2	36	37,425	
2025	1	6	0	0	0	0	0	1	1	9	37,434	128
Total # pilots surveyed	6,763	4,122	5,288	1,637	3,950	1,322	3,194	6,712	4,446	37,434		

Due to high turnover rates at the time of publication, accurate retirement figures for Eastern are not available.

*PFEs not included in this chart

Chapter 5
ASPECTS OF THE AIRLINE JOB

The Schedule, With Focus on the Majors

Pilots for the major airlines fly from 10 days to as many as 20 short days per month, depending upon their seniority and the type of equipment they fly.

In most cases, the pilots have a 75- to 85-hour maximum that can be flown each month. This does not necessarily mean actual flight hours, but may include credit time. For example, in most cases pilots are awarded one hour of flight time for each two hours on duty when this "credit time" exceeds that duty period's actual flight time. Actual flight time for any one month could be as low as 55 hours, but with the credit time the pilot would reach the maximum of 75 hours. The ratio of flight pay for on-duty time and trip time (time away from home) is called duty rig and trip rig, respectively. Trip rigs usually are paid at a ratio of 1:3 or 1:4, so that you are paid for one hour of flight pay for every three or four hours you are away from your domicile. Duty rig, on the other hand, is paid at the ratio of 1:2, i.e., you are paid for one hour of flight time for every two hours on duty (must be in uniform and at the airport).

In addition to flight time, you are given expense pay or "per diem" for every hour you are away from home. On the average, major airlines pay approximately $1.50 per hour per diem. Per diem is tax-free and represents between $360 and $480 each month on top of your base salary.

A typical work schedule includes flying 80 hours a month (block-to-block: push-back from the gate to pull-up at the gate). This represents about 10 to 20 days of flying a month, for an average of 15 working days. The total hours on duty will be close to 160 hours a month, and the time spent away from home will range from 240 to 320 hours a month. "Hard time" represents actual flight time and taxi time (time it takes for the aircraft to get to the active runway for takeoff and back to the gate after touchdown).

Normally, the pilots who are on reserve (on call) are allowed 10 or 12 days free of duty each month. Pilots on reserve usually come from the bottom of the seniority list, but not exclusively, and are allowed to use portable beepers in order to meet the requirements for being on call. Reserve pilots usually are on 24-hour call (in some cases only 12 or 13 hours) and usually are required to be within one to two hours from the airport.

A comparative note: Pilots for major and national airlines fly longer legs, probably averaging at least two hours or more, whereas pilots with regional carriers will fly short hops, usually less than one hour in length, but will do several flights per day. With all of the major airlines, time free of duty is generous, and job conditions are excellent.

The Pay, Jet Airlines

Airline pilots are paid according to the position flown (captain, first officer or flight engineer), the type of aircraft flown, the speed of the aircraft, and the maximum certified gross weight of the aircraft. Pay also is determined by day or night and domestic or international flying. As an example, as a DC-9 captain, you might be paid $80 per hour for flying. In addition, you might be paid 3¢ per hour for each thousand pounds of gross weight. For a DC-9-30 this is about 108,000 pounds, which comes out to an additional $3.24 per hour.

Pilots usually are paid per mile flown as well. Mileage is computed by incorporating a contract-designated speed, such as 550 miles per hour, yielding an additional $16.50 per hour. Usually, night flying pays about $3 per hour more than day flying.

Airline B-scale & Parity Point	Starting no overtime monthly	2nd year pay & position monthly	10th year pay & position monthly	Maximum CPT. pay and position annual	Flight Hours on which pay is based per month
American $-9 yrs or CPT	1,800 B-727 FE	3,400 MD-80 FO	7,300 DC-10 FO	154,000 B-747	75
Continental None	1,685 B-727 FE	3,292 B-727 FO	6,457 B-727 CPT	102,000 All CPT's	85
Delta $-5 yrs	1,800 B-727 FE	2,658 B-727 FE	7,324 B-727 FO	169,879 L-1011	75
Eastern $-5 yrs	1,450 B-727 FE	2,258 B-727 FE	5,002 B-727 FO	121,548 DC-10	86
Federal Express None	3,750 B-727 FE	4,000 B-727 FE	10,500 B-727 CPT	160,800 DC-10	84
Northwest $-5 yrs	1,900 B-727 FE	3,690 B-727 FO	11,229 B-727 CPT	182,400 B-727	80
Pan Am $-5 yrs	1,500 B-727 FE	2,669 B-727 FO	4,910 B-727 FO	115,000 B-747	80
TWA $-5 yrs	1,968 B-727 FE	2,624 DC-9 FO	7,827 MD-80 CPT	132,576 B-747	80
United	1,919	2,345	6,792	161,976	80
USAir $-5 yrs	1,638 B-727 FE	2,800 B-727 FO	7,920 DC-9 FO	146,782 B-727	85
Major Average	1,941	2,974	7,526	144,696	81

In all, the grand total would be approximately $99.74 per hour for a DC-9 captain flying daytime duty. Since the normal maximum is about 75 hours per month, this DC-9 captain could expect to make approximately $7,480.50 per month. A base pay also may be added to this figure. Pay increases will range from zero to 10 percent per year. Longevity pay will top out at 12 years. Rates will vary depending on the airline.

First officers normally are paid a flat rate during the first year (probation); in the second year, they start on a percentage pay scale. Usually in the second year, a first officer makes about 50 percent of captain's pay. During the third year, first officers are paid approximately 50 to 60 percent of captain's pay, with pay increases each year up until about nine to 12 years with the company, depending upon the airline.

Flight engineers also normally are paid approximately 42 percent of captain's pay after the first year. The rate is about 45 to 52 percent in the third year, with longevity increases thereafter. In some cases flight engineers are paid 80 to 90 percent of the first officer's pay.

Second-year pay will vary according to the equipment and position that you are flying. The figures shown in the following chart will vary plus or minus $200 per month, depending upon the airline. The figures are approximate and are calculated based on a 75-hour month for turbojet aircraft and 80 hours per month for turboprop aircraft.

Representative Salary Ranges for Major/Turbojet Airlines

	Start Salary (annually)	2nd Year (annually)	10th Year (annually)	Max Capt. (annually)
Average	$22,020	$35,346	$85,284	$136,843
Low End	$17,400	$25,356	$52,500	$71,000
High End	$24,000	$57,480	$140,400	$166,500

Third-year pay will be approximately 18 percent higher than second-year pay with the airlines, assuming you are flying in the same aircraft and crew position. After the third year, longevity increases will be approximately two percent per year. In addition, you may expect zero to 10 percent annual pay increases for cost-of-living adjustments.

Overall, your earning power at the major airlines is substantial. The latest Delta B-scale contract pays $65,000 in the sixth year (first A-scale year) for a B-727 flight engineer.

CAREER EARNING MODEL

(Assume you live to be 80)

5 years as a flight engineer at $42,000/year =	$ 210,000
5 years as a first officer at $65,000/year =	$ 325,000
20 years as a captain at $107,000/year =	$2,140,000
Total career earnings =	$2,675,000
20 years' retirement at 60 percent of $107,000/year =	$1,284,000
Total lifetime earnings =	$3,959,000
Non-retirement benefits, equal to 15 percent of career earnings =	$401,250
Total lifetime pay and benefits =	$4,360,250

The B Scale

The B scale or two-tier pay scale is a system under which new employees earn less for doing the same job as the more senior employees. The first B scale implemented in the industry was at American Airlines in 1984, where new-hire pilot pay was 50 percent less than the original pay. This was to be a non-merging scale, that is, the 50 percent less was to be forever. At the time the B scale was adopted, American was planning a massive expansion and transition program.

With the upcoming retirements and American's positioning to hire hundreds of pilots, the theory was that eventually everyone would be on the B-scale.

Within 18 months of its inception, under pressure from its pilots' union, American had to readjust its B scale, which has been changed twice since that time. Today, most airlines have a B scale; however, most are between 60 and 80 percent of A scale and merge with A scale within five to nine years of hire, or upon a pilot's reaching the captain's position.

Eventually, the B scale at most airlines will be brought up to merge with the A scale in the fifth year of a pilot's employment.

Pilots should not judge the outcome of the new pay system before it has a chance to settle down. Market pressures are constantly pushing salaries up. To turn away from a career when the average income is more than $80,000 a year and rising is premature. Overall, you can expect a continuing increase in total pilot compensation.

Seniority

Seniority is not a merit promotion system; it is a time-in-service system. Your seniority number will become one of the most important numbers in your career. Usually, it is established by date of hire or by the date that you complete your training. Normally, the oldest pilot in each class is assigned the lowest seniority number.

Your seniority will determine several things: bidding for vacation, for monthly trip schedules, for higher status (such as first officer or captain), for domicile, and so on. Your number will change as pilots above you leave the company. For example, if you are hired as number 2,000 for the company and 200 pilots above you retire, you would then move up to 1,800. You cannot enhance your seniority number by superior performance or by knowing the "right people." Your date of hire is permanent, and you will normally carry it with you for the rest of your career. A rare and controversial exception to permanency of seniority number can arise with merging airlines or after extended furlough periods.

One of the most important functions of your seniority number comes into play when a company decides to furlough. When this happens, company management starts at the bottom of the seniority list with its furloughing and moves up until the pilot groups are reduced to the size needed to operate the desired reduced schedule.

Such variables as airline financial health, union representation, the management track record of a carrier, and quality of life underscore the need for careful selection of an employer. If you get disgusted and leave, or if you are laid off, you will have to start all over at the bottom of the seniority list of your new employer. And even if you are merely furloughed because the airline for which you fly could not weather a recession other than by reducing its schedules and payroll, you may suffer the economic consequences of a period of scrambling for enough income to pay the bills until recalled. Then, too, there is the possibility that your airline employer will never recover sufficiently to place you back on its active pilot rolls.

The lesson: Research your potential career goal employer well.

The Training

Initial flight engineer or first officer training will include a week of company indoctrination training, three to six weeks of ground school and simulator training, and 25 hours of initial operating experience (IOE), which includes a check ride with an FAA check airman. This schedule is standard among all the majors. National and turbojet carriers also will follow this training schedule for their pilots. Once checked out, you will be required to go to recurrent training. The requirement for recurrent training is twice a year for captains and once a year for first officers and flight engineers. The FAA or company check airman can at any time board the airplane unannounced and conduct a check ride.

Training for an upgrade in position on the same aircraft (e.g., B-727 first officer to B-727 captain) consists of four to seven days of ground school and a simulator aircraft checkout with an FAA or company check airman. Requirements for upgrade training in the same position on new aircraft are the same as initial training, including a three- to six-week ground school, simulator, IOE and check ride. The one-week company indoctrination training is not a part of recurrent training.

Those Furloughs

Furloughs usually are the result of a cutback in service by the airline because of an economic downturn or other market factors. Sometimes furloughs are caused by the

Don't Wait for the Gold Watch

[This sidebar was condensed from an article by Teresa Greer, editor of *Piloting Careers* Magazine.]

Whoever you fly for, don't wait around until the day on which you receive your gold watch to ask about the company retirement plan.

Employee pension/retirement plans often make up the major portion of a pilot's retirement income. This situation comes about because some pilots fail to take any steps on their own to assure that they will not face straitened circumstances in retirement. In some cases, there is no great harm done: The company has a fine pension/retirement plan, and the pilot is taken care of quite well.

Suppose, however, the company for which you work does not have a first-rate employee retirement plan? You do not need retirement day to tell you what every glance at your wrist watch should proclaim: You can't stay young forever.

If your company's retirement program is not first-class, you need to be aware of its deficiencies and make up for these with a supplementary private plan.

To illustrate generally how a good plan works: A pilot collects pension pay at 60 percent of the average maximum captain's wages of $133,000, receiving about $79,800 a year. Medical, dental and life insurance benefits, allocated at 7.5 percent of retirement income, potentially increase retirement compensation by $5,985 a year. If all benefits are used in a given year, the total compensation for that year would be $85,785; assuming an individual sickly enough to collect all medical and dental benefits and still lucky enough to live 20 years past retirement, total compensation over 20 years would come to a little more than $1.7 million.

Eight of the 11 major airlines offer a dual retirement program consisting of an "A" fund, or defined benefit plan, which promises an employee a specific monthly payout upon retirement; and a "B" fund, or defined contribution plan, to which the company contributes a specific percentage of the employee's salary each pay day.

Among national, turbojet and regional airlines, profit sharing, stock purchases and 401(k) plans are popular vehicles for either the sole re-

Major Airline Pilot Retirement Pay Comparison - *Piloting Careers* Magazine, April 1989

Airline	Final Year Monthly Pay	Defined Benefit Monthly Pay	Defined Contribution Monthly Pay	Total Retirement Pay/ Mo. (No Pilot Contributions)	Total Retirement Pay/ Mo. If Pilot Contributes 4%
American	$12,333	$3,742	$1,241	$4,983	$6,639
Continental	$6,500	$2,509	$0	$2,509	$3,525
Delta	$13,265	$7,586	$0	$7,586	$10,250
Eastern	$8,127	$2,041	$925	$2966	$4,200
Federal Express	$10,000	$3,399	$0	$3,399	$4,813
Northwest	$12,400	$6,020	$0	$6,020	$7,723
Pan Am (A-300)	$8,085	$0	$3,403	$3,403	$4,587
TWA	$9,739	$2,508	$3,803	$6,311	$7,694
United	$11,449	$4,050	$3,575	$7,625	$9,214
USAir (B-767)	$11,579	$6,385	$0	$6,385	$8,012

Assumptions
- Amounts stated are in 1988 dollars.
- Amounts are based on a pilot having a 30-year career after being hired Jan. 1, 1989, retiring at age 60, and having a spouse of the same age as himself. The chart is based on working 10 years as a B-727 FE, 10 years as a B-727/L-1011 FO, and 10 years as a DC-10/L-1011 Capt. (except where aircraft differs as noted for Pan Am and USAir). Pay is based on 75 flight hours a month.
- Social Security figures are not included.
- The surviving spouse will receive 50 % of the defined benefit plan and 100% of defined contribution pay.
- Inflation increases 5 % per year and income increases equal to inflation.
- Defined contribution accounts earn 10% per year.
- Plans are fully funded and company owes plan nothing (unlike the old Braniff).
- Pilot's 4% contribution means 4% of his annual salary.

tirement plan or for the "B" plan.

Most of the major airline "A" fund programs are calculated using both the employee's number of years of service to the company and the final average earnings (FAE), usually determined by selecting an employee's highest average wages during any consecutive 36 calendar months occurring within the last 120 months (10 years) preceding the date of retirement. For example, United's formula is 1.39 percent of the FAE times the number of years an employee has worked for the company. Northwest's "A" fund formula is 60 percent of the FAE if the pilot has 25 years or more of employment with the company. (See "Major Airline Pilot Retirement Pay Comparison" chart on page 40).

Depending on the airline (and such factors as its retirement formula and ongoing pay scale), a retiring B-747 captain with 30 years of service would collect annual "A" fund retirement pay over the next 15 years ranging from $49,815 to nearly $90,000. (Federal law limits the amount distributed without penalty from "A" fund retirement plans to $98,064 a year, indexed.)

Most airlines also have a "B" fund retirement plan that involves company contributions or, in a few cases, profit sharing. United's "B" fund is a savings/investment plan to which United contributes 9 percent of the pilot's annual compensation. A United captain with 30 years in service thus would draw (even without contributing any of his or her pay) about $1,006,564 from the "B" fund simply from United's contribution plus 6 percent interest. Like many "B" fund plans, United's allows a pilot to add up to 10 percent of his or her annual compensation to the plan and have this money placed in a variety of investment funds. This aspect of the "B" fund could be beneficial to those pilots who have difficulty saving money.

Usually, the pilot receives a monthly allocation from the "A" fund retirement pay and is denied access to the entire amount at once. Eight of 12 "B" fund programs in 1989, however, allowed the pilot to receive his or her retirement money in one lump sum, which could be reinvested in a private retirement program. Most retirees roll over their lump sum payments into another retirement program; this way, they are taxed only on the amounts they withdraw for monthly living expenses rather than on the entire lump sum.

Airlines that offer profit sharing as all or part of the retirement program are Continental, Federal Express, Airborne Express, Braniff, Evergreen and Southwest. The limitation to such programs is that if the company is not profitable, there is no retirement money. Continental's September 1988 institution of an "A" fund plan was a recognition that its profit-sharing plan could not carry the retirement load by itself. American has a profit-sharing plan that is used as part of an incentive program; the profit sharing does not replace American's "A" and "B" fund retirement programs but is an "extra."

Not all pilots have the privilege of being 30-year employees of an airline when they retire from it. An example is the ex-military pilot who is hired by an airline when he is 45. He or she can serve the airline only 15 years before reaching the mandatory retirement age of 60 and most likely will receive only about 40 to 60 percent of the "A" fund retirement of a 30-year employee. Pilots who perceive that they fit into the category of relatively short-term employees should have another retirement program to rely on, such as military retirement or a private IRA account.

As each pilot's circumstances are different from just about every other pilot's, it behooves the individual to examine company policies, project his or her future earnings, calculate the probable retirement benefits, and take such remedial action as appears wise. A wise precaution is a periodic check on the health of the pension plan.

replacement of many smaller aircraft with fewer larger ones, a fleet change that reduces the total number of pilots required. Furloughed pilots have recall rights. This means that the company must recall any pilots who are on furlough before hiring new pilots. Most pilot contracts stipulate "recall rights" — the maximum number of years you can be on furlough before the company can remove you from the seniority list. Retention ranges from five years to an unlimited number of years, depending upon the airline. Pilots often are recalled even after the recall rights have expired, based on the needs and desires of the company.

Companies without unions may or may not offer furlough rights. The decision of management prevails in these cases. Sometimes pilots are released without recall rights. (More on furloughs — and being ready for one — in chapter 21 of this book.)

Probation

The probationary period for most of the major carriers is from 12 to 15 months. This is the time when the company is allowed to observe you and decide whether or not you are living up to its standards. No statistics are available, but it is estimated that the primary reason for not making it through probation is the inability to work with other crew members. Other reasons given for dismissal are lying on the employment application (hiding flying violations), stealing, drug and alcohol abuse, tardiness, lack of flying proficiency, etc. About 5 percent of newly hired pilots do not make it through probation. As the qualifications of new-hires drop, there tends to be more attrition during the first year due to inability to perform cockpit duties to airline standards.

Domiciles

Companies establish official domiciles or bases for all pilots. Your domicile is the city where your trips will begin and end. The company will expect you to report at a specified time before departure (usually one hour), do a professional job, and represent the company well.

Many airline pilots who handle scheduled flights live in cities other than their official domiciles. Their situation is referred to as "commuting" and is fairly widespread. At the present time, none of the airlines requires that you reside in your domicile; however, pilots who are on reserve usually will find it necessary to live in the same city as their domicile because of the number of days they will spend on call (18-20 days a month). Moreover, commuting for many airline pilots will be impossible during the first six to 12 months because they may not have pass privileges at that point. Finally, the conditions of a pilot's reserve schedule may prevent him or her from living more than an hour away from the airport; this stipulation is to ensure that the pilot can adhere to short-notice trip alerts.

Airline Pilot Unions

Eighty percent of the nation's airline pilots are represented by the Air Line Pilots Association (ALPA). The remainder are represented by other unions or are non-union companies.

There are some in-house unions. These are unions with membership made up exclusively of pilots working for a particular airline. American Airlines, Southwest and Federal Express are three large companies with pilots represented by in-house unions. The airline division of the Teamsters also represents some airlines.

Historically (and continuing today), ALPA has been the organization which has done the most to ensure flying safety, good pilot working conditions, a degree of governmental oversight of the airlines, and excellent pay and benefits for pilots. The benefits of a strong national union include not only protection of pay scales, work rules and jobs, but the investigation of air accidents and of airline non-compliance with FARs, as well as the funding of labor battles that could not be handled by a single-company union acting alone. Conversely, the Allied Pilots Association (APA), American Airlines' in-house pilot union, has argued that it can focus better on the needs of its own membership without worrying about far-flung agendas that sometimes may conflict with local interests. And the airline division of the Teamsters Union has the advantage of being able to mobilize not only an airline's pilots, but its flight attendants, mechanics and ground service personnel, all of whom it represents at various carriers.

With 80 percent of pilots represented by ALPA, however, the odds are that any given pilot will wind up at an airline with an ALPA chapter. Assuming this to be your case, in your first year with

ALPA, you can apply for apprentice membership and pay no dues. As an apprentice member, you enjoy all of ALPA's benefits; however, you are not eligible to vote until you are off probation and are an active dues-paying member of ALPA. After your first year, you are eligible for active ALPA membership, and you will pay a small percentage of your gross pay in dues each month.

During your probationary year, you will not be asked to join the company union. Once off probation, you will receive an invitation.

When an application for ALPA membership is submitted within 90 days of date of eligibility, the fee is $25. If the application is submitted later, the fee is $50.

The dues rate for active union members is based on 2.35 percent of income for ALPA members and one percent for the Allied Pilots Association (APA, the union at American Airlines). Assessments by the Board of Directors may be issued at any time. Union dues are paid using any of the following procedures:

- Monthly dues through your airline's payroll deduction plan.

- Annual payment in advance, payable directly to the union.

- Monthly dues payable directly to the union.

Training Contracts

There are some airlines that will require you to sign a training contract. The contracts normally are $8,000 to $12,000, depending on the airline's training program. If you leave the company during your first year of employment, you will owe a prorated amount of your total training cost.

Very few of the pilots who have signed training contracts and left the airline have been taken to court. The airlines will contact you about payment and try to work out a mutual agreement, but will not necessarily take you to court. Most union contracts specifically forbid charging pilots for training. The cost of collecting a training contract probably exceeds the value of the contract to the company, especially if the pilot is out of state.

Employee Benefits

1. *Medical & Dental.* Most airlines offer excellent medical and dental protection for the pilot and the pilot's family. The medical and dental plans are paid for by the company and will cover 80 to 100 percent of the costs, with most providing a maximum out-of-pocket expense for the pilot of anywhere from $500 to $1,000 each year. This eliminates the risk of catastrophic losses due to illness or injury.

2. *Retirement.* All major airlines and many lesser ones offer retirement programs, with the bigger companies offering both a company retirement plan and a voluntary plan, usually a 401(k) with various fund programs in which you can invest your money. For company retirement plans, see the sidebar, "Don't Wait for the Gold Watch," page 40.

   A 401(k) program, which most airlines offer, is a tax-deferred retirement plan in which the employee contributes to a fund. In a 401(k), you contribute a percentage of your salary to the fund; your employer is not required to, but generally will either match your contribution or put up a percentage for each dollar you contribute to your account. The maximum contribution is determined by Internal Revenue Service (IRS) regulations.

   The employee has various investment options when participating in a 401(k) plan. Among these are keeping the funds in a savings account and making investments, which may include both conservative and high-risk investment vehicles. The interest earned and payoffs are determined by the type of investment an individual makes. The vestment period is determined by the plan the company agrees to: A fund can be fully vested immediately or after as many as seven years. If you choose to leave the company before the fund is vested, you are entitled to withdraw all the money you have contributed to the fund, but no more, and the employer's contribution, if any, goes back to the company. If you withdraw the money after the vestment date, all of the money belongs to you. Your contributions are not taxed until your retirement, or until you withdraw the money prior to retirement.

The Management Option

When major or national airlines hire a line pilot, they are looking for a line pilot, not a management candidate. However, this stance has more to do with the attitudes and outlook expected of the pilot applicant than with long-range goals of the airline. No one in management is ever disappointed when a pilot displays an aptitude for managerial duties, and there are many fine career possibilities for a pilot in management.

Since the universities and colleges with aviation programs always teach aviation management, pilots who pass through those programs theoretically should be good managerial candidates. Not everyone with an MBA, however, is a good manager, and the same holds true for graduates of aviation programs.

Regional airlines may look at a pilot's management abilities a bit more quickly than the larger airlines do. The smaller airlines have to make do on fewer resources, and the gung-ho pilot with a positive attitude about the company and some administrative ability is likely to find that management opportunities do exist.

The first management position that comes open for a pilot generally is the assistant chief pilot's position. The next step may be chief pilot on an aircraft type, as Chief Pilot/Jetstream 31s. At some regional airlines, the title of Chief Pilot, with no qualifier behind it, may encompass the entire flight operation; at others, the individual in broad charge of the flight operation will have a more high-sounding title, such as Vice President/Flight Operations.

At regional airlines, a principle found in many other professions often applies: In order to advance beyond a certain level, you may have to switch airlines. For example, a static situation may occur when the next step up is occupied by someone who has been with the airline since its inception and is not likely to leave.

At the level of the majors and nationals, it sometimes is true that most promotions occur from within. Delta Air Lines and Federal Express are examples of airlines which have prided themselves on using their own pools of talent to fill positions as they come open.

At the larger airlines, because of the scale and complexity of operations, a wider variety of opportunities exists for a pilot to move into management, but the process may take longer than at a smaller carrier.

At both the regional and major levels, one of the remarkable developments of deregulation has been the entrepreneurial spirit with which numerous airline employees have "jumped ship" to begin airlines of their own: One thinks of Donald Burr, who left Texas Air to start People Express; Hap Paretti, who left Texas Air to begin Presidential Airways; Mike Brady, who left Metro Airlines to found Phoenix Airline Services/Express Airlines I, a feeder for Northwest Airlines; and Roy Hagerty, who left Atlantic Southeast Airlines (ASA) to acquire a failing airline and turn it into CCAIR, Inc., a Piedmont/US Air feeder. Pilots tend to have an independent streak, and in some pilots that streak is a bit wider than in others. Not every entrepreneurial pilot has the hubris necessary to go out and start up an airline, but highly independent pilots do often prefer to use their managerial skills in starting their own outside businesses, which they run in their time off from flying. Still others prefer to use their administrative abilities for the pilot union of their airline.

Nor is management of any kind an option that every pilot cares to consider. Many prefer to be pilots, period, and enjoy their time off. For those with managerial aspirations, however, the airline industry is a ripe field for advancement, challenge and even entreneurship.

Bases for Major and National Airlines

Airlines*	Anchorage, AK	Appleton, WI	Atlanta	Baltimore	Berlin, W. Germ.	Boston	Bradley, CT	Charlotte, NC	Chicago, IL	Cincinnati	Cleveland	Dallas, TX	Denver, CO	Detroit	Ft. Lauderdale	Ft. Wayne, IN	Greensboro, NC	Guam	Honolulu	Houston	Indianapolis	Kansas City	Las Vegas	Los Angeles	Louisville, KY
Airborne Express																									
Air Wisconsin		•														•									
Alaska Airlines	•																								
Aloha																			•						
American						•			•			•												•	
American Trans Air						•			•					•							•		•		
America West																									
Arrow Air																									
Braniff												•			•							•			
Continental													•					•	•	•				•	
Delta			•			•			•	•		•			•				•					•	
DHL										•															
Eastern			•			•			•																
Evergreen			•										•											•	•
Federal Express																									
Flying Tigers						•	•						•									•		•	
Hawaiian																			•					•	
Midway									•																
Northwest														•											
Pacific Southwest																								•	
Pan Am					•																				
Piedmont				•				•									•								
Southwest												•								•					
TWA																								•	
United									•		•		•												
UPS																									•
USAir						•																			
World				•																					
Zantop																									

* Major airlines are shown in bold text.

	Memphis, TN	Miami	Minneapolis	Moline	Newark, NJ	New Orleans	New York	Oakland, CA	Ogden, UT	Orlando, FL	Philadelphia	Phoenix	Pittsburgh	Portland, OR	Raleigh, NC	Salt Lake City	San Antonio, TX	San Diego	San Francisco	Seattle	St. Louis	Syracuse, NY	Warner Robins, GA	Washington, DC	Wilmington, OH	Ypsilanti, MI	Airlines
																								•			Airborne Express
				•																							Air Wisconsin
																				•							Alaska Airlines
																											Aloha
							•							•			•	•						•			**American**
							•																				American Trans Air
												•															America West
		•					•																				Arrow Air
																											Braniff
					•																			•			**Continental**
		•				•								•		•			•	•							**Delta**
		•					•																				DHL
		•					•			•	•													•			**Eastern**
		•			•		•		•	•				•					•								Evergreen
	•																										**Federal Express**
							•				•			•				•	•			•					**Flying Tigers**
											•							•	•								Hawaiian
		•																									Midway
	•		•				•													•							**Northwest**
																			•								Pacific Southwest
		•					•												•								**Pan Am**
		•																				•					**Piedmont**
												•															Southwest
							•														•						**TWA**
																											United
																											UPS
													•											•			**USAir**
								•																			World
									•								•						•			•	Zantop

3. *Profit Sharing.* Profit-sharing options vary from airline to airline and are not available at some of them. However, profit-sharing plans at such major carriers as American, Continental, Federal Express and TWA are potentially a significant bonus to a pilot's income, depending on the airline's profit picture. Federal Express is an example of an airline that has been successful in using profit sharing, employee ownership in the company, and other motivational tools to improve the company's bottom line and to create a work force enthusiasm that comes back to employees in the form of larger profit-sharing bonuses. (In some cases, profit-sharing plans can backfire on an airline, e.g., at People Express.)

4. *Travel.* All major carriers offer free and reduced-rate travel for their pilots. In many cases there will be a waiting period before you are allowed to use passes. You will find that the passes are very liberal and will be more than enough to satisfy your desire to travel. You will receive passes on other carriers as well as your own airline. The amount you pay for a pass on another airline will vary, but 90 percent, 75 percent and 50 percent discounts are available. When traveling on a 90 percent or 75 percent pass, you must travel on a standby basis. These rates are available for you and eligible family members. All major airlines except Delta have jump seat privileges for pilots providing no-cost travel on a space-available basis. Some companies require you to be in uniform to ride the jump seat.

5. *Loss-of-License Insurance.* Many major carriers provide loss-of-license insurance for their pilots in case they ever fail to pass their Class I medical. The benefits range from $1,000 per month for 46 months to half-pay for the rest of the pilot's life. Many pilots purchase, on their own, supplemental loss-of-license insurance that will provide up to $150,000 tax-free in a lump sum or in monthly payments should medical problems prematurely end their flying careers.

Terms Involved in Contracts

Whether your airline is unionized or not, you will work under a contract. You owe it to yourself, therefore, to be aware of some of the terms associated with contracts and with the unions that represent pilots in contract negotiations. Here are several frequently encountered names, words and phrases:

- AFA: Association of Flight Attendants*

- AFL-CIO: American Federation of Labor-Congress of Industrial Organizations*

- ALPA: Air Line Pilots Association

- APA: Airline Pilots Association (at American Airlines)

---

* Such organizations as the AFA, AFL-CIO and IAM become important to pilots when a pilot union desires to present a united front with flight attendants or mechanics and baggage handlers, etc., as when Eastern's pilots honored an IAM picket line in 1989.

- Back-to-work agreement: An agreement, generally a one-time application, governing the terms and conditions of the return to work of striking employees. It may, for example, provide for termination or transfer of permanent replacements to make room for returning employees.

- Binding arbitration: A contractual agreement to submit a dispute concerning the terms and conditions of the contract or interpretation of the contract to a neutral third party for a decision. Such arbitration is legally binding and is subject to extremely limited judicial review.

- Cooling-off period: A 30-day period called by the National Mediation Board to allow both parties to reconsider their positions, during which time no changes are made in the contract and a legal strike cannot be called.

- FEPA: Federal Express Pilots Association

- IAM: International Association of Machinists & Aerospace Workers*

- IBT: International Brotherhood of Teamsters

- Local Executive Council (LEC): A local governing body for an ALPA chapter, representing the pilots within a local grouping, usually at a domicile.

- Master Executive Council (MEC): Three members from each LEC in an airline represented by ALPA make up the MEC, or central pilot governing body, of that airline.

- Mediation: The use of a neutral third party as a buffer in a labor dispute in order to settle the dispute.

- National Mediation Board: A board established under the Railway Labor Act to intervene on its own initiative, or at the request of any party in a labor dispute, to mediate the dispute or to interpret a contractual provision.

- Permanent replacement pilot: A pilot hired as a permanent employee to replace an employee on strike. A back-to-work agreement may provide that a permanent replacement will be displaced by a returning striker. If the permanent replacement is displaced, his rights will be determined by his individual contract with the company.

- Railway Labor Act: The federal statute governing labor relations in the airline and railroad industries.

- Scope clause: The extent of the legal obligation of the employer to recognize the union as a representative of its employees. The scope clause may cover a subsidiary or another airline of an employer in a particular case. Scope clauses are used to ensure that all aircraft owned or operated by the company or its subsidiaries are flown by union pilots or maintained by union technicians.

- Self-help: A broad term generally describing the activity of the employer who attempts to operate during a strike.

- SWAPA: Southwest Airlines Pilots Association

- Temporary replacement: An individual who is hired to replace strikers only for the duration of the strike.

Chapter 6
THE REGIONAL AIRLINE FLYING JOB

In 1989 there were approximately 6,983 airline pilots flying non-jet aircraft. The regional and commuter segment of the aviation industry has been growing at a variable annual rate of from 10 to 100 percent, and the regional/commuter airlines have been hiring 3,000 to 4,000 per year. Some of the reasons for this growth are technological advances, general acceptance of commuters by the passengers, and deregulation of the industry. Contributing to the rapid hiring pace are the vacancies created as many regional/commuter pilots move up to larger airlines.

The Regional Airline Association (RAA) has estimated that more than 61 million passengers a year will be carried by its member airlines (commuters and regionals) by 1997. Furthermore, not all of the airlines that fit into the category of small turboprop passenger or cargo carrier belong to the RAA. The total flying activity by small airlines is even greater, therefore, than RAA numbers would suggest.

The fleet for this segment of the airline industry has grown dramatically in both size and sophistication, and will continue to do so. There is an increased percentage of larger turboprop and smaller jet equipment being operated by the regional carriers. Many manufacturers are spending millions of dollars designing and producing aircraft specifically for the commuter market. The new breed of turboprop aircraft varies in size from the six-passenger Piper to the 50-passenger Boeing/de Havilland Dash 7 to the 68-passenger Aerospatiale-Aeritalia ATR 72. In addition, small jet aircraft, such as the Canadair RJ, a stretched 48- to 52-passenger derivative of the Challenger business jet, have hit the commuter and express package markets. All of these aircraft are fuel efficient and designed for short-haul, high-cycle service. And manufacturers keep adding more aircraft to the drawing board, each designed for a specific segment of the commuter field.

With these new aircraft comes better acceptance of the commuter airlines by the passengers. The new planes look more like airliners. Flight attendants are being added to improve the level of service and safety. Published schedules are adhered to by the carriers. Tickets are sold by agents at counters just as at major carriers. Flight crews are wearing uniforms and insignia. All of these things give the passenger more confidence in the commuters and increase public acceptance of air travel by regional/commuter airline.

From the pilot's point of view, these aircraft are increasingly the best of training grounds for moving up to the Boeing, McDonnell Douglas, and Airbus aircraft operated

Block Time Circles

- 1 and 2 hour regional jet block time circles around Memphis
- 1 hour turboprop block time (200 mi.) circles around competitive hubs

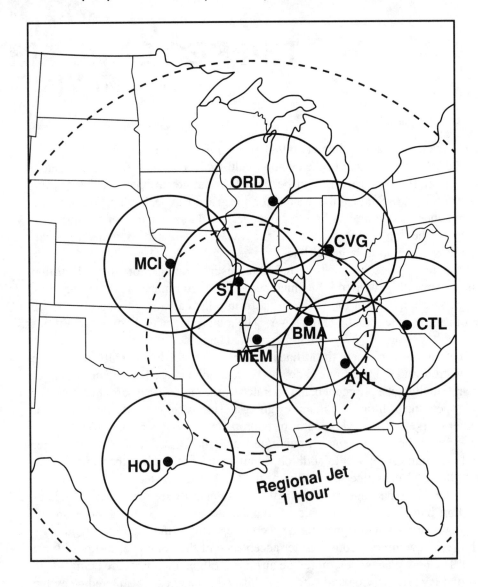

The striking evolution in regional airliners is the trend toward equal sophistication and speed with major-carrier aircraft. Canadair, maker of the Regional Jet, a 52-seat airplane with Mach .08 speed, extends the effective range of regional airline flying so that a Regional Jet operating out of the Memphis airport, for example, can penetrate the one-hour feed markets of eight other hub airports. Such aircraft as the Canadair Regional Jet, the Embraer EMB-145 jet, the Saab 2000 turboprop, and the Embraer CBA-123 pusherprop also make possible long "thin" (low-traffic-volume) O & D routes that previously could not be undertaken by either regional or major airlines. The major and national airlines could not fly such routes because they could not board enough passengers to make their huge airplanes pay off; the regionals could not fly them because they had no planes capable of flying that far without a fuel stop or without exhausting their passengers with the excessive duration of flights.

by major and national airlines. The "glass cockpit" (i.e., cockpit with all-electronic display systems), sophisticated aircraft systems, and the flight data recorder and cockpit voice recorder have come to all of the new-generation regional/commuter airplanes. A couple of major airlines have gone out of their way to make the cockpit environment of pilots at their feeder airlines consistent with their own cockpit environments, e.g., Texas Air has standardized equipment and cockpits on its three basic feeder aircraft (ATR 42, Brasilia and Beech 1900), spending close to $300,000 per aircraft on additional avionics for the Beech 1900s, to provide a true glass cockpit designed to ease a pilot's transition to jets. In addition, many of the regional/commuter airlines are flying under the same FAR Part 121 regulations as the majors. All of these factors add up to a major airline-style piloting environment except for aircraft payloads, length of flight segments, pay scales and a few other adjustments.

As noted, deregulation helped the commuter industry. When major carriers were allowed to pull out of their unprofitable short-haul markets, the commuters moved in to provide needed air service to smaller communities. Commuter aircraft are designed to be profitable in these lower-passenger-volume and shorter-trip markets. Thus, in commuter-to-major feed relationships, both carriers have benefited. For example, the commuter takes a passenger to a larger hub airport, where he can board one of the airlines for the long portion of his trip. A passenger arriving at a large hub can transfer to a commuter and continue to his final destination, which often is not served by a major carrier. Because of the efficiencies of this system, the concept of major-regional airline networks has taken off, and a major carrier either owns a commuter partner outright; owns a percentage of the company; or has a contract with the smaller airline. With the success of partnership hubbing, both ownership of commuters and feed contracts with commuters have spread to national airlines (e.g., both Alaska and Midway own commuter carriers; Braniff and overnight courier DHL utilize extensive contract feeder networks; and America West operates its own turboprop feeder flights to its jet hubs at Phoenix and Las Vegas).

The passenger carrier contracts take the form of code-sharing agreements that permit the commuter airline to operate under the major's two-letter designator, becoming a Delta Connection, Northwest Express, American Eagle, United Express, USAir Express, or other trade-named feeder. The contracts also provide for joint fare arrangements that give the commuter carrier a portion of the national or major's long-haul fare to compensate for the fact that feeder fares are lower than commuter O&D fares. The joint fares are equitable for the major carrier because the feeder arrangements make possible flights that otherwise could not be filled, as Piedmont Airlines was one of the first to recognize. When Piedmont decided to fly non-stop from Charlotte to San Francisco, there were many who scoffed. "Charlotte," they said, "is not a big enough city to support such a flight." "True enough," Piedmont said, "but it is not Charlotte alone that is filling up these airplanes; it is Charlotte PLUS all the little towns from which our feeders are bringing us passengers." Piedmont turned out to be correct.

The major-regional relationship has been an important contributing factor in the rapid growth of the regional/commuter airline industry. The major airlines also could be the best reason why the commuter airline industry will not go away: Such airline companies as Texas Air and AMR have substantial investments in regional/commuter airlines and have shown a willingness to recognize that the true value of their feeder networks is the protection they give against damaging incursions by other large airlines at hubs which they control. (The profits these small feeders are able to generate are negligible in the whole income picture for an AMR/American, and sometimes are non-existent.) According to Regional Airline Management Systems of Golden, Colo., nearly every jet carrier in the United States has now built its entire foundation and staked its future on the operation of its hubs.

Pilot Qualifications

Commuter pilots come from all areas of aviation and have a diversified flying background. Their flight experience ranges from 500 hours and a minimum of multi-engine time to over 19,000 hours, most of which is multi-engine time. Of the regional airline pilots hired in 1988, 58 percent had the ATP license, 82.3 percent had a general aviation background, and 59 percent had a four-year college degree; the average total flight time was 3,142 hours (277 hours in jets and 571 hours in turboprops). Ages ranged from 20 to 53, with the average age being 32.

Company pilot requirements are as different as the flight crew members themselves. Some commuters will hire copilots with fairly low time and upgrade them as they build their experience in company aircraft; other commuters have pilot qualifications that are more rigid. Usually, commuter airlines hire copilots who are sufficiently skilled to upgrade to captain in a short time. The reason for the rapid advancement is a combination of rapid company expansion and the drain on the pilot force from hiring by major and national airlines. The expansion and attrition rates for regional/commuter airlines are so high that these carriers do not have the luxury of letting their flight crews build time with them; yet, during the industry expansion of the late 1980s, they increasingly were faced with the costly necessity of training pilots to fly their equipment.

Insurance restrictions greatly influence hiring criteria, and minimum qualifications are usually determined by the guidelines set by the insurance carrier. Most commuter airlines are reluctant to hire pilots with qualifications below the insurance company's requirements because the company could end up having to pay increased insurance premiums. On the other hand, in order to attract and retain highly qualified pilots, the commuter airlines find that they must offer salaries that are competitive among all companies industry-wide and may be higher than they can afford to pay.

Most recently, there has been an exception to the insurance restrictions under which certain waivers are issued for hiring pilots with lower qualifications but who have a training background of known excellence. For example, FlightSafety International graduates receive lower insurance rates, and students graduating from an ab initio program also might get lower insurance rates. These waivers have a limited value for the airlines. Even though commuter airlines could reap some insurance benefits by hiring newly trained pilots who have graduated from well-known flight schools, these pilots could never comprise the majority hired. Because of their low flight time, chances are that when the opportunity came to upgrade, they would not meet the 1,500-hour flight time requirement for the ATP license. Therefore, the company would end up with pilots who could not fill its captains' seats. Companies that hire recent flight school graduates will probably do so in small numbers, and these pilots will be a part of the mix of low- and high-time line pilots.

To be qualified to fly for a commuter airline, you should get as much total flight time, pilot-in-command time and multi-engine time as possible.

The ATP certificate is a critical rating to have. Like the major carriers, many commuter airlines will hire pilots without it, but until you qualify for and receive your ATP, you will be unable to fly as a captain and build pilot-in-command time. If a company flies single-pilot flight operations, an ATP is mandatory. Also, some companies hire pilots as captains, not as first officers. Thus, an ATP could mean money in your pocket immediately.

Many commuters shy away from hiring pilots with a flight engineer rating or FE written exam because pilots with this license are qualified to fly for a major airline and are likely to leave the commuter soon for a job with a major carrier. When the cost of interviewing and training is considered, few commuters can afford such a loss. As a result, discussing such qualifications with prospective regional/commuter employers may not be in your best interests.

Another pilot qualification that is becoming increasingly important is a college education. At this time, a degree is not usually necessary, and most commuters will hire pilots without it. However, with many companies acquiring more sophisticated aircraft, the trend toward requiring higher education levels for pilot applicants is growing. As an executive with a commuter airline remarked, "We're looking for a person who's not afraid of work and study"; one gauge of the pilot's work and study habits, he noted, is educational track record.

The Schedule

Pilots for commuters can expect to do a lot of flying under current regulations. The number of days per month you can expect to fly, as well as the number of hours per month, varies greatly among companies. Some of the factors that affect this are the type of flying (scheduled passenger runs or charters), union contracts, and work rule agreements. Hours per month may range from around 60 to 75 up to 110 to 120. As of mid-1989, FAR Part 135.265 restricted a commuter or regional airline pilot flying under Part 135 to a maximum of 120 hours of flight per month or 1,200 hours a year (34 hours within any seven-day period), while under Part 121,* a pilot was restricted to a maximum of 100 hours a month or 1,000 hours a year of flight time. A new-hire also may expect to be on reserve as long as he or she is in the bottom 20 to 25 percent of the seniority list, much as with the large carriers.

The Pay

Improvements in pay and benefits are occurring as the smaller companies seek to slow the exodus of pilots to the major airlines. As a company matures and grows, its pay and benefits improve.

Pay varies with the type of agreement the pilots have with the company. Some have

---

* FAR Part 135 includes a number of smaller operations (air taxi, U.S. mail), but the primary distinction between Parts 135 and 121 for commercial air transport purposes is that a Part 135 operator is limited to using aircraft with a maximum capacity of 30 seats or a maximum payload of 7,500 pounds. If an operator wishes to use larger aircraft, it must qualify under the more stringent Part 121 rules. (Data taken from 1989 FARs.)

a base pay plus a set amount per hour. Some have a guaranteed base or the total of the pay per hour, whichever is greater. Others are paid on a weekly or monthly rate. Generally, as with all jobs, the larger the company and equipment, the higher the pay. The chart below shows the average salary according to position and aircraft.

AVERAGE SALARY, COMMUTER PILOT				
	Start Salary (annually)	2nd Year (annually)	10th Year (annually)	Max/Capt. (annually)
Average	$14,664	$19,740	$34,320	$34,320+
Low End	$ 8,400	$11,700	$19,200	$19,200+
High End	$24,996	$31,800	$57,480	$57,480+

Seniority

Seniority systems vary among commuters. These systems generally fall into two categories. The first is almost identical to the one described for the major carriers. The second depends more on your qualifications and the company's hiring practices.

At a company that establishes seniority on the basis of qualifications, if you are hired into a captain's position, you may immediately be senior to all the first officers without working your way up, or you may fly as a junior captain until your overall seniority allows you to move up the captain's step system. If hired as a first officer, you may move up to captain ahead of first officers hired earlier if you meet the experience or qualification requirements for captain before they do.

In other words, this second category of seniority system applies to all captains as a separate group and all first officers as a separate group, but not to all pilots as a whole.

Training

Initial training consists of three to four weeks of ground school with written tests, oral exams, and actual aircraft flying with a check airman (instructor pilot). The length of training varies among companies. Most regional/commuter carriers have not made simulator training part of their programs, but some do, and as the number of available simulators grows (at such training centers as those of FlightSafety International), so do the number of airlines offering simulator training. All companies must conduct recurrent training: every 12 months for both captains and first officers, with proficiency checks coming every six months for captains and once a year for first officers.

When you are upgrading to the captain's position on the same aircraft you have been flying, training will consist of three to four days of ground school and an aircraft oral exam and check ride with an FAA or company check airman.

For upgrading to captain or transitioning to new aircraft, training will be the same length as initial training: two to three weeks of ground school and tests, actual aircraft experience, and an oral exam and check ride with an FAA or company check airman.

Advancement Opportunities

By virtue of the rapid growth and 50 percent attrition rate, upgrades to captain and larger (or, at least, different) aircraft are possible within the first year at many commuter airlines.

Among the major/regional airline networks, a new "farm club" concept has been established. Pan Am and Pan Am Express (owned by Pan Am) and Northwest and Express Airlines I (a subsidiary of Atlanta-based Phoenix Airline Services, Inc.) were the first carriers to institute the farm club concept. Continental was not far behind in establishing the same system with Britt Airways and Rocky Mountain Airways (both owned by Continental's parent company, Texas Air). With these companies, a pilot flying for the commuter network has the opportunity to move up to fly for the major carrier.

The concept of the farm club is new and its future uncertain. As the consolidation period of deregulation comes to an end, more and more companies can be expected to implement this concept. Its purpose is to encourage younger pilots to consider the regional airlines as a step along a complete career path leading to a job with a major airline. The effect of this concept could be slower, more controlled attrition and less opportunity for quick upgrades.

Furloughs

Like major airline pilots, commuter pilots may be furloughed or laid off depending on the needs of the company. These needs are affected by the economy, the financial condition of the company, the addition or subtraction of aircraft, and the viability of the major airline with which a commuter or regional carrier has a code-sharing feeder agreement. (A regional airline that had to furlough pilots because of problems encountered by its major airline partner was Eastern Metro Express in 1989. All of Eastern Airlines' unions struck the carrier, forcing it into Chapter 11 reorganization. The sudden suspension of the vast bulk of Eastern's operations dealt a serious blow to Eastern Metro Express, which saw most of its business evaporate overnight.)

If your pilot group is represented by a union, you will be furloughed, as opposed to being laid off. This means you will retain your seniority number for a specified time period, and when the company needs pilots again, you will be recalled in order of your seniority. Some non-union commuters offer these rights to their pilots, too.

With most non-union companies, you will be laid off, as opposed to being furloughed. This means that the job does not have to be offered to you when it again becomes available. If it is offered, you will be rehired with a new, higher seniority number (the higher the number, the lower the pilot on the seniority pecking order).

Bases for Turbojet Airlines

Airlines	Anchorage, AK	Appleton, WI	Atlantic City, NJ	Austin, TX	Boise, ID	Boston	Bradley, CT	Bridgeport, CT	Carlsbad, CA	Chicago, IL	Dallas, TX	Dayton, OH	Denver, CO	Detroit	Elco, NY	Ft. Lauderdale	Ft. Wayne, IN	Groton, CT	Guam	Honolulu	Indianapolis	Jacksonville, FL	Kansas City
Airlift Int'l																							
Aspen Airways													●										
Buffalo Airways																							
Business Express						●	●	●										●					
Challenge Int'l																							
Emerald Air			●	●																			
Express One											●												
Five Star						●																	
Flight Int'l									●													●	
Florida Express																							
Global Int'l																							●
Gulf Air						●				●				●									
Horizon Air					●																		
Interstate						●																	
Key Airlines																							
Lockheed																							
Markair	●																						
Mid Pacific																			●	●			
Midwest Express		●																					
Orion Air												●											
Presidential																							
Reeve Aleutian	●																						
Rich Int'l																							
Rosenbalm												●	●			●	●						
Royal West																							
Ryan Int'l												●											
Skyworld													●										
Southern Air Tpt.																	●						
Spirit of America												●		●							●		
Suncoast																●							
Sun Country																							
Sunworld Int'l																							
Tower Air																							
Agro Air																							

	Kelly AFB, TX	Las Vegas	Los Angeles	Louisville, KY	Miami	Milwaukee	Minneapolis	Naples, FL	Newport News, VA	New York	Oakland, CA	Ontario, CA	Orlando, FL	Pago Pago	Philadelphia	Portland, OR	Sacramento, CA	Salt Lake City	San Diego	San Francisco	Saudi Arabia	St. Louis	Tuscon, AZ	Washington, DC	**Airlines**
					●																				Airlift Int'l
																									Aspen Airways
																●									Buffalo Airways
																									Business Express
					●																				Challenge Int'l
																									Emerald Air
																									Express One
																									Five Star
								●	●																Flight Int'l
													●												Florida Express
																									Global Int'l
															●						●				Gulf Air
																●									Horizon Air
	●			●						●	●														Interstate
		●																						●	Key Airlines
																				●					Lockheed
																									Markair
																									Mid Pacific
						●																			Midwest Express
			●									●													Orion Air
																								●	Presidential
																									Reeve Aleutian
				●																					Rich Int'l
			●									●				●		●	●	●			●		Rosenbalm
		●																							Royal West
			●																						Ryan Int'l
																		●							Skyworld
				●													●								Southern Air Tpt.
																									Spirit of America
																									Suncoast
							●																		Sun Country
		●																							Sunworld Int'l
										●															Tower Air
				●																					Agro Air

Probation

Commuter probation varies from three months to a year, depending on the company. Normally during this period the pay will be lower, and you may not receive full company benefits or union protection.

Domicile

Companies establish official domiciles or bases for all pilots. Your domicile is the city where your trips begin and end. The company will expect you to report at a specified time before departure (usually one hour), do a professional job, and represent the company well.

Commuting

Major airline pilots often are able to commute to work while living in a city other than the one in which they are based.

Commuter pilots usually are unable to do this because of the smaller size of their company's route system (in comparison to larger carriers) or because of company regulations that require pilots to live within a specified distance of the domicile (sometimes a pilot must live within so many minutes or hours of the airport). Sometimes, commuter pilots are able to fly to domicile using their privileges with the major airline partner of the company for which they work.

Unions

Not all commuters have unions. Some commuters have an in-house union or pilot association, but these are not nationally affiliated organizations. ALPA is a national organization and at mid-1989 represented approximately 20 commuter airlines. ALPA representation has been expanding rapidly as ALPA efforts to organize the regional airline industry continue. Some commuters have no organization to represent the pilots as a group.

Employee Benefits

1. *Medical & Dental.* Medical and dental benefits will vary. Some companies will offer packages almost identical to those of the major carriers. Much of this is dependent on the size of the company and whether or not it has a union contract.

2. *Retirement.* About half of all commuter airlines offer a retirement program, the most common being a 401(k). A 401(k) program is a retirement plan in which the employee and, usually, the employer contribute to a fund. [See Chapter 5 for explanation of 401(k) funds.]

3. *Stock Option/Profit Sharing.* A majority of commuter airlines offer stock option or profit-sharing programs, or both.

4. *Travel.* Most commuter airlines have pass privileges for employees and their families on the company aircraft. Company-issued passes generally are free. Some companies do charge, but the charge is minimal: either 25 percent of the full fare or a flat rate, e.g., $45 per ticket. The majority of the commuter companies have jump seat privileges for their pilots. Many also have reduced-fare agreements with other companies, including major carriers, especially the major airlines with which they are affiliated. Most interline agreements will enable you to buy tickets for 90 percent, 75 percent or 50 percent less than the normal full ticket fare by showing your company ID at the ticket counter.

Loss-of-License Insurance

This insurance, which pays you a lump sum or annuity monthly payment if you lose your FAA medical certificate, may not be available to you through your company if you are a commuter pilot. Some regional/commuter airlines are starting to provide this coverage for their pilots, but more often the insurance must be purchased by the pilot, not the company.

Chapter 7
THE CORPORATE FLYING JOB

An estimated 10,000 pilots fly cabin class twins or larger.

The equipment involved in corporate flying encompasses a wider range of aircraft than that perhaps of any other segment of the aviation industry. A corporate airplane may be a Cessna 172; it may be a B-727. Although the corporate segment of aviation does include single-engine aircraft operations, this chapter will be addressed primarily to flight operations using at least a cabin class twin or helicopters.

When considered against the goal of gaining valuable overall flight time, the amount of flying available in the corporate segment is very limited. Corporate pilots accumulate flight time slowly: The average monthly flight time accrual is 20 to 30 hours.

When major airlines are hiring, there are more corporate positions open than normal since many corporate pilots are hired by the airlines, leaving vacancies in corporate flight departments. Yet the corporate field is hard to penetrate simply because it is a system that operates through a close-knit network. Usually, openings for corporate flying jobs are not advertised. Generally, a pilot is hired upon referral by another pilot.

Corporate pilots have varied backgrounds. Some pilots have come from the military, while others have come up through the civilian ranks. In many cases, getting the job is more "Who do you know?" or being in the right place at the right time than just meeting the minimum requirements. Most corporations prefer experience in the aircraft they fly, but this does not exclude a pilot from being hired if he does not have the experience. Personality and knowing the right people can overcome some lack of experience.

Being hired by a Fortune 500 company often is more difficult to accomplish than being hired by a major airline. Mailing lists of corporate operators are sold in most aviation publications, creating a tremendous flow of resumes and letters. The companies cannot handle the flow of paper, so by and large, it is ignored. In most cases, corporations prefer to hire people already living in the area where the flight department is based; management has less fear of losing such individuals to other corporate flight departments or to an airline.

With respect to attracting and retaining pilots, corporate job conditions play an important role in a pilot's making a career as a corporate aviator. Those items important to an airline pilot may not be as important to the corporate pilot (e.g., pass privileges). The corporate pilot's lifestyle is different, and this job may not be for everybody. It does, however, offer some interesting opportunities that appeal more to some people than does airline flying.

Qualifications

Although a commercial license with an instrument and multi-engine rating is all that the FAA requires, an ATP is generally preferred by most corporate operations. As with most types of flying, the more ratings, the better. Most corporations also prefer a type rating in a large jet or turboprop aircraft, especially if they are flying jet equipment. Corporations tend to shy away from pilots with Flight Engineer written exams or ratings because of the possibility that they may leave for an airline when the chance comes.

The Schedule

Some corporate flight departments are operated similarly to the flight operations of small airlines. They have a number of scheduled routes, with only a few unscheduled flights in relation to normal total flying per month. The pilots have scheduled flights and scheduled days off. They also are rotated through "on call" or "reserve" for those last-minute, unscheduled trips that occasionally come up.

On the other hand, most corporate operations have very few prescheduled trips. If you fly for one of them, you will remain on call during most of the month. Scheduled days off are fewer and more difficult to arrange. This does not mean you will fly every day, but being on standby does restrict your activities. Usually, the bigger the flight department, the closer the scheduling is to that of an airline.

Since corporate flight operations are run on a businessman's schedule, layovers are few. In most cases, a pilot is home every night, and flying on holidays is rare. A corporate pilot usually can expect more waiting time at the destination. If company executives are flown in for a meeting, a pilot may be expected to wait for hours until the meeting adjourns and the executives are off to another meeting or returning home.

Occasionally, some of these waiting periods may turn into company-paid vacations. If there is an extended meeting (say two or three days) and there is room on the plane, the corporation may allow you to bring your spouse along. Once you arrive and the plane is parked, you are given a time for the return flight and then released for the rest of the time to enjoy yourself. Although not all companies do this, it is a nice benefit when available.

The Pay

This varies as widely as the type of equipment flown and the area of the country in which the flight department is headquartered. Generally, the pay is highest in the Northeast and lowest in the Southeast and matches the cost of living in each area.

Seniority

Although most corporations have a seniority system, it usually is not as rigidly followed as the systems at airlines. Promotion usually is based on merit, not seniority.

Corporate Pilot Pay

Jet:Captain	Average '87 W2 Wages	'87 Wage Range 1000's	Average '88 W2 Wage
Gulfstream 2/3	61,645	40-85K	67,150
Falcon 900/50	56,750	42-67K	61,125
Canadair Challenger 600/601	67,095	56-86K	76,135
Lockheed JetStar	66,900	48-79K	72,125
Falcon 200/20	49,487	26-80K	53,480
BAe 125-400/-600/-700/-800	53,667	44-68K	59,332
Cessna Citation 3	53,389	39-79K	56,600
Lear 55	50,135	25-67K	53,244
Falcon 100/10	47,840	30-63K	49,600
IAI Westwind 1/2	44,606	30-67K	51,271
Lear 35/36	46,792	30-75K	48,263
Lear 23/24/25	31,333	22-40K	34.820
Cessna Citation 1/2	47,575	33-89K	52,125
Sabreliner	53,778	39-89K	56,712

Jet: Co-Pilot	Average '87 W2 Wages	'87 Wage Range 1000's	Average '88 W2 Wages
Gulfstream 2/3	48,160	36-60K	50,362
Falcon 900/50	43,000	43K	49,100
Canadair Challenger 600/601	38,300	37-40K	42,230
Lockheed JetStar	40,800	37-45K	45,100
Falcon 200/20	39,500	37-42K	42,650
BAe 125-400/-600/-700/-800	38,800	32-52K	46,966
Lear 55	42,500	43K	47,500
Falcon 100/10	35,267	24-56K	36,970
IAI Westwind 1/2	35,000	31-37K	37,800
Lear 35/36	29,220	17-60K	33,710
Beechjet/Diamond	25,767	21-32K	N/A
Cessna Citation 1/2	30,647	20-45K	32,133
Sabreliner	37,800	24-60K	40,125

Corporate Pilot Pay

Turboprop: Captain	Average '87 W2 Wages	'87 Wage Range 1000's
Fokker F27	49,333	38-57K
Gulfstream I	41,625	23-51K
Fairchild Merlin 300	33,000	27-35K
Beech King Air 300/200/100	38,588	24-65K
Piper Cheyenne 3/2/1	29,950	20-36K
Beech King Air 90	35,999	26-47K
Gulfstream Turbo Commander	37,333	32-45K
Cessna Conquest 2/1	33,750	25-42K
Mitsubishi MU2	27,580	19-36K

Turboprop: Co-Pilot	Average '87 W2 Wages	'87 Wage Range 1000's
Beech King Air 300/200/100	28,167	21-34K
Mitsubishi MU2	19,500	17-22K

Corporate Pilot Pay

Reciprocating: Captain	Average '87 W2 Wages	'87 Wage Range 1000's
Mojave/Chieftan	42,000	42K
Cessna 401/402/404	32,233	30-36K
Beech Baron	30,000	30K
Cessna 305/310/337	44,500	42-47K
Piper Aztec	25,600	26K
Single Engine	28,500	23-45K

Helicopters: Captain	Average '87 W2 Wages	'87 Wage Range 1000's
Sikorsky S76	49,117	44-55K
Bell 222	32,000	32K
MBB BK117	25,000	25K
Agusta 109	35,000	35K
MBB BO105	41,000	41K
Bell 206	39,748	26-60K
Aerospatiale AS350	38,000	25-57K
Hughes 500	30,500	21-40K

* Printed with permission from the April, 1988 issue of *Professional Pilot* magazine. The complete 1988 Salary Guidelines may be ordered by sending $5.00 to: Professional Pilot, 3014 Colvin Street, Alexandria, VA 22314.

Advancement Opportunities

Upgrade in seat position and aircraft once again depends on the size and needs of the company. The larger the department, the more its upgrade policies will tend to parallel those of a major airline, where all pilots are upgraded according to seniority.

Some companies will require their pilots to fly as first officer on all fleet aircraft before being upgraded to captain. Other companies qualify all their pilots as captain, but only a few pilots will actually fly the position. Then again, a pilot may be captain-qualified on some of the company aircraft and first officer-qualified on the rest.

In corporate aviation, being pilot-in-command is not necessarily the premier job sought by line pilots. Most career corporate pilots aspire to achieve such administrative positions as chief pilot or director of flight operations.

With many corporations, being a pilot will not be your only full-time duty. Corporate pilots usually have to perform additional, non-flying duties, such as keeping the aircraft clean and supplied with whatever the executives desire. Companies that do not hire flight attendants may expect you to act in this capacity. Your duties may include getting the coffee, doughnuts, meals, drinks, newspapers, magazines, etc. And your company may expect you to fill a corporate position as aviation department manager as well as fly the aircraft. Some pilots also have to be aircraft mechanics or supervise maintenance performed by others.

Many corporations allow pilots to cross-train out of flying into non-aviation-related fields if they are qualified and so desire.

Probation

This period varies among companies but usually ranges from three months to a year.

Domiciles

Companies establish official bases for all pilots. Your base is the city or airport where your trips will begin and end. It may or may not be at the corporate headquarters. Many corporate flight departments are in different states from the company headquarters.

Most companies will require that you live within a certain distance from the base. This distance usually is measured by time (most commonly one hour). The company will expect you to report on time, so it is best to leave yourself plenty of room for the unexpected, such as bad weather, car problems, etc.

Unions

Most corporate pilots are not represented by unions.

Employee Benefits

1. *Medical & Dental.* Most corporations provide major medical insurance, but only about half offer dental insurance. There is usually a life insurance policy that goes along with the medical benefits. Any potential employer should be asked about these items.

2. *Retirement.* Many of the big corporations (Coca Cola, Southern Bell, etc.) offer a complete benefits package, including retirement programs.

3. *Profit Sharing & Stock Options.* Whether a company offers a stock option or profit sharing will vary. Many of the larger corporations offer these benefits to their employees. Such programs are a chance for the pilot to share in the profits of the corporation and buy a limited number of stock shares, usually below their market value.

4. *Travel.* Space-available travel on company aircraft is offered to you and your family by many corporations. Restrictions vary greatly, so you will have to determine what is available from a company for which you are interested in flying. Corporate flight departments do not have interline agreements with commercial airlines, so reduced-rate travel on airlines is not possible. Likewise, corporations do not maintain jump seat privileges for pilots traveling on scheduled air carriers.

5. *Loss-of-License Insurance.* This insurance pays you a specified amount of money (either in a lump sum or in a monthly payment) if you cannot maintain a Class I or II medical. It is available through a limited number of insurance companies. Corporations usually do not pay for this coverage.

   One disadvantage of this type of insurance is that it will not pay if you are unable to pass the company physical but still are able to pass a Class I or II medical.

Other Factors

Knowing corporate executives can be either good or bad depending on your job performance and ability to "get along with the brass." As a corporate pilot, you may have more contact with the top executives in the company than do most of the people in the field, and this can work to your advantage.

Chapter 8
HELICOPTER AND OTHER FLYING JOBS

With recent advances in technology, the helicopter segment of the aviation industry is expected to expand rapidly. These aircraft are being used more and more for corporate transport and have a future in commuter airline operations; they are used heavily by the oil, timber and agriculture industries. The new helicopters are capable of single-pilot, IFR operations and have cruise speeds in the 200 mph range. Late-1980s programs expected to expand the role of rotor equipment considerably were the military and civilian developments of a tilt-rotor aircraft. This machine is able to combine the hovering capability and vertical takeoffs and landings of helicopters with the horizontal flight of airplanes and can reach cruise speeds of close to 300 mph.

Advances in mechanical monitoring of helicopters are reducing maintenance costs significantly, and this development also is helping to expand the role of these aircraft.

A large number of currently employed helicopter pilots came from the military; most were trained by the Army during the Vietnam conflict. These pilots had 1,100 to 1,200 hours of rotary time, mostly turbine, when they separated. Since the end of the conflict, the number of military pilots available has greatly decreased.

Qualifications

Pilots who wish to fly helicopters professionally have two options other than the military in order to become qualified. The first option is to obtain private and then commercial ratings, then find employment and build time flying as an instructor, flying charters, etc. One point to consider is that it is cheaper to get the fixed-wing rating first and then add the helicopter rating. The same hours and experience requirements that apply to fixed-wing operations hold true for helicopter operations except that you do not need the instrument rating for the helicopter ATP.

For pilots who already have fixed-wing ratings, an additional rating can be obtained by getting instruction in a helicopter and passing a check ride. However, many companies require a minimum number of hours in both helicopters and the aircraft type used by the company, in addition to the total flight time minimum.

While many companies require only the commercial and instrument ratings, additional ratings are preferred. Depending on the operation, an ATP may be required.

Unlike many airplane operations, a bonus is paid for additional ratings. For example, base pay may be calculated on a pilot's having a commercial license. Bonuses are paid for instrument, instructor, and mechanic's ratings. Additional bonuses may be paid for an ATP and for a set number of hours in a specific aircraft.

Aspects of the Helicopter Flying Job

In the past the offshore segment of the industry (flying for the oil producers, e.g., Exxon, Mobil, British Petroleum) provided most of the helicopter flying jobs. With most of these operations, you will have a set schedule (two weeks on duty and two weeks off is common). Almost all the captains have an IFR (or instruments) rating. Flying time runs approximately 50 hours per month. Depending on the operation, pay can be very good or rather mediocre, e.g., flying duty for North Sea oil rigs has high pay commensurate with the hazardous duty.

In agricultural flying, the job is dependent on the crops. The work increases as the crops start growing and decreases during the harvest. It is not unusual for an agriculture pilot to be out of work during the winter months or to work in different geographic regions.

Agricultural flying also can mean a lot of travel — following the crops as the growing season progresses. Since many pilots are independent, they must find a new job each season. Stability is not one of the attributes of this type of flying.

Good news for helicopter pilots is that more corporations are utilizing helicopters for executive business flights, in some cases simply as a shuttle from the company's landing pad to the airport, in others as a way to avoid airport congestion completely.

Another source of jobs for helicopter pilots is with metropolitan police forces. In these positions, you must not only be well-qualified, but must also become a police officer. If you do not make it through police training, you lose the job regardless of your piloting qualifications.

Other opportunities flying helicopters can be found in news and traffic reporting, aerial photography/photomapping, pipeline patrol and aerial sightseeing tours. The TV news job is a glamorous one and often pays quite well, but you will have to learn to be a good newscaster as well as an aviator.

As avionics and systems of helicopters have developed so that they parallel the glass cockpits of airliners, the accomplished helicopter pilot has looked more attractive to airlines (by late 1989, American, Continental and Eastern all had tentatively begun taking a new look at the helicopter pilot). The best route from helicopter flying to a major or national airline remains that of acquiring a fixed-wing multi-engine rating, getting hired by a commuter airline, and building at least 500 hours of multi-engine time.

Employee Benefits

Pay for helicopter pilots may range from $10,000 to $60,000 per year, depending on the equipment flown and the type of operations. Pay for flying turbine equipment generally starts in the $16,000 to 18,000-per-year range.

Seniority, furloughs, probationary periods, domiciles, unions, and benefits are dependent on the operation you are flying for and are as varied as the number of corporations and companies that hire helicopter pilots. If you are considering taking a job with a helicopter operator, you should discuss these things with the chief pilot or the other line pilots before signing a contract.

AVERAGE SALARY, HELICOPTER PILOTS				
	Start Salary (annually)	2nd Year (annually)	10th Year (annually)	Max/Capt. (annually)
Average	$24,888	$28,608	$38,328	$38,328+
Low End	$13,560	$18,000	$27,600	$27,600+
High End	$33,000	$50,400	$60,000	$60,000+

Other Opportunities in the Aviation Market

1. *Start-Up and "Upstart" Airlines.* A start-up airline is any new airline. The term "upstart" came into vogue in the early years of deregulation when such start-up carriers as People Express and New York Air had an immediate competitive impact on the pricing of airline fares and on the contest for market share.

   At start-up airlines, the potential for rapid growth and mergers is excellent, and pay and benefits usually improve as an airline matures. The emerging airlines, however, are risky. People Express, New York Air, Air Atlanta and several other start-ups have perished or have been folded into larger airlines. Other start-ups, notably Midway and America West, have turned into thriving carriers. It is predicted by many that after the consolidation phase of deregulation, only 20 percent of the start-ups from the first 10 years of deregulation will survive.

2. *FBOs with Package Feed Operations.* This field is a seldom-noticed result of deregulation. Fixed-base operations, which frequently have a very stable, experienced mechanic corps, have proved better able than regional/commuter airlines to meet the 100 percent reliability demands of large cargo/package operations like Federal Express, Flying Tigers, DHL and Airborne. Today, most of the feed carriers to major cargo companies are former FBOs that have evolved into large, workable, knowledgeable companies and have been working with the majors and nationals for a number of years.

   An example of a flourishing small package feeder is Mid-Atlantic Freight, a division of Atlantic Aero, an FBO based at Greensboro Triad International Airport in North Carolina. Another is Murray Aviation, based at Ypsilanti, Mich., which flies CASA 212s, MU-2s and Learjets while serving not only such overnight package operations as DHL and UPS, but Ford, General Motors and Chrysler (carrying automotive parts) and several air freight forwarders. An operation like Mid-Atlantic Freight, which now flies coast to coast into various hubs, might not be attractive to a pilot planning to move on to a major airline because it operates only the Cessna Caravan, a single-engine turboprop (if you have major airline ambitions, you need multi-engine time). But several of the cargo feed operations fly aircraft that could help pave your way to a major airline. And even though its feeders use the Caravan, Federal Express has hired a number of pilots from its small package feed partners.

3. *Overseas Flying.* There are a growing number of opportunities in the overseas market; however, several factors should be considered. In most cases, foreign air carriers will require that you have wide-body experience and/or type rating in the aircraft they operate (e.g., B-747, B-727, L-1011 and DC-10). If you are employed as a co-pilot, you may receive your type rating outside the United States. However, the opportunity to be upgraded or fly larger equipment may be limited. Captains and professional flight engineers (PFEs)* in transport jets, especially wide-bodies, are in great demand.

Opportunities are expected to improve due to the upcoming deregulation of the European airline industry in 1992. This will result in expansion throughout Europe, and the expansion which began in the late 1980s throughout the Pacific Rim will accelerate in the 1990s. Both regions lack an established supply of military and general aviation pilots. Since the United States has the largest pool of pilots, it is expected that Europe will draw from the U.S. pilot supply to meet its short-term needs and possibly its long-term needs as well.

Usually, flying for foreign carriers is considered to be contract work with few or no employee benefits and especially no retirement. Pay, however, was rising rapidly in the late 1980s. There used to be tax advantages in working outside the United States for a foreign employer, but new tax laws limit tax-free income to $70,000.

Job security is another aspect to be considered. You may be forced to return to the U.S. market during hard times when no alternate jobs are open. The most important factor: While away, you will lose touch with the U.S. airline market.

Flight/Simulator Training

General aviation-based training was very slow from 1985 to 1988, but is gradually improving. Simulator training companies like FlightSafety and Simuflite are expanding and profitable. Both of these firms vastly increased their training capabilities during a rapid expansion period of the late 1980s. So far the overall number of jobs is small, but it is growing.

---

* PFE or Professional Flight Engineer. This is a profession separate from piloting; a PFE is not allowed to advance to a pilot seat, and PFEs have their own unions, seniority systems, etc. A PFE at a major airline is required to have both a full FE Turbojet rating and an Airframe & Powerplant mechanic's license.

Chapter 9
EDUCATION, TRAINING, RATINGS, EXPERIENCE

Two primary educational and training routes are open to the pilot: civilian or military.

Let's assume for the moment that your career goal is a seat with a major airline. What are your options for education, training and experience?

Such airlines as Delta, American and Northwest still prefer military pilots and hire primarily from the pool of ex-military aviators. Even so, you should opt for flying with a branch of the military only if you desire a military career as such. The military flying option is a slower route to the major airlines today. If you want to be a military pilot, fine; if what you want is to be an airline pilot, you can get there quicker as a civilian — and quick is good. It locks up your seniority position sooner.

With thousands of civilian-trained airline pilots having proved the worth of civilian career channels, some airline recruiters actually prefer the flexibility of civil aviation. If a civilian candidate is offered a job, two-weeks notice can be given to the current employer, whereas a military pilot must complete his service obligation. The biggest factor, however, is supply and demand: The supply of pilots separating from military service cannot keep pace with commercial pilot demand; pilots with civil flying backgrounds are now filling the majority of openings with major airlines.

Those civil backgrounds are highly varied. There are numerous avenues to a seat with a major airline.

Ab Initio Programs

Airline managements responded in the late 1980s to a weakening of the pool of quality airline pilot candidates by fostering "farm programs," "track systems," *ab initio* programs, and "transition" training curricula. All such plans recognized that large numbers of pilot backgrounds were inadequate for airline flying. They started from the premise that a pilot candidate needed to be brought from some Point A to the Point B of "airline-qualified."

Ab initio is Latin for "from the beginning." The ab initio program trains the zero-time pilot aspirant, taking the individual through an intensive and comprehensive regi-

Financial Aid Programs

A four-year college degree is not an absolute "must" to be hired by a major airline or some other prime employer, but you should regard it as one of the big guns you need before commencing your job hunt in earnest.

As the listings beginning on page 87 show, large numbers of two- and four-year colleges and universities are offering special programs designed to help a future pilot prepare for a flying career. Quite a number of these schools have demonstrated an aggressive commitment to aviation training.

If you are preparing to begin your education, write or call any of the dozens of colleges offering aviation programs and ask for the complete brochure or package that the college offers, including its catalogue. After selecting a few that seem to fit your needs, visit the schools that interest you most. You need the visits to get a good idea of the facilities, atmosphere, staff, physical layout, equipment and general personality of the institutions you are considering.

The best indication of a school's commitment to aviation is its flight department. If the flight department is well-equipped, with simulators, recent-vintage aircraft, a plentiful fleet relative to the size of the student body, a good-sized instruction staff, an apparently fine maintenance program, and good marks from the FAA, you can be fairly well assured that your money and time will not be wasted there.

The local Flight Standards Office of the FAA, which has to inspect and oversee any FAA-approved school, can be of great help in evaluating a flight department.

Things to check for: good simulators, a provision for plenty of ground time with instructors, ample work space, a good dispatch department, single- and multi-engine aircraft for advanced training, and reasonable access to facilities that assist with instrument flying. Ask around among professional aviators about the reputation of any school at which you are thinking of enrolling.

Having to fight for the attention of an under-staffed faculty or being obliged to use over-utilized equipment can make your pursuit of an education difficult. Make sure the school you choose is adequate in all respects.

Then decide.

But there may be one more hitch: money. The finer colleges and universities may cost you as much as $60,000 to $70,000 (or even more) for a full four-year degree with basic flight training. The least expensive of associate degrees (two-year) can top $25,000 after flight training fees have been added.

Don't despair. Financial aid is widely available for airline career candidates at all universities with aviation schools (for example, 85 percent of the students at Embry-Riddle Aeronautical University receive financial aid). Frequently given loans and grants include:

• The Federal Pell Grant Program from the Federal Department of Education (with no repayment required for this tuition and support money).

• The Student Secondary Education Opportunity Grant, administered on-campus (no repayment required).

• The Guaranteed Student Loan Program of the Federal Department of Education, handled through local lending institutions and state guarantee agencies (low interest, extended repayment period, e.g., $10,000 loan with 120 repayments).

• Perkins Loans, formerly called the National Direct Student Loan Program, administered on-campus (even lower interest, extended repayment period, e.g., $10,000 loan with 120 repayments).

• The Plus Loan Program, which assists those students who do not qualify under the Guaranteed Student Loan Program (it allows their parents to pursue the loan for them).

These five programs are explained in a United States Department of Education booklet, *The Student Guide: Five Federal Financial Aid Programs, '88-'89*. The booklet can be obtained from almost any college or university.

Some states have financial aid programs of their own, e.g., Colorado Student Incentive Grant (CSIG), Colorado Student Grant (CSG), Colorado Work-Study Program — Need (CWSN), Colorado Work-Study Program — No-need (CWSNN). Check these out with your state department of education.

Federal and state financial assistance programs are not the only assistance available to aviation students. There are a number of scholarships available specifically to students in an aviation-related major.

A partial listing of such aviation scholar-

ships, compiled by the University Aviation Association, is provided below, along with some eligibility criteria and contact names and addresses for those desiring to pursue these avenues of assistance.

Aviation students are encouraged to apply both for scholarships and for federal and state financial assistance programs in all cases in which they meet eligibility requirements.

Some colleges and universities may have scholarships of their own that are open specifically to aviation students. Contact the aviation department or financial aid office of each specific college to inquire about scholarship possibilities.

men that prepares him or her for airline flying. By the time an individual emerges from the program, he or she will be qualified to fly for a regional airline.

Ab initio programs did not start in the United States, but St. Louis, Mo.-based TWA was involved in one of the first, helping Saudia, the Arabian carrier, set up a pilot training program in which FlightSafety International also became involved. Several European airlines utilized ab initio programs before anyone in the United States decided to attempt similar training regimens on behalf of the U.S. airline industry. When the 1980s brought the first signs of a shortage of airline-qualified pilots, the airline community saw the need for a more reliable civilian way of producing qualified pilots than the haphazard situation then prevalent. What bothered many in airline management was that a candidate technically could have accumulated the ratings and experience necessary to fly for a turbojet airline — could even "look great on paper" — yet bomb out in the testing and interviews for an airline job. The quality line from candidate to candidate was erratic. The solution, some felt, was a learning environment that was controlled from the beginning by a major airline.

Early results of this thinking included: a joint project of Northwest Airlines and its sister company, Northwest Aerospace Training Corp. (NATCO), with the University of North Dakota "to create and operate an aviation training center to graduate airline-level pilots for future aviation requirements"; a less elaborate ab initio program involving United Airlines and Southern Illinois University at Carbondale; Eastern Airlines' Pilot Entry Program (PEP), a partnership between Eastern and colleges in Florida, Louisiana, Texas and Colorado, to provide "a defined career path to employment as a pilot with the major airlines"; and a program begun by several United Airlines captains in conjunction with AMR Training, also with the goal of producing full-blown airline pilots.

Typically, these programs predicate that the student will graduate from the university or college with approximately 300 hours of flying time, a Commercial Pilot Certificate with Instrument Pilot and Multi-Engine privileges, and the Flight Engineer

Schools Offering

Name	Address	Telephone	Degrees Offered	Cost
Anoka Ramsey Community College	11200 Mississippi Blvd. NW Coon Rapids, MN 55433	(612) 427-2600	AS, Applied Science *student must take some courses in-house	$30.50/credit hr. $15/registration $150/qtr.books& supplies
Bridgewater State College	Bridgewater, MA 02325	(508) 697-1200	Ph.D., Education & School Adm.	$80/credit hr. $45/registration (due to change)
CA State Univ. Dominguez Hills	1000 E. Victoria St. Carson, CA 90747	(213) 513-3743	MA, Arts of Humanities	$110/unit (30 units)
Central Michigan University	School of Extended Learning Rowe Hall Mt. Pleasant, MI 48859	(517) 774-3865	MA, Science & Administration	$146/credit hour
Columbia Union College	External Degree Dept. Flower Ave. Tacoma Park, MD 20012	(301) 891-4155	Bachelor of Arts	$117/ semester hr.
Dixie College	255 S. 700 East St. St. George, UT 84770	(801)673-4811	AS, Professional Flight, Prof. Flight Mgmt., Aviation Maintenance, Inflight Services	$380/resident $800/non-resident *student must take 2 qtrs. in-house
Embry-Riddle Aeronautical University	Dept. of Independent Studies 600 S. Clydemore Blvd. Daytona, FL 32114	(904) 239-6000	Bachelor, Professional Aeronautics, B.S. in Aviation Business Adm.	$130/semester hour
Embry-Riddle Aeronautical University	3200 N. Willow Creek Rd. Prescott, AZ 86301	(602) 776-3728	AS & BS, Professional Aeronautics, Aviation Business Adm.,	$130/credit hr. (does not include books)
Empire State College	2 Union Ave. Saratoga Springs, NY 12866	(518) 885-1763	Associate and Bachelor degrees in numerous fields	$693.50/quarter full-time $372.25/quarter half-time $47.35/hour
Goddard College	RR. 2, Box 235 Plainfield, VT 05667-9989	(802) 454-8311	MA, MPA, BA single flexible program, MA of Fine Arts	$2917/semester grad $6957/semester-residency $2613/undergrad
Nicholls State University	University Station Dept. Aeronautical & Life Science Technology Thibodaux, LA 70302	(504) 447-3386	AS, Aeronautical Science BS in related field while instructing	$800/semester (12+ hrs.) $18,000/2 yr. flt. training program

External Degree Programs

Name	Address	Telephone	Degrees Offered	Cost
Norwich University	Graduate Program Vermont College Montpelier, VT 05602	(802) 223-8750	MA, Arts	$7000/year
Nova University	3301 College Ave. Ft. Lauderdale, FL 33314	(305) 475-7300	Doctor of Education MA, Public Admin., Health Services	$18,000 total cost
St. Mary's College	2510 Park Ave. South Minneapolis, MN 55987	(612) 874-9877	MA, Human Development and Education	$175/credit
Syracuse Univ.	Independent Study Degree Program 610 E. Fayette St. Syracuse, NY 13244-6020	(315) 443-3284	BA in Liberal Studies, Business Admin., and Food Systems Mgmt; Masters in Business Admin. and Social Science, MA in Illustration and Design	$199 undergraduate $325graduate/credit hr.
Thomas A. Edison State College	101 W. State St. CN 545 Trenton, NJ 08625	(609) 984-1100	AS, Applied Science Tech. BS, Science	
Univ. of Oklahoma	Coll. of Liberal Studie 1700 ASP Ave. Norman, OK 73037	(405) 325-1061	Bachelors and Masters in Liberal Studies	In-state $3410 BA $1635 MA Out-of-state $6770 BA $3220 MA
University of the State of New York	Cultural Education Ctr. Albany, NY 12230	(518) 474-3703	Bachelors in Business Admin. and Nursing	$375 enrollment fee $200 maint. fee
W. Illinois Univ.	Non-Traditional Program #5 Horrabin Hall Macomb, IL 61455	(309) 298-1929	Bachelors of Arts	$66/semester hr.

Deferment Summary: Perkins Loans and GSL/PLUS/SLS

Deferment Condition	Perkins	GSL	PLUS	SLS
Study at a postsecondary school (half-time * deferments for GSL, PLUS, and SLS are allowed only if borrower has obtained a GSL, PLUS, or SLS for the same enrollment period§)	while at least half-time *	while full-time half-time *	while full-time £ or half-time *£Ω	while full-time £ or half-time *£
Study at a school operated by the Federal Government	no	while full-time	while full-time £	while full-time £
Study in an eligible graduate fellowship program, or a rehabilitation training program for the disabled	no	while full-time	while full-time £Ω	whole full-time £
Peace Corps or ACTION Programs, or comparable full-time volunteer work for a tax-exempt organization	up to 3 years	up to 3 years	no	up to 3 years £
Active duty membr of U.S. Armed Forces or service in the Commissioned Corps of U.S. Public Health Service	up to 3 years	up to 3 years	no	up to 3 years £
Active duty membr of National Oceanic and Atmospheric Administration Corps §	up to 3 years	up to 3 years	no	up to 3 years £
Temporarily totally disabled, or can't work because you're caring for a temporarily totally disabled spouse or other dependent §	up to 3 years	up to 3 years	up to 3 years £	up to 3 years £
Full-time teacher in a public or nonprofit private primary or secondary school the U.S. Department of Education has determined is in a teacher shortage area §	no	up to 3 years	no	up to 3 years £
Eligible internship deferment *	up to 2 years	up to 2 years	no	up to 2 years £
Unemployment	at school's discretion	up to 2 years	up to 2 years £	up to 2 years £
Mother of preschool age children, who is going to work (or back to work) at a salary no more than $1.00 over the minimum wage §	up to one year	up to one year	no	up to one year £
Parental leave deferment *	up to 6 months §	up to 6 months	no	up to 6 months £

*See Glossary
£ Deferments are for principal only.
Ω Deferments are for periods during which student or parent is engaged in eligible study.
§ For new borrowers only.
§§ For Perkins borrowers, deferment for dependents other than a spouse is only for new borrowers.

(FE) written examination passed. Some of the programs go even further in providing opportunity for qualifications.

All of the surviving programs have curricula that call for the student to acquire considerable aviation technical and management knowledge as well as tested flying skills. A good example of how an *ab initio* program works is the United Airlines plan.

United's *ab initio* program in conjunction with Southern Illinois University at Carbondale (SIUC) involves a four-year flight program for a B.S. in aviation management. The *ab initio* program is incorporated into SIUC's overall flight program, admitting a small number of students into concurrent SIUC and United schooling. Per semester, the program takes not more than 15 of up to 300 SIUC flight training students, chosen as they enter their junior year.

To be accepted into the United/SIUC *ab initio* training, a student must apply from within SIUC's aviation management program, have a minimum grade point average (GPA) of 2.5, pass a Class I physical, and have earned an Associate Degree in Aviation Flight. The 2.5 GPA must be maintained during the course of the program. Students accepted into the program receive both a ground school on one of United's airplanes at the airline's Denver Training Center and a simulator evaluation of flight skills in that aircraft. Perhaps as many as a third of the handful of students in the *ab initio* program also will have the chance to earn a flight engineer rating in one of United's aircraft. The Northwest/ NATCO/University of North Dakota program is distinguished by the depth of financial commitment. A $6 million flight training center at the University of North Dakota (UND) campus, operated jointly by NATCO and CAS, is a multi-purpose facility for research on air safety and airline operations and for the training of pilots for Northwest Airlines and other flight customers. The program includes two advanced training phases: High-Performance Transition Training exposes students to turboprop and light jet operations and provides a link for pilots moving directly into regional airlines; Transport Category Aircraft Training builds on the transition phase, allowing students to qualify as flight engineers and/or first officers on heavy jet aircraft. Twenty to 30 percent of the curriculum consists of computer-based instruction, and computer literacy is required of all NATCO students. First-class FAA medical condition is a prerequisite for the program.

Ab initio programs assume that the regional/commuter airlines will continue to be the main civilian training ground for major airline pilots. This "training ground" role is being intensified, not diminished, by the various programs to increase the supply of airline qualified pilots. *Ab initio* and so-called "transition" training will have to send pilots first to regional airlines, then on to majors.

Track Systems

A natural career channel was established by Northwest Airlines not only by sponsoring the *ab initio* program with NATCO and the University of North Dakota, but also by moving to set up with Express Airlines I (the airline subsidiary of Phoenix Airlines Services, Inc. in Atlanta) a "track system" for pilots. Under this program, still developmental in late 1989, a pilot hired by Express Airlines I, which feeds Northwest Airlines at such large hubs as Memphis and Minneapolis/St. Paul, was to be given a Northwest Airlines seniority number so that if he later was chosen as a pilot by Northwest, he already would have begun building his time under Northwest's pay, benefits and

Flow Chart

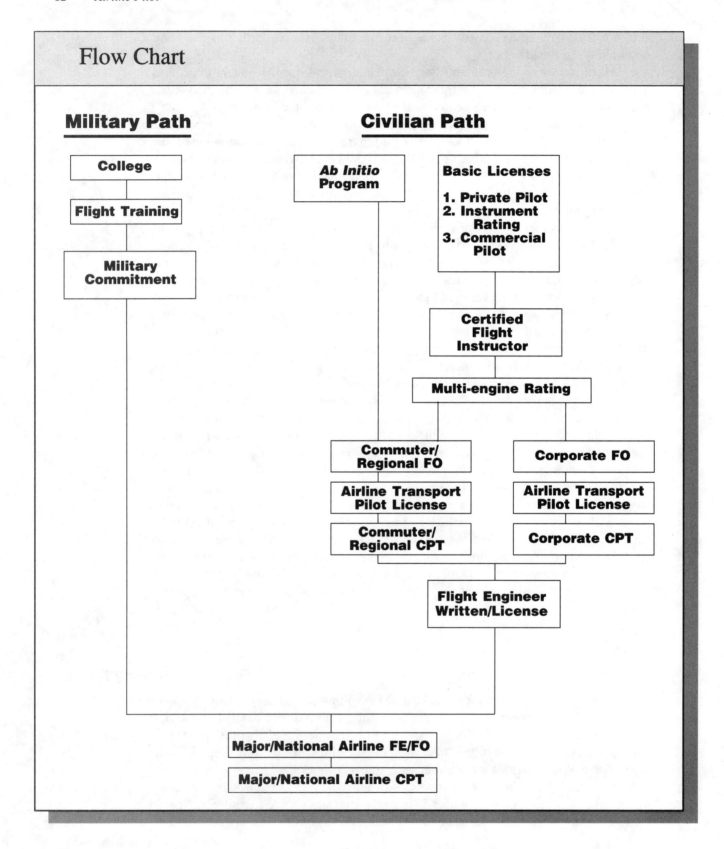

Military Path

College

Flight Training

Military Commitment

Civilian Path

Ab Initio Program

Basic Licenses

1. Private Pilot
2. Instrument Rating
3. Commercial Pilot

Certified Flight Instructor

Multi-engine Rating

Commuter/ Regional FO

Airline Transport Pilot License

Commuter/ Regional CPT

Corporate FO

Airline Transport Pilot License

Corporate CPT

Flight Engineer Written/License

Major/National Airline FE/FO

Major/National Airline CPT

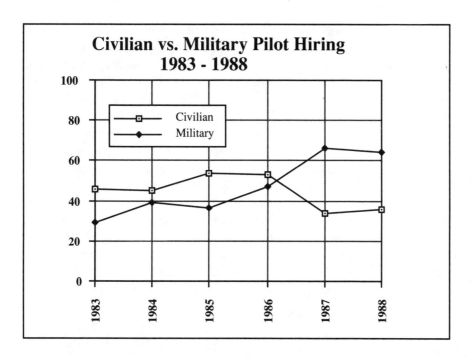

promotion schemes. This track system was to operate both independently of and in conjunction with the ab initio program; that is, a good student coming out of the University of North Dakota program would be able to take a job with Express Airlines I immediately upon graduating, but the regional airline would not be restricted, of course, to these students in filling its pilot needs.

Other early track programs were those at Pan Am/Pan Am Express and Continental/Continental Express. These were not acting in conjunction with an *ab initio* program.

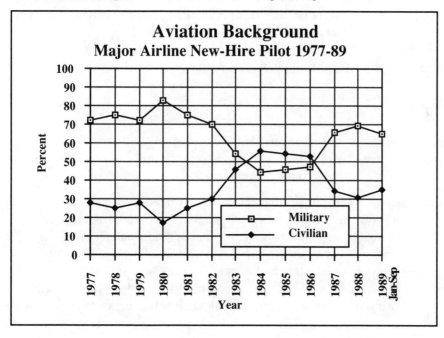

Both programs, however, assigned a major airline seniority number to pilots hired by the regional/commuter carriers (the number being awarded after probation). The regional establishing a track system with Pan Am was Ransome Airlines, bought by Pan Am and utilized as Pan Am Express. The regionals having track systems with Continental were Britt Airways and Rocky Mountain Airways, both bought by Texas Air and used as Continental Express. Continental refers to its regional airline track system as its Pilot Development Program. "Farm system" is another term for a track program.

The advantage of such career tracks for the regional airlines is stabilization of the pilot corps; for the majors, the advantage is in having pilots tied into a maturity program that will enlarge the supply of quality jet airline pilot candidates.

It should be noted that some regionals have grown so big that they have become in effect "pilot feeders" for their major partners as well as passenger feeders. Pilots with Fresno, Calif.-based WestAir can work their way up through several turboprop types into the British Aerospace BAe 146 turbojet, and from there to a seat with a major airline, often United. Pilots with Seattle, Wash.-based Horizon Airlines stand in a similar relation to national carrier Alaska (the two airlines, Alaska and Horizon, are owned by the same holding company).

"Transition" Programs

"Transition" is a technical FAA piloting term, referring to the move up from one aircraft type to another, but it also has been applied to a kind of program initiated by TWA and FlightSafety International. The so-called transition program provides yet another avenue from zero time to an airline job. TWA and FlightSafety designed their program to move graduates of college aviation schools from a green student state to the status of a qualified Fairchild Metro first officer. As with the other programs, the good student pilot is made ready for a regional/commuter airline job, not for a seat with a major or national airline. The pilot then gains his or her turbine time and Part 135 or 121 flying experience while working for the regional airline.

Ab initio, transition and track programs keep popping up, and these can be expected to play an increasing role in pilot supply for the majors.

Other Routes to a Job

Although the *ab initio* route is an efficient one, it probably will never prove to be the single best route to a major airline for all pilots. Several factors will prevail in creating more than one pool of aviators for national and major airline pilot recruiters.

- Sheer numbers will dictate that the airlines spread their nets over a wider population than the *ab initio* programs can cover. If the pool of retiring military pilots cannot keep up with airline hiring needs (and it cannot), then the much smaller pool of fully qualified *ab initio* pilots cannot hope to do so, even after *ab initio* programs multiply and mature.
- Individual preference will continue to be a big factor. Many persons still have a powerful yen for a stint as a military pilot before moving on to civil aviation.

Others have a built-in bias against having their careers stage-managed from day one, preferring a more individualistic course of action.

- Academic and financial barriers will keep many pilot candidates out of the *ab initio* programs. Only the ablest students are chosen for the programs, but a great many individuals who fall below the level of academic performance demanded by these programs ultimately will make excellent airline pilots. Similarly, the majority of candidates cannot come up with the $50,000 to $90,000 price of the most extensive *ab initio* programs. Some of these may find the free training offered by the military to be the best educational avenue available to them, even though this choice means giving Uncle Sam eight years of military service. Other students may prefer the civilian route of training at a flight school or a local airport, then building time through instructing and miscellaneous low-paying flying jobs before latching on with a regional airline, where multi-engine time can be built rapidly. (The latter group can recover some of their training costs from paid flying jobs even as they are working toward being hired by a regional airline.) And there are paths that fall somewhere between the "high road" of *ab initio* programs and the "low road" of flight school or local airport training, e.g., a pilot might attend one of the many four-year colleges or universities with an aviation program, then get accepted into a transition program of the FlightSafety/TWA type. Moreover, an important question suggests itself: "Who is to say that if you take the 'high road' and I take the 'low road,' I'll not be in Scotland (i.e., the desired major airline position) before ye?"

- Along the same lines, the enormous investment involved in most *ab initio* programs may never be recouped by many students because they may never be hired by a major airline. As currently operated, *ab initio* programs are funded by the students, and there is no guarantee of a job offer from the sponsoring airline once a student completes such a program. Then, too, a risk associated with the health requirements for *ab initio* programs is that the Class I medical, utilized by the program administrators as a health standard, is far less rigorous than the medical requirements of major airlines. The FAA Class I medical is concerned with a pilot's health for six months at a time, whereas airline hiring personnel need to predict a pilot's health over a 30-year time span. A student may pass the Class I with flying colors, then be rejected by a major airline as a health risk. (This factor suggests that a pilot candidate considering the costly *ab initio* route should take the trouble to undergo a full airline-type medical examination before plunking down all that money.)

If you are one of the vast majority who, for whatever reasons, are opting for non-*ab initio* avenues to their career objectives, you will find the alternatives virtually infinite. First, you get to choose from hundreds of educational possibilities. Then you get to choose from more possible combinations of additional training and experience than you can count.

The military option deserves a few words:

Many pilots have found the armed forces attractive both as a career and as an initial step toward becoming an airline pilot. At one time, the major and national airlines selected 75 percent of their new-hire pilots from this pool of highly trained, experienced pilots. For the first six months of 1989, according to FAPA's tracking of airline hiring, the figure had slipped to 67 percent, and civilian career paths are expected to account for an increasing share of major and national airline hiring in coming years.

If you are considering going into the armed forces for pilot training, note the following:

1. A four-year college degree is required (except in the Army).

2. You must be in an officer training school (OCS) prior to your 27th birthday; you must begin pilot training prior to reaching 27 years and six months of age.

3. A commitment of several years of military service after pilot training is required. The Air Force requires eight years; the Navy, seven; the Coast Guard and Marines, four; and the Army, three.

4. Pilot training lasts 12 to 18 months.

5. You may join the Air National Guard or Reserves (Reserve Components) and obtain your military pilot training under their auspices. By this means, you can receive the same training that an active-duty pilot receives without incurring the active-duty service commitment. Your reserve service commitment after completion of pilot training is five years. Two negative factors apply: Reserve component pilot openings are few, and pilots with previous military experience have an edge in filling them. If you do not have previous military experience, your best bet (a long shot) for filling one of these openings is to join the Reserves as a non-pilot and hope to be chosen for training.

One source of training deserves special note: For the pilot taking an "independent" route to the majors, there is in Atlanta a career counseling firm, Future Aviation Professionals of America (FAPA), from which in-depth training in how to pass muster in simulator and other tests at the airlines is available. FAPA also provides instruction in how to pursue a job with an airline. FAPA's services apply equally well to military and civilian airline pilot candidates.

For information on financing your education and on certificates and experience required by the airlines, see the sidebar, "Financial Aid Programs," and Chapter 10, "What It Takes: Ratings, Background."

Following are two lists. The first is a list of collegiate aviation schools in the United States. The second is a list of FAA-approved training schools.

FAA Approved Schools

Editor's note: The following list should not be considered an endorsement by FAPA. Since the FAA has not updated its list of approved flight schools since 1987, this list is a compilation of several previous and current lists. Please let us know of any errors or omissions. Other FAA-approved flight programs are included as part of the "Collegiate Aviation Schools" on page 112.

ALABAMA

- **Auburn University Aviation,** 700 Airport Rd., Auburn, AL 36830.

- **Dixie Air,** P.O. Box 1370, Tuscaloosa, AL 35401.

- **Edwards Aircraft,** Rte. 1, Box 26, Enterprise, AL 36330.

- **Gold Dust Flying Service,** 305 Airport Rd., Jacksonville, AL 36265.

- **Redstone Arsenal Flying Club,** Bldg. 118, Redstone Arsenal, AL 35809.

ALASKA

- **Action Helicopters,** 507 W. Northern Lights Blvd., Anchorage, AK 99503.

- **Aero Tech Flight Service,** 1100 Merrill Field Dr., Anchorage, AK 99501.

- **Alaska Air Academy,** 2301 Merrill Field Dr., Anchorage, AK 99501.

- **Alaska Flying Network,** Rte. 2, Box 1621, Soldotna, AK 99669.

- **Alaska Flying Network Inc.,** 403 N. Willow NR 1, Kenai, AK 99611.

- **Anchorage Air Center,** 2301 Merrill Field Dr., Anchorage, AK 99501.

- **Aviation Company,** 3762 S. University Ave., Fairbanks, AK 99709.

- **Aviation North,** P.O. Box 671528, Chugiak, AK 99567.

- **Club 1 Flight Group,** 403 N. Willow, Kenai, AK 99611.

- **Eielson Aero Club,** Eielson AFB, AK 99702.

- **Elmendorf Aero Club,** Hgr. 7, Anchorage, AK 99506.

- **Flight Safety Alaska Inc.,** 1740 E. 5th Ave., Anchorage, AK 99501.

- **Ft. Richardson Flying Club,** P.O. Box 5-364, Anchorage, AK 99505.

- **Ft. Wainwright Flying Club,** P.O. Box 35062, Ft. Wainwright, AK 99703.

- **High Tech Helicopters,** 1931 Merrill Field Dr., Anchorage, AK 99501.

- **Lazy Mountain Aviation,** P.O. Box 157, Palmer, AK 99645.

- **Mat-Su Bush Flying,** P.O. Box 2327, Palmer, AK 99645.

- **Ptarmigan Aviation Inc.,** 1935 Merrill Field Dr., Anchorage, AK 99501.

- **VernAir,** 1704 E. 5th Ave., Anchorage, AK 99501.

- **Wilbur's Flight Operations,** 1740 E. Fifth Ave., Anchorage, AK 99501.

- **Mustang,** 3901 Lindberg, Jonesboro, AR 72401.

ARIZONA

- **Arizona Flight School Inc.,** 2020 Clubhouse Dr., Prescott, AZ 86301.

- **Chandler Air Service,** Chandler Municipal Airport, Chandler, AZ 85224.

- **FlightSafety International,** 6870 S. Plumer Ave., Tucson, AZ 85706.

- **Hudgin Air Service,** 1732 E. Valencia, Tucson, AZ 85706.

- **Litchfield Aviation,** Phoenix-Litchfield Airport, Goodyear, AZ 85338.

- **North-Aire,** Prescott Municipal Airport, Prescott, AZ 86301.

- **Sawyer School of Aviation,** 2602 E. Sky Harbor Blvd., Phoenix, AZ 85034.

- **Superstition Air Services,** 4766 Falcon Dr., Mesa, AZ 85205.

- **Unicorn Balloon Company of Arizona Inc.,** 7406 E. Butherus Dr., Scottsdale, AZ 85260.

ARKANSAS

- **Central Flying Service,** Adams Field, Little Rock, AR 72202.

- **Central Flying Service Inc.,** Rt. 4 Box 10, Arkadelphia, AR 71923.

- **International Air,** Rt. 6, Box 148, Russellville, AR 72801.

- **Morey's Flying Service,** 3501 Hudson Rd., Rogers, AR 72756.

CALIFORNIA

- **Above All Aviation,** 1501 Cooke Place, Goleta, CA 93117.

- **Accelerated Ground Training,** 19531 Airport Way S., Santa Ana, CA 92707.

- **Aero Tech Academy,** 1745 Sessums Dr., Redlands, CA 92373

- **Air Center International Inc.,** 2103 Airport Dr., Bakersfield, CA 93308.

- **AirFlite,** 2700 E. Wardlow Rd., Long Beach, CA 90807.

- **Airline Training Institute,** 795 Skyway, San Carlos, CA 94070.

- **Air Trails,** 280 Mortensen Ave., Salinas, CA 93905.

- **Alpha Aviation,** 16303 Waterman Dr., Van Nuys, CA 91406.

- **American Aerobatics,** 820-D E. Santa Maria St., Santa Paula, CA 93060.

- **American Flyers ATE of California,** 2701 Airport Ave., Santa Monica, CA 90405.

- **Aris Helicopters LTD,** 1138 Coleman Ave., San Jose, CA 95110.

- **Aviation Training,** 21593 Skywest Dr., Hayward, CA 94541.

- **Aztec Air,** 4310 Donald Douglas Dr., Long Beach, CA 90808.

- **Balloon Excelsior School,** 1241 High St., Oakland, CA 94601.

- **Balloons of Woodland,** 1233 E. Beamer, Woodland, CA 95695.

- **Bates Foundation for Aeronautical Education,** Harvey Mudd College, Claremont, CA 91711.

- **Berg-Branham Flying Service,** 16425 Hart St., Van Nuys, CA 91406.

- **Bridgeford Flying Service Inc.,** 2030 Airport Rd., Napa, CA 94558.

- **Cal-Ag-Aero,** P.O. Box 939, Tulare, CA 93275.

- **California Aviation,** 2701 Airport Ave., Santa Monica, CA 90405.

- **California Wings Inc.,** 4025 Kearney Villa Rd., San Diego, CA 92123.

- **Capitol Sky Park Flying School,** Executive Airport, Sacramento, CA 95822.

- **Chrysler Aviation,** 7120 Hayvenhurst Ave., Ste. 309-311, Van Nuys, CA 91406-3836.

- **Consolidated Aviation Corp.,** 961 W. Alondra Blvd., Compton, CA 90220.

- **Eagle Aviation,** 4307 Donald Douglas Dr., Long Beach, CA 90808.

- **El Cajon Flying Service,** 1825 N. Marshall Ave., El Cajon, CA 92020.

- **El Monte Flight Service,** 5001 N. Santa Anita Ave., El Monte, CA 91731.

- **El Toro Marine Aero Club,** MCAS, El Toro, Santa Ana, CA 92709.

- **Executive Aero Systems,** P.O. Box 11557, Tahoe Paradise, CA 95708.

- **Executive Aviation Services,** 3521 E. Spring St., Long Beach, CA 90806.

- **Executive Flyers Inc.,** 6151 Freeport Blvd., Sacramento, CA 95822.

- **Fallbrook Air Service,** 2141 S. Mission Rd., Fallbrook, CA 92028.

- **Flight Associated Activities,** 6920 Vineland Ave., N. Hollywood, CA 91605.

- **Flight Operations Inc.,** 5999 Freeport Blvd., Sacramento, CA 95822.

- **Flight Trails,** 2188 Palomar Airport Rd., Carlsbad, CA 92008.

- **Flying Country Club Marketing,** 2555 Robert Fowler Way A, San Jose, CA 95148.

- **Flying J Aviation,** 6717 Curran St., San Diego, CA 92173.

- **General Air Services,** 200 Sally Ride Dr., Concord, CA 94520.

- **GHKC Inc.,** 2188 Palomar Airport Rd., Carlsbad, CA 92008.

- **Gibbs Flite Center,** 3717 John J. Montgomery Dr., San Diego, CA 92123.

- **Golden Gate Piper,** 603 Skyway, San Carlos, CA 94070.

- **Golden State Aviation,** 1640 N. Johnson Ave., El Cajon, CA 92020.

- **Great American Balloon Company Inc.,** 1112 Wrigley Way, Milpitas, CA 95035.

- **Gunnell Aviation,** 3000 Airport Ave., Santa Monica, CA 90405.

- **Harbor Aviation,** 4225 Donald Douglas Dr., Long Beach, CA 90808.

- **Hiser Helicopters Inc.,** 1969 Aviation Dr., NR C, Corona, CA 91720.

- **Horizon Helicopter,** 7443 Murieta Dr., Rancho Murieta, CA 95683.

- **IASCO Flight Training Center,** 100 IASCO Rd., Napa, CA 94558.

- **Lake Tahoe Aviation,** P.O. Box 7323, S. Lake Tahoe, CA 95731.

- **Lancer Aviation,** 1900 Joe Crosson Dr., El Cajon, CA 92020.

- **Lenair Aviation Inc.,** 19531 Airport Way South, Santa Ana, CA 92707.

- **Long Beach Flyers,** 2901 E. Spring St., Long Beach, CA 90806.

- **M&S Aviation,** 4137 Donald Douglas Dr., Long Beach, CA 90808.

- **Marin Air Services,** 351 Airport Rd., Novato, CA 94947.

- **Martin Aviation Inc.,** 19331 Airport Way South, Santa Ana, CA 92707.

- **Mazzei Flying Service,** 4955 E. Anderson, Fresno, CA 93727.

- **National Air College,** 3760 Glenn H. Curtis Rd., San Diego, CA 92071.

- **Navajo Aviation,** 145 John Glenn Dr., Concord, CA 94520.

- **North American Airline Training Group,** 7120 Hayvenhurst Ave., Ste. 100, Van Nuys, CA 91406.

- **North Island Navy Flying Club,** P.O. Box 12, San Diego, CA 92135.

- **Pacific Air College,** 2901 E. Spring St., Long Beach, CA 90808.

- **Pacific States Aviation,** 51 John Glenn Dr., Concord, CA 94524.

- **Parflite,** 6651 Flight Rd., Riverside, CA 92504.

- **Patterson Aircraft Co.,** Executive Airport, Sacramento, CA 95822.

- **Phillips Flying,** P.O. Box 2000-31, S. Lake Tahoe, CA 95705.

- **Professional Airline Systems,** 111 Sequoia, Ste. B, Carlsbad, CA 92008.

- **Renken's Executive Flying Club,** 2026 Palomar Airport Rd., Carlsbad, CA 92008.

- **Rose Aviation,** 3852 W. 120th St., Hawthorne, CA 90250.

- **Rosemead Adult School,** 9063 E. Mission Dr., Rosemead, CA 91770.

- **Sierra Academy of Aeronautics,** Bldg. L-130, Earhart Rd., Oakland, CA 94614.

- **Skyhawk Aviation,** Corona Municipal Airport, Corona, CA 91720.

- **Skyway Aviation,** 795 Skyway, San Carlos, CA 94070.

- **Southwest Skyways,** 25321 Bellanca Way, Torrance, CA 90505.

- **Steck Aviation,** 6949 Curran St., San Diego, CA 92173.

- **Sussex Aviation,** 7535 Valjean Ave., Van Nuys Airport, Van Nuys, CA 91408.

- **Trans Bay Airways Corp.,** 620 Airport Dr., Ste. 1, San Carlos, CA 94070.

- **TransOcean Aviation,** Oakland Int'l Airport, P.O. Box 2166, Oakland, CA 94621.

- **Travis AFB Aero Club,** W. Hangar Ave., Travis AFB, CA 94535.

- **Type Rating Training,** 116 W. Grand Ave., El Segundo, CA 90245.

- **Valenti Aviation,** 1601 W. Fifth St., Oxnard, CA 93030.

- **Vindar Aviation,** P.O. Box 747, Novato, CA 94947.

- **Western Aviation Inc.,** 3717 John J Montgomery Dr., San Diego, CA 92123.

- **Western Helicopters,** 1670 Miro Way, Rialto, CA 92376.

- **Western Sun Aviation,** 2025 N. Marshall Ave., El Cajon, CA 92020.

COLORADO

- **Air Carrier Int'l. Flight Academy,** Jefferson County Airport, Broomfield, CO 80020.

- **Arnautical Inc.,** United Airlines Flight Training Center, Stapleton Int'l Airport, Denver, CO 80207.

- **Aviation Adventures Aloft Inc.,** 2200 Airway, Ft. Collins, CO 80524.

- **Denver Air Center,** Jefferson County Airport, Broomfield, CO 80020.

- **Durango Air Service,** P.O. Box 2117, Durango, CO 81301.

- **Emery School of Aviation,** 661 Buss Ave., Greeley, CO 80631.

- **Flower Aviation of Colorado,** 31201 Bryan Cir., Pueblo, CO 81001.

- **Hoffman Pilot Center,** Executive Office Bldg., Ste. 7, Broomfield, CO 80020.

- **Judson Flying School,** Rte. 3, Box 121, Longmont, CO 80501.

- **Monarch Aviation,** Walker Field, Grand Junction, CO 81501.

- **Northern Colorado Aviation,** 625 Buss Ave., Greeley, CO 80631.

- **P.C. Flyers,** 13000 E. Control Tower Rd., Englewood, CO 80112.

- **Peterson AFB Aero Club,** P.O. Box 14123, Bldg. 104, Peterson AFB, CO 80914.

- **Propilot Proficiency Center,** 715 Locust St., Denver, CO 80220.

- **West Aire,** 1245 Aviation Way, Colorado Springs, CO 80916.

- **Wings of Denver Flying Club Inc.,** 7625 S. Peoria St., Englewood, CO 80112.

CONNECTICUT

- **Action Air,** Groton/New London Airport, Groton, CT 06304.

- **Bluebird Aviation Corp.,** Danbury Municipal Airport, Danbury, CT 06810.

- **Centerline South Inc.,** Brainard Airport, Hartford, CT 06114.

- **Chester Airport,** Winthrop Rd., Chester, CT 06412.

- **Coastal Air Services,** Groton-New London Airport, Groton, CT 06340.

- **Interstate Aviation,** 82 Johnson Ave., Plainville, CT 06062.

- **Johnnycake Aviation Services Inc.,** 529 Burlington Rd., Harwinton, CT 06791.

- **Kelaire,** Sikorsky Memorial Airport, Stratford, CT 06497.

- **Meriden Airways,** 213 Evansville Ave., Meriden, CT 06450.

- **Northeast Flight Training Center,** Hgr. 2, Ellington, CT 06029.

- **Northstar Aero Services Inc.,** Rt. 83, P.O. 457, Ellington Airport, Ellington, CT 06029.

- **Shoreline Aviation,** 1362 Boston Post Rd., Madison, CT 06443.

- **Staples High School,** 70 N. Ave., Westport, CT 06880.

- **Waterford Flight School,** Waterford Airport, Waterford, CT 06385.

- **Windham Aviation Inc.,** P.O. Box 136, Willimantic, CT 06226.

DELAWARE

- **Dawn Aeronautics Inc.,** NR 2, 120 Old Churchmans Rd., New Castle, DE 19720.

- **FlightSafety International,** P.O. Box 15003, Greater Wilmington Airport, Wilmington, DE 19850.

- **Kent County Vo-Tech. Center,** P.O. Box 97, Woodside, DE 19980.

DISTRICT OF COLUMBIA

- **Jet America International,** Washington National Airport, Washington, DC 20001.

FLORIDA

- **Ace Flying School,** 3244 Capital Circle Southwest, Tallahassee, FL 32304.

- **Aeroservice Int'l. Training Centers Inc.,** 1499 N.W. 79th Ave., Miami, FL 33126.

- **Aero Sport Flight Center,** P.O. Box 1719, St. Augustine, FL 32084.

- **Air Line Aviation Academy Inc.,** 400 Herndon Ave., Orlando, FL 32803.

- **Air Valdosta,** 2612 Madison Hwy., Valdosta, FL 32601.

- **ATE of Florida,** 5500 NW 21 Terrace, Bdlg. 4, Ft. Lauderdale, FL 33309.

- **ATE of Florida,** 1006 NE 11th St., Pompano Beach, FL 33060.

- **Bay Aviation,** 1000 Jackson Way, Panama City, FL 32405.

- **Bill Shields Aviation Inc.,** 855 St. Johns Bluff Rd., Jacksonville, FL 32225.

- **Boca Flight Center Inc.,** 3900 Perimeter Rd., Boca Raton, FL 33431.

- **Braunig Aeromarine,** 1832 Spruce Creek Blvd., Daytona Beach, FL 32014.

- **Carib Aviation,** 14250 SW 129th St., Miami, FL 33186.

- **Cav Air,** 5500 NW 21st Terrace, Ft. Lauderdale, FL 33309.

- **Craig Air Center,** 855 St. Johns Bluff Rd., Jacksonville, FL 32225.

- **Craig Flight School Inc.,** Craig Airport, Jacksonville, FL 32225.

- **Crescent Airways,** 7501 Pembroke Rd., W. Hollywood, FL 33023.

- **Crystal Aero Group,** P.O. Box 2050, Crystal River, FL 32629.

- **Eagle Flight Center Inc.,** 1624 Bellvue Ave., Daytona Beach, FL 32014.

- **Eglin Aero Club,** P.O. Box 1588, Eglin AFB, FL 32542.

- **Ferguson Flying Service,** Ferguson Airport, Pensacola, FL 32506.

- **First Coast Flight Center Inc.,** Rt. 3, Box 38, St. Augustine, FL 32084.

- **Flight Management Inc.,** 855 St. Johns Bluff, Jacksonville, FL 32225.

- **FlightSafety International,** P.O. Box 2708, Vero Beach, FL 32960.

- **Florida Flight Academy Inc.,** 7601 Airport Blvd., Sarasota, FL 34143.

- **Gardens Aviation,** P.O. Box 12642, Lake Park, FL 33403.

- **Gateway Aviation,** 365 Gold Knight Blvd., Titusville, FL 32780.

- **Gulf Atlantic Airways,** 4305 NE 49th Dr., Gainesville Regional Airport, Gainesville, FL 32601.

- **Hollywood Flying Service Inc.,** 7750 Hollywood Blvd., Hollywood, FL 33024.

- **Huffman Aviation Int'l.,** 400 E. Airport Ave., Venice, FL 34285.

- **Island City Flying Service,** 1900 S. Roosevelt Blvd., Key West, FL 33040.

- **Jax Navy Flying Club,** Bldg. 841, Jacksonville, FL 31121.

- **Kendall Flying School,** P.O. Box 557516, Miami, FL 33155.

- **Korman Aviation Inc.,** 3751 NW 145 St., Opa Locka, FL 33054.

- **L.T. Aero,** 14532 SW 129th St., Miami, FL 33186.

- **Lauderdale Aviation Inc.,** 7501 Pembroke Rd., Hollywood, FL 33023.

- **McArthur High School,** 6501 Hollywood Blvd., Hollywood, FL 33054.

- **Miami Helicopter Service,** Bldg. 147, Opa Locka Airport, Opa Locka, FL 33054.

- **Milton T. Aviation,** P.O. Box 742, Milton, FL 32570.

- **Miracle Strip Aviation,** P.O. 159, Destin, FL 32541.

- **North Florida Aviation Seminars,** 3300 Wilderness, Middlebury, FL 32068.

- **Palatka Aviation,** Kay Larkin Airport, Palatka, FL 32077.

- **Pensacola Aviation Center,** P.O. Box 2781, Pensacola, FL 32503.

- **Phoenix East Aviation,** 561 Pearl Harbor Dr., Daytona Beach, FL 32014.

- **Pompano Air Center,** 1401 NE 10th St., Pompano Beach, FL 33060.

- **Quincy Aviation Services Inc.,** Quincy Airport, Quincy, FL 32351.

- **Roberts Flying Service,** P.O. Box 1011, Lakeland, FL 33802.

- **Savco Flying,** 7750 Hollywood Blvd., Hollywood, FL 33024.

- **South Dade Aviation Services,** 28700 SW 217 Ave., Homestead, FL 33030.

- **Sowell Aviation Co.,** P.O. Box 1490, Panama City, FL 32401.

- **Technical Aviation Service,** 5553 NW 36th St., Ste. C, Miami Springs, FL 33166.

- **Tidwell,** AC, Star Rt. 2, Box 9068, Tallahassee, FL 32304.

- **Topp Air,** St. Petersburg-Clearwater Airport, Clearwater, FL 33520.

- **Tursair,** P.O. Box 85, Opa Locka Airport, Opa Locka, FL 33054.

- **Tyndall Air Force Base Aero Club,** P.O. Box A, Bldg. 540, Tyndall AFB, FL 32403.

- **Venice Flying Service,** 220 E. Airport Ave., Venice, FL 33595.

- **Volusia Aviation Service,** Regional Airport, Daytona Beach, FL 32014.

- **West Florida Helicopters,** Albert Whitted Airport Hangar, St. Petersburg, FL 33701.

- **Wordair International Inc.,** 14532 SW 129th Terrace, Miami, FL 33186.

- **Wings International,** P.O. Box 3288, Ft. Pierce, FL 33454.

- **World Aircraft Flight Operations,** 7501 Pembroke Rd., W. Hollywood, FL 33023.

GEORGIA

- **Airline Transport Professionals,** 3948 Aviation Circle, Ste. 110, Atlanta, GA 30336.

- **Augusta Aviation,** Daniel Field, Augusta, GA 30909.

- **Aviation Atlanta Inc.,** 1951 Airport Rd., Chamblee, GA 30341.

- **Butler Aviation-Savannah,** P.O. Box 22637, Savannah, GA 31403.

- **Diamond Aviation Flight Academy,** Statesboro Municipal Airport, Statesboro, GA 30458.

- **Epps Air Service,** Peachtree-DeKalb Airport, Atlanta, GA 30341.

- **Gulfstream Learning Center,** P.O. Box 2307, Savannah, GA 31402.

- **Holland Flying Service,** Valdosta Municipal Airport, Valdosta, GA 31601.

- **Peachtree-DeKalb Flight Academy,** 1954 Airport Rd., Chamblee, GA 30341.

- **Quality Aviation,** 1951 Airport Rd., Atlanta, GA 30341.

- **Robins Air Force Base Aero Club,** Bldg. 184, Robins AFB, GA 31098.

- **Southeastern Flight Academy,** Herbert Smart Downtown Airport, Macon, GA 31201.

HAWAII

- **Associated Aviation Activities,** 218 Lagoon Dr., Honolulu, HI 96819.

- **Kona Flight Services,** P.O. Box 2067, Kailua-Kona, HI 96740.

IDAHO

- **Aero Technicians,** P.O. Box 7, Rexburg, ID 83440.

- **Clark's Air Service,** P.O. Box 56, Nampa, ID 83651.

- **Flight Service,** P.O. Box 38, Caldwell, ID 83605.

- **Pocatello AV Center,** 17 Star Rte.- Airport, Pocatello, ID 83201.

ILLINOIS

- **Air Institute & Service,** Southern Illinois Airport, Carbondale, IL 62901.

- **AMCorp.,** P.O. Box 553, Lansing, IL 60438.

- **Associated Air Activities,** P.O. Box 158, Lansing, IL 60438.

- **Aviation Training Enterprises,** American Flyers, DuPage Airport, W. Chicago, IL 60185.

- **Clark Aviation,** Bloomington Normal Airport, Bloomington, IL 61701.

- **Dixon Aviation,** Walgreen Field, Dixon, IL 61021.

- **Elliot Flight Center,** Quad City Airport, Box 26, Moline, IL 61265.

- **Frasca Air Services Inc.,** 1402 E. Airport Rd., Urbana, IL 61801.

- **Galt Flying Service,** 5112 Greenwood Rd., Wonder Lake, IL 60097.

- **George J. Priester Aviation,** Pal-Waukee Airport, Wheeling, IL 60090.

- **T.K. Aviation,** 4943 W. 63rd St., Chicago, IL 60638.

- **Tufts-Edgcumbe,** Elgin Airport, Box 557, Elgin, IL 60120.

- **Vincennes University Aviation,** Lawrenceville Vincennes Municipal Airport, Lawrenceville, IL 62439.

INDIANA

- **Aretz Flying Service,** 180 Aretz Lane, LaFayette, IN 47905.

- **Chambers Aviation Inc.,** Rt. 18, Box 127, Indianapolis, IN 46234.

- **Franklin Flying Field,** R.R. 3, Box 58, Franklin, IN 46131.

- **Griffith Aviation,** 1705 E. Main St., Griffith, IN 46391.

- **H & D Aviation,** Hulman Regional Airport, Terre Haute, IN 47803.

- **Helicopter Airways of Indiana,** 1401 N. Rangeline Rd., Carmel, IN 46032.

- **Indianapolis Aviation,** 10565 Allisonville Rd., Indianapolis, IN 46060.

- **LaFayette Aviation,** Hgr. 5, Purdue University, LaFayette, IN 47906.

- **Sky Harbor,** 7700 W. 38th St., Indianapolis, IN 46254.

- **Sunrise Aviation,** 2572 CR 60, Auburn, IN 46706.

- **Tri-State Aero,** 6101 Flightline Dr., Evansville, IN 47711.

IOWA

- **Balloons Over Iowa Ltd.,** 1900 Blue Place, Carlisle, IA 50047.

- **Charles City Aeronautics,** Municipal Airport, Charles City, IA 50616.

- **Denison Aviation,** Municipal Airport, Denison, IA 51442.

- **Haps Air Service,** Municipal Airport, Ames, IA 50010.

- **Iowa City Flying Service Inc.,** Municipal Airport, Iowa City, IA 52240.

- **Johnson Aviation,** Box 986, Newton, IA 50208.

- **Marshalltown Aviation,** Municipal Airport, Marshalltown, IA 50158.

- **P&N Corp.,** McBride Airport, Marion, IA 52302.

- **Remmers-Tomkins Flight Service,** P.O. Box 373, Burlington, IA 52601.

- **Storm Flying Service,** R.R. 2, Webster City, IA 50595.

- **Straley Flying Service,** Municipal Airport, Clinton, IA 52732.

- **Tibben Flight Lines,** Municipal Airport, Cedar Rapids, IA 52401.

- **Wathan Flying Service,** P.O. Box 1368, Municipal Airport, Cedar Rapids, IA 52406.

KANSAS

- **Capitol Air Service,** Manhattan Municipal Airport, Manhattan, KS 66502.

- **Coffeyville Aircraft,** Municipal Airport, Coffeyville, KS 67337.

- **Craig's Aero Service,** Sherman Field, Ft. Leavenworth, KS 66027.

- **FlightSafety International Inc.,** Citation Learning Center, 1851 Airport Rd., Wichita, KS 67277.

- **Ft. Riley Flying Club,** 359 Curant Ct., Ft. Riley, KS 66442.

- **K.C.H. School of Aeronautics,** One Executive Aero Plaza, Olathe, KS 66062.

- **Kansas City Piper,** P.O. Box 1850, Olathe, KS 66061.

- **Ken Godfrey Aviation Inc.,** 3600 Sardou, Topeka, KS 66616.

- **Lawrence Aviation,** Rte. 3, Lawrence, KS 66044.

- **McConnell Aero Club,** McConnell AFB, Wichita, KS 67221.

- **Moores Midway Aviation Inc.,** 2812 Hein Ave., Salina, KS 67401.

- **Prairie Air Service,** Rt. 1, Box 86-23, Benton, KS 67017.

KENTUCKY

- **Ayer Flying Service,** Owensboro-Daviess Co. Airport, Owensboro, KY 42301.

- **Don Davis Aviation,** R.R. 2, Box 28, Henderson, KY 42420.

- **Elizabethtown Flying Service,** Ben Floyd Field, Elizabethtown, KY 42701.

- **Kentucky Flying Service,** Bowman Field, Bldg. T-30, Louisville, KY 40205.

LOUISIANA

- **Airtaix Aviation,** Williams/Mitchell Hgrs., New Orleans, LA 70126.

- **Deridder Aircraft Corp.,** 2132 Blankenship Dr., Deridder, LA 70634.

- **Fleeman Enterprises,** 5410 Operations Rd., Monroe, LA 71201.

- **Lincoln Services,** S. Farmerville St., Ruston, LA 71270.

- **McMahan Aviation Inc.,** Nanco Flight Training Center, 5106 Operations Rd., Monroe, LA 71203.

- **Nicholls Aviation Inc.,** P.O. Box 1222, Thibodaux, LA 70302.

- **Pelican Aviation Corp.,** P.O. Box 2008, New Iberia, LA 70560.

- **Southern Aviation Corp.,** 1400 Airport Dr., Shreveport, LA 71107.

- **Tiger Air Center,** 5520 Operations Rd., Monroe, LA 71201.

MAINE

- **Central Maine Flying Service,** De Witt Field, Old Town, ME 04468.
- **Central Maine Vocational Technical Inst.,** 1250 Turner St., Auburn, ME 04210.
- **Lebanon Airport Development Corp.,** Lebanon Municipal Airport, West Lebanon, ME 03784.
- **Maine Instrument Flight School,** P.O. Box 2, Augusta, ME 04330.

MARYLAND

- **Aero Flight Ltd.,** 7940 Airpark Dr., Gaithersburg, MD 20879.
- **ATC Flight Training Center,** 6709 CPL Frank Scott Dr., College Park, MD 20740.
- **Baltimore Aviation Service,** Baltimore Airpark, White Marsh, MD 21162.
- **Cumberland Airlines,** P.O. Box 1611, Cumberland, MD 21502.
- **Eastern Flying Service,** Back River Neck Rd., Baltimore, MD 21221.
- **Frederick Aviation Inc.,** Frederick Municipal Airport, Frederick, MD 21701.
- **Freeway Airport,** 3900 Church Rd., Mitchellville, MD 20716.
- **Gibson Aviation,** 7940 Airpark Dr., Gaithersburg, MD 20760.

- **Maryland Airlines Co.,** P.O. Box 577, Easton, MD 21601.
- **McDonald Flying Service,** St. Mary's County Airport, California, MD 20619.
- **Professional Flight Service,** 9550 Allentown Rd., Oxon Hill, MD 20022.
- **Suburban Airservice,** 520 Brock Bridge Rd., Laurel, MD 20810.

MASSACHUSETTS

- **Amity Aerotech Institute,** Worcester Municipal Airport, Worcester, MA 01602.
- **Aviation East Inc.,** Norfolk Airport, Norfolk, MA 02056.
- **Aviation Training Academy,** Sterling Airport, Sterling Junction, MA 01565.
- **Cape Cod Aero Marine,** George Ryder Rd., Chatham, MA 02633.
- **City Aviation,** Lafleur Airport, Northhampton, MA 01060.
- **E.W. Wiggins Airways,** Norwood Municipal Airport, Norwood, MA 02062.
- **Executive Flyers Aviation,** 1st Floor Civil Air Terminal, Bedford, MA 01730.
- **Fitchburg-Colonial Aviation,** Fitchburg Municipal Airport, Fitchburg, MA 01420.
- **Hyannis Aviation,** Barnstable Municipal Airport, Hyannis, MA 02601.
- **King Services of Aviation,** Taunton Municipal Airport, E. Taunton, MA 02718.
- **New England Flyers Air Service,** Beverly Airport, Beverly, MA 01915.

- **Northeastern Air Services,** Barnes Municipal Airport, Westfield, MA 01085.

- **Quonset Flight Center Inc.,** Airport Tower Bldg., North Kingstown, MA 02852.

- **Patriot Aviation Corp.,** State Terminal Bldg., Bedford, MA 01730.

- **Robert's Aviation,** Metro Airport, Palmer, MA 01069.

- **Tew-Mac School of Aeronautics,** Main St., Tewksbury, MA 01876.

- **Yankee Aviation,** Plymouth Municipal Airport, Plymouth, MA 02360.

MICHIGAN

- **AMR/Northern Air School of Aeronautics,** P.O. Box 380, Kent County Int'l Airport, Grand Rapids, MI 49588.

- **American Christian Aviation Inst.,** 1525 Airport Rd., Pontiac, MI 48054.

- **American Wings and Wheels Inc.,** P.O. Box 7275, Flint, MI 48507.

- **Andrews University Aviation,** Andrews Airport, Berrien Springs, MI 49104.

- **Anglin Flying Service,** G-3101 W. Bristol Rd., Flint, MI 48507.

- **Ann Arbor Aero Services,** 4320 State Rd., Ann Arbor, MI 48104.

- **Annas Airways,** 1675 Airport Rd., Pontiac, MI 48054.

- **Aviation Group Inc.,** 1525 Airport Rd., Pontiac, MI 48054.

- **Aviation Services Inc.,** 5580 Airport Rd., Mt. Pleasant, MI 48858.

- **Brooks Aero,** 1243 S. Kalamazoo St., Marshall, MI 49068.

- **D.J.s Flying Service,** 48000 Tyler Rd., Belleville, MI 48111.

- **Drake Aviation Company Inc.,** Oakland Pontiac Airport, Pontiac, MI 48054.

- **Flight One,** 1510 Main, Owosso, MI 48867.

- **Flytel Aviation,** Exec Terminal, Ste. 114, Detroit, MI 48213.

- **Grand Rapids School,** 1331 Franklin SE, Grand Rapids, MI 49506.

- **Great Lakes Aero,** 1232 Roods Lake Rd., Lapeer, MI 48446.

- **Grosse Ile Flight Services,** 9505 Groh Rd., Grosse Ile, MI 48138.

- **Hansen Flying Service Inc.,** 3999 W. Seaman Rd., Alma, MI 48801.

- **Jacobs Flying Service,** Lenawee County Airport, Adrian, MI 49221.

- **Jet Services,** Mettetal Airport, Canton, MI 48187.

- **Kal-Aero,** 5605 Portage Rd., Kalamazoo, MI 49002.

- **Macomb Aviation Corp.,** 59819 Indian Trail Rd., New Haven, MI 48048.

- **McKinley Executive Corp.,** 1851 W. Maple Rd., Troy, MI 48084.

- **Merillat School of Aviation,** 5447 Rogers Hwy., Tecumseh, MI 49286.

- **Michigan Aero Corporation,** 12401 Conner Ave., Detroit, MI 48205.

- **Olsen Flight Service,** 11499 Conner, Rm. 114, Detroit, MI 48213.

- **Prentice Aircraft,** 2495 Cadmus Rd., Adrian, MI 49221.

- **Price Aviation,** 618 Silver Lake Rd., Linden, MI 48451.

- **R.J. Helicopters,** 51125 Pontiac Trail, Wixom, MI 48096.

- **Roisen Enterprises Inc.,** 719 Airport Dr., Ann Arbor, MI 48104.

- **Shal Aero,** 9505 Groh Rd., Grosse Ile, MI 48138.

- **Skybolt Aviation,** G-3101 W. Bristol Rd., Flint, MI 48507.

- **Spicer Flying Service,** Executive Terminal, Ste. 103, Detroit, MI 48213.

- **Tradewinds Aviation,** 6545 Highland Rd., Pontiac, MI 48054.

MINNESOTA

- **Aerodrome,** Austin Municipal Airport, Austin, MN 55912.

- **Call O Wild Air,** Rte. 5, Mankato Airport, Mankato, MN 56601.

- **Cirrus Flight Operations,** 2289 County Rd. J, Blaine, MN 55432.

- **Crystal Shamrock,** 6000 Douglas Dr. N., Minneapolis, MN 55429.

- **Flight Training Center Inc.,** 9960 Flying Cloud Dr., Eden Prairie, MN 55343.

- **Flying Scotchman,** 6300 Zane Ave. N., Brooklyn Park, MN 55429.

- **Instrument Flight Training,** 590 Bayfield St., St. Paul, MN 55107.

- **St. Cloud Aviation Inc.,** P.O. Box 1599, St. Cloud, MN 56302.

- **Skyline Flite Inc.,** 2289 County Rd. J, Minneapolis, MN 55432.

- **Suburban Hennepin County Vo-Tech,** 9200 Flying Cloud Dr., Eden Prairie, MN 55344.

- **Thunderbird Aviation,** 14091 Pioneer Trail, Eden Prairie, MN 55343.

- **Thunderbird Aviation of Crystal,** Crystal Airport, Crystal, MN 55429.

- **Wings,** St. Paul Downtown Airport, St. Paul, MN 55107.

MISSISSIPPI

- **Cotton Belt Aviation,** Rte. 1, Box 482, Greenwood, MS 38930.

- **Delta Flying Service Inc.,** P.O. Box 365, Walls, MS 38680.

- **Merigold Flying Service,** P.O. Box 307, Merigold, MS 38759.

- **Mississippi School of Aviation,** 556 W. Ramp, Jackson, MS 39209.

- **Victory Aircraft,** Jackson County Airport, Pascagoula, MS 39567.

MISSOURI

- **Archway Aviation,** 3127 Creve Coeur Mill Rd., St. Louis, MO 63141.

- **BJ's Pilot Ground School,** 250 Richards Rd., Ste. 266N, Kansas City, MO 64116.

- **Cape Central Airways,** P.O. Box 99, Cape Girardeau, MO 63701.

- **Dick Hill Helicopters and Flying Inc.,** Airpark South, Rt. 2, Ozark, MO 65721.

- **FlightSafety International,** 6161 Aviation Dr., St. Louis, MO 63134.

- **Hal Aviation Inc.,** P.O. Box 524, Malden Air Base, Malden, MO 63863.

- **Kansas City Aviation Center,** Johnson County Executive Airport, Olathe, MO 66061.

- **Mizzou Aviation,** P.O. Box 846, Joplin, MO 64801.

- **Rankin Aircraft,** Rankin Airport, Rte. 3, Maryville, MO 64468.

- **Roederer Aviation,** Spirit of St. Louis Airport, Chesterfield, MO 63017.

- **St. Charles Flying Service,** 3001 Airport Rd., St. Charles, MO 63301.

- **School of the Ozarks Inc.,** General Delivery, Point Lookout, MO 65726.

MONTANA

- **Cody Aero Service Inc.,** 3213 Duggleby Dr., Cody, MT 82414.

- **Dillon Flying Service,** P.O. Box 188, Dillon, MT 59725.

- **Lynch Flying Service,** Billings Logan Int'l. Airport, Billings, MT 59101.

- **Sunbird Aviation,** Box 808, Belgrade, MT 59714.

- **Valley Aviation,** R.R. 4032, Great Falls, MT 59401.

NEBRASKA

- **AirKaman of Omaha,** P.O. Box 19064, Omaha, NE 68119.

- **Linaire Inc.,** Lincoln Municipal Airport, Lincoln, NE 68524.

- **Lincoln Aire,** Lincoln Municipal Airport, Lincoln, NE 68524.

- **Lincoln Aviation Institute,** Municipal Airport, Lincoln, NE 68524.

- **Midway Aviation,** P.O. Box 1844, Kearney, NE 68847.

- **Midwest Airways,** RFD 1 Municipal Airport, Plattsmouth, NE 68048.

- **Offutt Aero Club,** P.O. Box 13234, Offutt AFB, NE 68113.

- **Scottsbluff Aviation Co.,** Rte. 2, Box 182J, Scottsbluff, NE 69361.

- **Sky Craft,** P.O. Box 477, Grand Island, NE 68801.

- **Trego Aviation,** P.O. Box 1226, N. Platte, NE 69101.

NEVADA

- **Aerleon,** 2772 N. Rancho Dr., Las Vegas, NV 89130.

- **Air Neva,** Cannon Int'l Airport, Reno, NV 89502.

- **Aviation Services,** 1880 Gentry Way, Reno, NV 89502.

- **Carson Tahoe Aviation,** 2600 E. Graves Lane, Carson City, NV 89701.

- **General Aviation Services,** 5425 Texas Ave., Reno, NV 89506.

- **Nevada Aero Flight Academy,** 2500 Graves Lane, Carson City, NV 89701.

- **Nevada Aviation Services,** 2772 Rancho Dr., Las Vegas, NV 89106.

- **Pacific Interstate Airlines Training Center,** 1515 East Tropicana, Las Vegas, NV 89119.

- **Winnemucca Air Service,** Municipal Airport, Winnemucca, NV 89445.

NEW HAMPSHIRE

- **Fern's Flying Service,** Concord Municipal Airport, Concord, NH 03301.

- **Lebanon Airport Development Co.,** Lebanon Regional Airport, W. Lebanon, NH 03784.

NEW JERSEY

- **Aviation Career Academy,** Rd. 7, Medford, NJ 08055.

- **Cherokee Aero Club,** 106B Sharon Rd., Robbinsville, NJ 08691.

- **Computer Flight,** 510-B Industrial Ave., Teterboro, NJ 07608.

- **McGuire AFB Aero Club,** P.O. Box 838, Wrightstown, NJ 08562.

- **Raritan Valley Flying School,** Princeton Airport, Princeton, NJ 08540.

- **Sandpiper Air Services,** Bldg. 101, Millville, NJ 08332.

- **Solberg Flight Training Center,** P.O. Box 250, Solberg Airport, Somerville, NJ 08876.

NEW MEXICO

- **Ed's Flying Service,** Alamogordo White Sands, Alamogordo, NM 88310.

- **Great Southwest Aviation Inc.,** P.O. Box 5700, Roswell, NM 88201.

- **J.M. Grimes Aviation,** Silver City-Grant County Airport, Silver City, NM 88062.

- **Kirtland AFB Aero Club,** Hgr. 333, Albuquerque, NM 87117.

- **Mesa Aviation Services,** P.O. Box 1105, Farmington, NM 87401.

- **North American Institute of Aviation,** P.O. Box 668, Las Cruces, NM 88004.

- **Southwest Aviation,** P.O. Box 387, Fairacres, NM 88033.

- **World Balloon Corp.,** 4800 Eubank NE, Albuquerque, NM 87111.

NEW YORK

- **Academics of Flight,** 43-49 45th St., Sunnyside, NY 11104.

- **Air Experts,** 2111 Smithtown Ave., Ronkonkoma, NY 11779.

- **ATE of New York,** General Aviation Terminal, Ronkonkoma, NY 11779.

- **Aviation High School,** Queens Blvd. & 36th St., Long Island City, NY 11101.

- **Board of Cooperative Education,** 610 Hicksville Rd., Bethpage, NY 11714.

- **Board of Cooperative Education,** 375 Locust Ave., Oakdale, NY 11769.

- **Brockway Air Inc.-NY,** Clinton County Airport, Plattsburgh, NY 12901.

- **Buffalo Air Field Mgmt. Company,** 4500 Clinton St., Buffalo, NY 14224.

- **Dunkirk Aviation Flight School,** Dunkirk Municipal Airport, Dunkirk, NY 14048.

- **East Hampton Flight Services,** P.O. Box 656, Wainscott, NY 11975.

- **East Hill Flying Club,** Tompkins County Airport, Ithaca, NY 14580.

- **Edison Technical & Occupational Education Center,** 655 Colfax St., Rochester, NY 14606.

- **Flying Nunns Aviation,** Clinton County Airport, Plattsburgh, NY 12019.

- **Gace Flying Club,** P.O. Box 335, Bethpage, NY 11714.

- **Greenland School of Aviation,** 1 Mill Rd., Latham, NY 12110.

- **Island Helicopters Inc.,** Island Heliport, North Ave., Garden City, NY 11530.

- **Mid County Flyers,** 2099 Smithtown Ave., Ronkonkoma, NY 11779.

- **Mid Island Flying School,** Long Island Macarthur Airport, Ronkonkoma, NY 11779.

- **Miller Aviation,** P.O. Box 564, Endicott, NY 13760.

- **Page Rochester Beechcraft Aero,** 1265 Scottsville Rd., Rochester, NY 14624.

- **Pan American Aviation Institute,** 74-09 37th Ave., Jackson Heights, NY 11372.

- **Perry's Flying Service,** Bldg. 128, Westhampton Beach, NY 11978.

- **Rensselaer Learning Systems,** One Rensselaer Dr., Pittford, NY 14534.

- **Richmor Aviation,** Columbia County Airport, Hudson, NY 12534.

- **Sair Aviation Flight School,** 1801 Walden Rd., Syracuse, NY 13211.

- **Schweizer Soaring School,** P.O. Box 147, Elmira, NY 14902.

- **Skies Unlimited,** 22 Sintsink Dr. E., Port Washington, NY 11050.

- **Sky-Life Foundation,** P.O. Box 699, Northville, NY 12134.

- **Wellsville Flying Service,** P.O. Box 641, Wellsville, NY 14895.

- **Westair Flying School,** Westchester County Airport, White Plains, NY 10604.

NORTH CAROLINA

- **Allison Aviation,** Rte. 4, Box 43, Homestead MHP, Greenville, NC 27834.

- **Atlantic Aero,** P.O. Box 19608, Greensboro, NC 27419.

- **Balloon Ascensions LTD,** Rte. 11, Box 97, Statesville, NC 28677.

- **Carolina Air Academy Inc.,** Elkin Airport, Elkin, NC 28621.

- **Catawba Valley Aviation Inc.,** Rt. 14, Box 94, Airport Rd., Statesville, NC 28677.

- **Cherry Point Marine Aero Club,** P.O. Box 918, Havelock, NC 28532.

- **Goldsboro-Wayne Aviation,** P.O. Box 386, Pikeville, NC 27863.

- **ISO Aero Service,** P.O. Box 1294, Kinston, NC 28501.

- **Seymour Johnson Aero Club,** Seymour Johnson AFB, Seymour Johnson, NC 27531.

- **Shelby Aviation,** P.O. Box 970, Shelby, NC 28150.

- **Tar Heel Aviation,** P.O. Box 911, Jacksonville, NC 28540.

OHIO

- **5-K Flights,** Hgr. W-10, Cleveland, OH 44135.

- **Aerospace Technology,** Stow, OH 44224.

- **Air Service Center,** 2820 Bobmeyer Rd., Hamilton, OH 45015.

- **AM-Air,** Youngstown Municipal Airport, Vienna, OH 44473.

- **American Flyers,** 6200 Riverside Dr., Cleveland, OH 44135.

- **Brookville Air Park,** 9386 National Rd., Brookville, OH 45309.

- **Cardinal Air Training,** Terminal Bldg., Lunken Airport, Cincinnati, OH 45226.

- **CAS Aviation Flite Center,** 28181 McCrady Rd., Circleville, OH 43113.

- **Central Skyport,** 4700 E. 5th. Ave., Columbus, OH 43219.

- **Choi Aviation,** Wadsworth Municipal Airport, Wadsworth, OH 44281.

- **Commonwealth Aviation,** P.O. Box 75052, Cincinnati, OH 45275.

- **Community Airport Corp.,** 2050 Medina Rd., Medina, OH 44256.

- **Executive Jet Aviation,** 625 N. Hamilton Rd., Columbus, OH 43219.

- **FlightSafety International Inc.,** 11600 W. Airport Service Rd., Swanton, OH 43558.

- **Galion Flight Training,** 8240 State Rte. 309, Galion, OH 44833.

- **Heyde Aviation Center Inc.,** 10646 County Rd., Napoleon, OH 43545.

- **Icarus Executive Service Inc.,** 523 1/2 N. Columbus St., Lancaster, OH 43130.

- **Kettering Adult School,** 3700 Far Hills Ave., Kettering, OH 45429.

- **Lawrence County Aviation,** Rte. 2, Box 369, S. Point, OH 45680.

- **Madison Aviation Center,** P.O. Box 287, London, OH 43140.

- **Sundorph Aeronautical Corp.,** Cleveland & Hopkins Int'l Airport, Cleveland, OH 44135.

- **Wings Inc.,** 6060 Mercury Dr., North Canton, OH 44720.

- **Wright Patterson AFB,** Bldg. 153, Area C, WPAFB, OH 45433.

OKLAHOMA

- **Aircraft Service Co.,** Harvey Young Airport, Tulsa, OK 74108.

- **Allied Helicopter Service,** P.O. Box 6216, Tulsa, OK 74148.

- **Delta Aviation,** 1802 W. Wright, Stillwater, OK 74075.

- **Exec Express Inc.,** 2020-4 W. Airport Rd., Stillwater, OK 74075.

- **Midland Flyers,** Miami Municipal Airport, Miami, OK 74354.

- **NEC/Spartan School of Aeronautics,** 8820 E. Pine, P.O. Box 582833, Tulsa, OK 74158-2833.

- **Oklahoma Helicopters,** 1700 Lexington, Rm. 108, Norman, OK 73069.

- **Pionair Flying Club,** 2810 N. Main, Altus, OK 73521.

- **Port Cherokee Seaplane Base,** Rte. 2 Grand Lake, Afton, OK 74331.

- **Redleg Flying Club,** Henry Post Airfield, Ft. Sill, OK 73503.

- **Sellers Aviation Co.,** P.O. Box 204, Enid, OK 73702.

- **Stevenson Aviation Service,** P.O. Box 1711, Muskogee, OK 74401.

- **Stillwater Flight Center,** 2020-3 W. Airport Rd., Stillwater, OK 74075.

- **Versatile Helicopters,** P.O. Box 1433-Downtown Ardmore, Ardmore, OK 73401.

OREGON

- **AAR Western Skyways,** Portland-Troutdale Airport, Troutdale, OR 97060.

- **Aurora Aviation,** P.O. Box 127, Aurora, OR 97002.

- **Cascade Flight Center,** The Dalles Municipal Airport, Dallesport, OR 98617.

- **Caveman Aviation,** 2280 Carton Way, Grants Pass, OR 97526.

- **Coos Aviation,** Airport Way, Coos Bay, OR 97459.

- **Eagle Flight Center,** Portland-Hillsboro Airport, Hillsboro, OR 97123.

- **Eugene Flight Center,** 28809 Airport Rd., Eugene, OR 97402.

- **Greenleaf Helicopters,** Pearson Airpark, Vancouver, OR 98661.

- **Hermiston Flight Center,** P.O. Box 814, Hermiston, OR 97838.

- **Hillsboro Helicopters,** 3301 A NE Cornell Rd., Hillsboro, OR 97124.

- **Horizon Aviation,** P.O. Box 509, Aurora, OR 97002.

- **Klamath Aircraft,** Municipal Airport, Oregon City, OR 97601.

- **Logan & Reavis Air,** Medford-Jackson County Airport, Medford, OR 97504.

- **McKenzie Flying Service,** 90600 Greenhill Rd., Eugene, OR 97402.

- **Mill Plain Flying Service Inc.,** 13912 E. Mill Plain Rd., Vancouver, OR 98684.

- **Mountain Air Helicopters,** 3510 Knox Butte Rd., Albany, OR 97321.

- **Ontario Flight Service,** P.O. Box 879, Ontario, OR 97914.

- **Pilot Personnel International,** 1600 Airway Dr., Lebanon, OR 97355.

- **Roseburg Skyways,** Municipal Airport, Roseburg, OR 97470.

- **Stone Aviation,** 3443 NE Cornell Rd., Hillsboro, OR 97124.

- **T and T Equipment Inc.,** 3565 NE Cornell Rd., Hillsboro, OR 97124.

- **Transwestern Helicopters,** P.O. Box R, Scappoose, OR 97056.

PENNSYLVANIA

- **Aero Flight,** Rd. 2, Box 292, Montoursville, PA 17754.

- **AG Rotors,** Box 578, Gettysburg, PA 17325.

- **Air Condor Helicopters,** 609 Ross Ave., New Cumberland, PA 17070.

- **Arner Flying Service,** Jake Arner Airport, Lehighton, PA 18235.

- **Beaver Aviation Service Inc.,** Beaver County Airport, Beaver Falls, PA 15010.

- **Braden's Flying Service,** 3800 Sullivan Trail, Easton, PA 18042.

- **Cap Aviation,** P.O. Box 3037, Reading, PA 19604.

- **Clark Aviation,** 201 Airport Rd., New Cumberland, PA 17070.

- **Diamond Flite Center Ltd.,** Delaware Airpark, Cheswold, PA 19936.

- **Flying Dutchman Air Service,** Buehl Field, Wood Lane, Langhorne, PA 19047.

- **Haski Aviation Co.,** New Castle Airport, New Castle, PA 16101.

- **Horsham Valley Airways,** 451 Caredean Dr., Horsham, PA 19044.

- **K C Leasing Inc.,** P.O. Box 12568, Pittsburgh, PA 15241.

- **Keystone Aero Services Inc.,** Wilkes Barre-Scranton Airport, Avoca, PA 18641.

- **Lancaster Aviation,** Rd. 3, Lititz, PA 17543.

- **Lincoln Flying Service,** N. Philadelphia Airport, Philadelphia, PA 19114.

- **Moore Aviation Service,** Beaver County Airport, Beaver Falls, PA 15010.

- **Moyer Aviation,** Box 275, Mt. Pocono, PA 18344.

- **New Garden Aviation,** P.O. Box 171, Toughkenamon, PA 19374.

- **Queen City Aviation,** 1730 Vultee St., Allentown, PA 18103.

- **Security Airways,** Rostraver Airport, Belle Vernon, PA 15012.

- **Summit Airlines,** Scott Plaza II, Philadelphia, PA 19113.

- **Steel City Aviation,** Allegheny County Airport, West Mifflin, PA 15122.

- **Stensin Aviation Inc.,** Beaver County Airport, Beaver Falls, PA 15010.

- **Titan Helicopter Services Inc.,** Millville Municipal Airport, Millville, PA 08332.

- **Turner Field,** 1435 Horsham Rd., Ambler, PA 19002.

- **Vee Neal,** Rd. 1, Box 397, Latrobe, PA 15650.

- **Wings,** Rd. 6, Mercer, PA 16137.

PUERTO RICO

- **National Aviation Academy Inc.,** Puerto Rico Int'l. Airport, San Juan, PR 00913.

- **Isla Grande Flying School and Services,** P.O. Box C, Hato Rey, PR 00919.

RHODE ISLAND

- **Corporate Air Charter,** Hangar 1, Warwick, RI 02886.

- **Helms Westerly Aviation,** Westerly State Airport, Westerly, RI 02891.

- **North Central Airways Inc.,** North Central State Airport, Lincoln, RI 02865.

- **Skylanes,** North Central State Airport, Lincoln, RI 02865.

SOUTH CAROLINA

- **Eagle Aviation Inc.,** 2861 Aviation Way, West Columbia, SC 29169.

- **Georgetown Aviation,** P.O. Box 463, Georgetown, SC 29442.

- **Midlands Aviation Corp.,** 1400 Jim Hamilton Blvd., Columbia, SC 29250.

- **North American Institute,** P.O. Box 680, Conway, SC 29526.

- **South Carolina Helicopters,** P.O. Box 636, Saluda, SC 29138.

- **Summerville Aviation,** 850 Greyback Rd., Summerville, SC 29483

SOUTH DAKOTA

- **B & L Aviation,** Rte. 2, Box 74-H, Rapid City, SD 57701.

- **Business Aviation,** 3501 Aviation Ave., Sioux Falls, SD 57104.

- **Falcon Aviation,** R.R. 2, Box 297, Yankton, SD 57078.

- **Miller Aviation,** Brookings Municipal Airport, Brookings, SD 57006.

- **Professional Flight Services,** 3701 N. Minnesota Ave., Sioux Falls, SD 57104.

- **Silver Wings Aviation,** P.O. Box 522, Rapid City, SD 57709.

- **Star,** R.R. 2, Box 396A, Spearfish, SD 57783.

TENNESSEE

- **Bolivar Aviation,** P.O. Box 376, Bolivar, TN 38008.

- **Flight Services,** 2787 N. Second St., Memphis, TN 38127.

- **Moody Aviation,** Box 429, Elizabethton, TN 37643.

- **Morristown Flying Service Inc.,** P.O. Box 1874, Morristown, TN 37816.

- **Red Aero,** 2488 Winchester, Rm. 307, Memphis, TN 38116.

- **Smyrna Air Center,** Hgr. 621, Smyrna Municipal Airport, Smyrna, TN 37167.

- **Southernair Inc.,** P.O. Box 470, Collegedale, TN 37315.

- **Stevens Beech Aero Club,** P.O. Box 17248, Nashville, TN 37217.

- **Volunteer Aviation,** P.O. Box 804, Alcoa, TN 37701.

- **Volunteer Flight Training,** 200 Airport Rd., Clarksville, TN 37040.

- **Williams Aviation,** P.O. Box 397, Springfield, TN 37172.

TEXAS

- **A.T. "Fess" Moore Ground School,** 8605 Lemmon Ave., Dallas, TX 75209.

- **Abilene Aero,** Rte. 2, Box 508, Abilene, TX 79601.

- **Acme School of Aeronautics,** Meacham Field, Ft. Worth, TX 76106.

- **Aero Academy,** 8244 Travelair, Houston, TX 77061.

- **Aero Dynamics,** 8036 Aviation Place, Dallas, TX 75235.

- **Aerocountry Aviation,** Rte. 1, Rockhill Rd., McKinney, TX 75069.

- **Air Academy,** 4576 Claire Chennualt, NR 7, Dallas, TX 75248.

- **Air Center II Inc.,** 4209 Airport Blvd., Austin, TX 78722.

- **Air Central Inc.,** Harlingen Industrial Airport, Harlingen, TX 78550.

- **Airline Crew Training,** P.O. Box 1814, Grapevine, TX 76051.

- **Airport Flying School,** 4511 Eddie Rickenbacker Rd., Dallas, TX 75248.

- **Alpha Aviation,** 8629 Lemmon Ave., Dallas, TX 75209.

- **Alpha Tango Flying Service,** 1110 99th Ave., San Antonio, TX 78214.

- **Amarillo Flying Service,** Rte. 7, Box 5, Amarillo, TX 79118.

- **American Air Academy,** Rte. 1, Denton Municipal Airport, Denton, TX 76205.

- **American Airlines Training Corp.,** American Airlines Flight Academy, DFW Airport, TX 75261.

- **American Flyers,** Location 26 N., Meacham Field, Ft. Worth, TX 76106.

- **Anglo-American (International),** 500 N.W. 38th St., Hgr. 30S, Ft. Worth, TX 76106.

- **Austin Businessjets,** 1801 E. 51st St., Austin, TX 78723.

- **Aviation Ground School,** Rm. B-18, Meacham Field Terminal, Ft. Worth, TX 76106.

- **Bay Area Aviation Inc.,** RWJ Airpark, Baytown, TX 77520.

- **Bell Helicopter Training School,** Trinity Blvd. & Norwood Dr., Ft. Worth, TX 76101.

- **Browning Aerial Services,** Robert Mueller Municipal Airport, Austin, TX 78767.

- **Channel Aviation Inc.,** Baytown Airport, Baytown, TX 77521.

- **Chaparral Aviation Inc.,** 4451 Glen Curtis Dr., Addison, TX 75248.

- **Cliff Hyde Flying Service,** 11015 W. Main, Laporte, TX 77571.

- **Cook's Flying Service,** Box 606, Iowa Park, TX 76367.

- **Cothron Aviation,** 5104 S. Collins, Rte. 3, Arlington, TX 76014.

- **Crew Pilot Training,** P.O. Box 6692, Kingwood, TX 77325.

- **D&J Flight Training,** 4514 Jacksboro Hwy., Wichita Falls, TX 76302.

- **Doc's Aviation Service,** 8650 Cardinal Lane, Smithfield, TX 76180.

- **Eagle's Nest Aero Club,** Servion H, Hangar NR 1, Dallas, TX 75232.

- **Eastex Aviation,** Gregg County Airport, Longview, TX 75601.

- **Executive Aircraft Services of Texas Inc.,** 12 FM 2347, College Station, TX 77840.

- **Fletcher Aviation,** 8904 Randolph, Houston, TX 77061.

- **Flight Proficiency Service,** P.O. Box 7510, Dallas, TX 75209.

- **Gene's Flight Club of El Paso,** 7301 Boeing, El Paso, TX 79925.

- **Goble Aviation,** Redbird Airport, Dallas, TX 75232.

- **Grayson Flying Service,** P.O. Box 668, Sherman, TX 75090.

- **Hank's Flite Center,** Box 6036, Midland, TX 79701.

- **Heli-Dyne Training Center,** 9000 Trinity Blvd., Ft. Worth, TX 76118.

- **Hunt Pan Am Aviation,** Brownsville Int'l Airport, Brownsville, TX 78521.

- **Jet East,** 7363 Cedar Springs, Dallas, TX 75235.

- **Jet Fleet Corp.,** 7515 Lemmon Ave., Dallas, TX 75209.

- **K and S Classic Inc.,** 4831 S. Hampton LB42, Dallas, TX 75232.

- **Majors Aviation Services,** P.O. Box 1907, Greenville, TX 75401.

- **McAllen Aviation,** 2812 S. 10th St., McAllen, TX 78504.

- **McCreery Aviation Co.,** P.O. Box 1659, McAllen, TX 78502.

- **McKinney Aviation,** McKinney Municipal Airport, McKinney, TX 75069.

- **Modern Aero of Texas,** Redbird Airport, Lock Box 37, Dallas, TX 75232.

- **North Dallas Helicopter Corp.,** 4576 Claire Chennault, Ste. 12, Dallas, TX 75248.

- **Pegasus Aeronautical Center,** Ste. 239, Meacham Field Terminal, Ft. Worth, TX 76106.

- **Precision Flight,** P.O. Box 57, Addison, TX 75001.

- **Qualiflight Training,** Location 1N, Meacham Field, Ft. Worth, TX 76106.

- **Randolph AFB Aero Club,** P.O. Box 494, Randolph AFB, TX 78148.

- **Redbird Flite Center Inc.,** Lock Box 10, Dallas, TX 75232.

- **Regional Aviation,** 3114 S. Great Southwest Pkwy., Grand Prairie, TX 75051.

- **Shierry Aviation Inc.,** 4515 Jacksboro Hwy., Wichita Falls, TX 76302.

- **Skybreeze Aviation,** P.O. Box 5771, Lubbock, TX 79414.

- **Skywings Flight Training,** Rm. 119, Meacham Field Terminal, Ft. Worth, TX 76106.

- **Stramel Aviation Inc.,** P.O. Box 863178, Plano, TX 75086.

- **Texas Aero,** Madison Cooper Airport, Waco, TX 76708.

- **Texas American Crew Training,** 8402 Nelms, Houston, TX 77061.

- **Tiger Aviation Services,** Kleberg County Airport, Kingsville, TX 78363.

- **Victoria Aviation Services,** Rte. 6, Bldg. 829, Victoria, TX 77901.

- **Wes-Tex Aircraft,** Rte. 3, Box 48, Lubbock, TX 79401.

- **Westwind Aviation,** 1003 McKeever, Rosharon, TX 77583.

UTAH

- **Alpine Aviation,** P.O. Box 691, Provo, UT 84601.

- **Central Utah Aviation,** P.O. Box C, Provo, UT 84601.

- **Color Canyons Aviation,** P.O. Box 458, Cedar City, UT 84720.

- **Intermountain Air College,** Salt Lake Int'l. Airport, Salt Lake City, UT 84116.

- **Interwest Aviation Corp.,** AMF Box 22063, Salt Lake City, UT 84122.

- **Logan Air Service,** P.O. Box 725, Logan, UT 84321.

- **Ogden Air Service,** 3909 S. Airport Rd., Ogden, UT 84401.

- **Sunwest Aviation,** 3909 Airport Rd., Ogden, UT 84067.

- **Thompson Beechcraft of Salt Lake City,** 369 N. 2370 W., Salt Lake City, UT 84116.

- **Wasatch Helicopter Training Center,** P.O. Box 435, Bountiful, UT 84010.

VERMONT

- **Montair Flight Service,** 1160 Airport Dr., S. Burlington, VT 05401.

VIRGINIA

- **Air Chesterfield,** 7511 Airfield Dr., Richmond, VA 23832.

- **Andrews Bolling Aero Club,** 76 ABG SSYA Hangar 2, Andrews AFB, VA 20331.

- **Colgan Airways,** P.O. Box 1650, Manassas, VA 22110.

- **Dulles Aviation,** P.O. Box 2169, Manassas, VA 22110.

- **Executive Air,** Woodrum Field, Roanoke, VA 24012.

- **Falwell Aviation Inc.,** P.O. Drawer 11409, Lynchburg, VA 24506.

- **Flight International,** Patrick Henry Airport, Newport News, VA 23602.

- **General Aviation,** P.O. Box 457, Municipal Airport, Danville, VA 24541.

- **Hanover Aviation Co.,** 604 Air Park Rd., Ashland, VA 23005.

- **Janelle Aviation,** Leesburg Municipal Airport, Leesburg, VA 22075.

- **Mid-Eastern Airways,** P.O. Box 15400, Chesapeake, VA 23320.

- **Norfolk Navy Flying Club,** Naval Air Station, Norfolk, VA 23511.

- **Virginia Aviation,** P.O. Box 4209, Lynchburg, VA 24502.

- **Waring Aviation,** P.O. Box 7925, Charlottesville, VA 22906.

WASHINGTON

- **Aircraft Specialties,** 101 E. Reserve, Vancouver, WA 98661.

- **Auburn Flight Service,** 506 23rd NE, Auburn, WA 98002.

- **Aviation Training and Research,** ASA Ground School, Seattle, WA 98108.

- **Cliff Howard's Aviation,** 6726 Perimeter Rd. S., Seattle, WA 98108.

- **Clover Park Vocational-Technical,** 4500 Steilacoom Blvd., S.W., Tacoma, WA 98499.

- **Fancher Flyways,** P.O. Box 412, Renton, WA 98055.

- **Felts Field Aviation,** P.O. Box 11877, Spokane, WA 99211.

- **FlightCraft,** 8285 Perimeter Rd. S., Seattle, WA 98108.

- **Flight Training Int'l,** 13424 N.E. 51st Place, Bellevue, WA 98005.

- **Galvin Flying Service Inc.,** 7205 Perimeter Rd., Seattle, WA 98109.

- **Inland Aviation,** P.O. Box 424, Ephrata, WA 98823.

- **Kenmore Air Harbor,** P.O. Box 64, Kenmore, WA 98028.

- **Kennewick Aircraft Service,** 6951 Grandridge Blvd., Kennewick, WA 99336.

- **Midstate Aviation,** 1101 Bowers Rd., Ellensburg, WA 98926.

- **S. Weymouth Naval Aero Club,** U.S. Naval Air Station, S. Weymouth, WA 02190.

- **Snohomish Flying Service,** 9807 Airport Way, Harvey Field, Snohomish, WA 98290.

- **Spanaflight,** 204-188th St. E., Spanaway, WA 98387.

- **Spokane Airways,** P.O. Box 19125, Spokane, WA 99219.

- **Yankee Country Flight Center,** 9115 NE 117th Ave., Vancouver, WA 98662.

WEST VIRGINIA

- **Lawrence County Aviation,** Marshall University, Huntington, WV 25703.

- **Rambar Aviation,** P.O. Box 4307, Parkensburg, WV 26104.

- **Valley Aero,** P.O. Box 768, Martinsburg, WV 25401.

WISCONSIN

- **Aerodyne,** 4800 S. Howell Ave., Milwaukee, WI 53207.

- **Carter Aircraft,** Rte. 3, Pulaski, WI 54162.

- **Central Wisconsin Aviation,** Central Wisconsin Airport, Mosinee, WI 54455.

- **Chaplin Aviation,** Rte. 1, County Trunk 0, Sheboygan Falls, WI 53085.

- **Fond Du Lac Skyport,** Rte. 5, Fond Du Lac, WI 54935.

- **Four Lakes Aviation Corp.,** 3606 N. Stoughton Rd., Madison, WI 53704.

- **G.A.K. Aviation,** 923 E. Layton Ave., Milwaukee, WI 53207.

- **Gibson Aviation Service,** 3800 Starr Ave., Eau Claire, WI 54701.

- **Gran Aire,** 9305 W. Appleton Ave., Milwaukee, WI 53225.

- **Heileman Air Services Ltd.,** 2709 Fanta Reed Rd., La Crosse, WI 54601.

- **Hodge Aero,** Rte. 7, Hwy. 51 S., Janesville, WI 53545.

- **Maxair,** Outagamie County Airport, Appleton, WI 54911.

- **Morey Airplane Co.,** Morey Airport, Middleton, WI 53562.

- **Sylvania Airport,** 2624 S. Sylvania Ave., Sturtevant, WI 53177.

- **Twin Ports Flying Service,** 4804 Hammond Ave., Superior, WI 54880.

WYOMING

- **Casper Air Service,** Natrona County Int'l. Airport, Casper, WY 82604.

Collegiate Aviation Schools

ALABAMA

- **ALABAMA AVIATION & TECHNICAL COLLEGE,** Dr. Sandra H. Flowers, Director of Institutional and Student Development, P.O. Box 1209, Ozark, AL 36361, (800) 624-3468.

- **AUBURN UNIVERSITY,** Dr. James C. Williams III, Head and Prof./Aerospace Engineering, 162 Wilmore Lab, Auburn University, AL 36849-5338, (205) 844-6800.

- **COMMUNITY COLLEGE OF THE AIR FORCE,** SMSgt. Darrel W. Kitchens, Program Administrator/Tech. Branch, Simler Hall (Bldg. 836), Maxwell AFB, AL 36112-6655, (205) 293-2041.

- **JACKSONVILLE STATE UNIVERSITY,** Dr. Reed, Jacksonville, AL 36265, (205) 231-4814.

- **NORTHWEST ALABAMA COMMUNITY COLLEGE,** Mr. Charles E. Harris, Dept. Head, P.O. Drawer 9, Hamilton, AL 35570, (205) 921-2528.

- **WALLACE STATE COMMUNITY COLLEGE,** Highway 31 S., Hanceville, AL 35077, (205)352-6403. Aviation contact: Mr. Bert Mackentepe, Chief Flight Instructor, P.O. Box 288, Vinemont, AL 35179, (205) 739-4452.

ALASKA

- **ALASKA BIBLE COLLEGE,** Mr. Dwayne King, Director of Development, Box 289, Glennallen, AK 99588, (907) 822-3201.

- **ANCHORAGE COMMUNITY COLLEGE,** Mr. Bob Pearson, Aviation Administration, 2811 Merrill Field Dr., Anchorage, AK 99501, (907) 276-3737.

- **ISLANDS COMMUNITY COLLEGE,** R.M. Griffin, Director, 1101 S.M.C. Blvd., Sitka, AK 99835, (907) 747-6653.

- **KETCHIKAN COMMUNITY COLLEGE,** Mr. Jerry Hok, Instructional Services, Ketchikan, AK 99901, (907) 225-6177.

- **KODIAK COMMUNITY COLLEGE,** Mr. Jack Bunting, Instructor, Aviation Dept., Box 946, Kodiak, AK 99615, (907) 486-4161.

- **MATANUSKA-SUSITNA COMMUNITY COLLEGE,** Mr. Hank Nosek, Instructor/Aviation, Box 899, Palmer, AK 99645, (907) 745-4255.

- **UNIVERSITY OF ALASKA - ANCHORAGE,** Mr. Ron Haney, Associate Professor/Aviation Administration, 3211 Providence Dr., Anchorage, AK 99508, (907)277-7591 or (907) 786-1800.

- **UNIVERSITY OF ALASKA SOUTHEAST,** Mr. Gene Hickey, Counseling Supervisor, Counseling, 11120 Glacier Hwy., Juneau, AK 99801, (907) 789-4439.

ARIZONA

- **ARIZONA STATE UNIVERSITY,** Mr. Laurence E. Gesell, Assistant Professor/ Dept. of Aeronautical Technology, Arizona

State University, Tempe, AZ 85287, (602) 965-7775 or (602) 965-9011.

- **COCHISE COMMUNITY COLLEGE,** Mr. Lee Oppenheim, Aviation Division Chairman, R.R. 1, Box 100, Douglas, AZ 85607, (602) 364-0302 or (602) 965-9011.

- **EMBRY-RIDDLE AERONAUTICAL UNIVERSITY AT PRESCOTT,** Dr. Peggy Baty, Associate Vice Chancellor/Academics, 3200 N. Willow Creek Rd., Prescott, AZ 86301, (602) 776-3728.

- **MOHAVE COMMUNITY COLLEGE,** Mrs. Dorene Jordan, Associate Dean/ Vocational Services, 1971 Jagerson Ave., Kingman, AZ 86401, (602) 757-4331.

- **NORTHLAND PIONEER COLLEGE,** Mr. Keith Leafdale, Instructor, P.O. Box 610, Holbrook, AZ 86025, (602) 524-6111.

- **PHOENIX COLLEGE,** Dr. Bert E. Griffen, Professor of Engineering, 1202 W. Thomas Rd., Phoenix, AZ 85013, (602) 285-7240 or (602) 965-9011.

- **PIMA COMMUNITY COLLEGE,** Mr. Anthony Guglielmino, Chairman, Aviation Dept., 1255 N. Stone Ave., Tucson, AZ 85709, (602) 884-6030.

- **SCOTTSDALE COMMUNITY COLLEGE,** Mr. Sylvester, Director of Admissions, Admissions Office, 9000 E. Chaparrel, Scottsdale, AZ 85253, (602) 423-6000.

- **YAVAPAI COLLEGE,** Mr. Larry Tiffin, Instructor, 1100 E. Sheldon, Box 6065, Prescott, AZ 86301, (602) 445-7300.

ARKANSAS

- **ARKANSAS TECH UNIVERSITY,** Russellville, AR 72801, (501) 968-0498.

- **HENDERSON STATE UNIVERSITY,** Dr. Jerry L. Robinson, Director of Aviation Programs, Box 7611, HSU, Arkadelphia, AR 71923, (501) 246-5511.

- **MISSISSIPPI COUNTY COMMUNITY COLLEGE,** Ms. Debora Williams, Chairperson, Applied Sciences Div., P.O. Box 1109, Blythville, AR 72316, (501) 762-1020.

CALIFORNIA

- **ANTELOPE VALLEY COLLEGE,** Mr. Jack Halliday, Aerospace Department, 3041 W. Ave. K, Lancaster, CA 93536, (805) 942-4022 or (805) 943-3241.

- **BAKERSFIELD COLLEGE,** Mr. Robin Davidson, Assistant Professor/Industrial Technology, 1801 Panorama Dr., Bakersfield, CA 93305, (805) 395-4571.

- **CALIFORNIA STATE UNIVERSITY,** Ms. Maureen A. Pettitt, Professor, 5151 State University Dr., Los Angeles, CA 90032, (213) 343-4550.

- **CERRO COSO COMMUNITY COLLEGE,** Dr. Paul Riley, Dean of Continuing Education, Office of Instruction, 3000 College Heights Blvd., Ridgecrest, CA 93555, (619) 375-5001.

- **CHABOTT COLLEGE,** Mr. Ali Saleh, Chairman/Technology & Engineering Division, 25555 Hesperian Blvd., Hayward, CA 94545, (415) 786-6852.

- **CHAFFEY COMMUNITY COLLEGE,** Mr. Lawrence X. Johnson, Aeronautics Coordinator, 5885 Haven Ave., Rancho Cucamonga, CA 91720, (714) 941-2350.

- **CHRISTIAN HERITAGE COLLEGE,** Mr. Gary F. Coombs, Chairman/Missions Dept., 2100 Greenfield Dr., El Cajon, CA 92019, (619) 440-3043.

- **CITY COLLEGE OF SAN FRANCISCO,** Mr. Vito Eiarfaglio, Aeronautics, San Francisco International Airport, Building 928, San Francisco, CA 94128, (415) 877-0161.

- **COLLEGE OF ALAMEDA,** Mr. Ralph Kearney, BAT Department, 555 Atlantic Ave., Alameda, CA 94501, (415) 748-2329.

- **COLLEGE OF THE REDWOODS,** Dr. Bill Hollenback, Associate Dean, Eureka, CA 95501, (707) 443-8411.

- **COLLEGE OF SAN MATEO,** Mr. S. Brad Banghart, Coordinator/Aeronautics Dept., 1700 W. Hillsdale Blvd., San Mateo, CA 94402, (415) 574-6275.

- **CUYAMACA COLLEGE,** Mr. Art McCoole, Aeronautics Program Coodinator, 2950 Jamacha Rd., El Cajon, CA 92010-4304, (619) 670-1980.

- **CYPRESS COLLEGE,** Mr. Chuck Gifford, Chairman/Aeronautics Dept., 9200 Valley View, Cypress, CA 90630, (714) 826-2220.

- **FOOTHILL COLLEGE,** Ms. Betty Hicks, Instructor, Middle Field Campus, 12345 El Monte Rd., Los Altos Hills, CA 94022, (415) 960-4600.

- **FRESNO CITY COLLEGE,** Ms. Lynn Ahrens, Director, Flight Science Dept., 1101 University Ave., Fresno, CA 93741, (209) 442-4600.

- **GAVILAN COMMUNITY COLLEGE,** Mr. Charles R. Price, Dept. Coordinator, 490 Skylane Dr., Hollister Municipal Airport, Hollister, CA 95023, (408) 637-1151.

- **GLENDALE COMMUNITY COLLEGE,** Mr. William L. Mallory, Dept. Chairman, 1500 N. Verdugo Rd., Glendale, CA 91208, (818) 240-1000.

- **KINGS RIVER COMMUNITY COLLEGE,** Mr. David Troehler, Dept. Chairman, Aeronautics, 995 N. Reed Ave., Reedley, CA 93654, (209) 638-3641.

- **LONG BEACH CITY COLLEGE,** Mr. Steven R. King, Professor/Aeronautics, Professional Pilot Dept., 4901 E. Carson St., Long Beach, CA 90808, (213) 420-4387.

- **MENDOCINO COLLEGE,** Mr. Bob Devinny, Instructor, Aviation, P.O. Box 3000, Ukiah, CA 95482, (707) 468-3005.

- **MERCED COLLEGE,** Mr. Jay Mayhue, Division Chairman/Industrial Tech., 3600 M Street, Merced, CA 95348, (209) 384-6172 or (805) 943-3241.

- **MIRA COSTA COLLEGE,** Mr. F. Bruce Stewart, Dean/Vocational Education & Applied Sciences, One Barnard Dr., Oceanside, CA 92056-3899, (619) 757-2121.

- **MONTEREY PENINSULA COLLEGE,** Mr. Jack Branson, Head/Aviation Dept., 980 Fremont St., Monterey, CA 93940, (408) 375-8603.

- **MT. SAN ANTONIO COLLEGE,** Mr. Wayne J. Lutz, Chairman/Aeronautics, 1100 N. Grand Ave., Walnut, CA 91789, (714) 594-5611, ext. 755.

- **MT. SAN JACINTO COLLEGE,** Mr. John Schuster, Coordinator/Aviation Program, 1499 N. State St., San Jacinto, CA 92383, (714) 658-3281.

- **NATIONAL UNIVERSITY,** Mr. Mead Massa, Dean/School of Aerospace Studies, 4141 Camino Del Rio S., San Diego, CA 92108, (619) 563-7402 or (619) 563-7100.

- **NORTHROP UNIVERSITY,** Dr. John P. Mattei, Dean/Institute of Technology, 5800

W. Arbor Vitae St., Los Angeles, CA 90045, (213) 337-4447 or (213) 337-4404.

- **OHLONE COLLEGE,** Ms. Jacqueline Waide, Professor, Air Transportation Tech., 43600 Mission Blvd., Fremont, CA 94539, (415) 659-6257.

- **ORANGE COAST COLLEGE,** Dr. Ernest W. Maurer, Dean/Division of Technology, 2701 Fairview Rd., Costa Mesa, CA 92626, (714) 432-5812.

- **PALOMAR COMMUNITY COLLEGE,** Mr. Jerry Houser, Aeronautical Science Coordinator, 1140 W. Mission Rd., San Marcos, CA 92069, (619) 744-1150, ext. 2518.

- **PASADENA CITY COLLEGE,** Mr. Bob Navarro, Director, Engineering Technology Dept., 1570 E. Colorado Blvd., Pasadena, CA 91106, (818) 578-7281.

- **SACRAMENTO CITY COLLEGE,** Mr. William Robinson, Aeronautics Dept., 3835 Freeport Blvd., Sacramento, CA 95822, (916) 449-7111.

- **SADDLEBACK COMMUNITY COLLEGE,** Ms. Carol Fowler, 28000 Marguerite Pkwy., Mission Viejo, CA 92692, (714) 831-4795.

- **SAN BERNARDINO VALLEY COLLEGE,** Mr. Frank Lopez, Head/ Aeronautics Dept., 701 S. Mt. Vernon Ave., San Bernardino, CA 92410, (714) 888-6511, ext. 1341.

- **SAN DIEGO MESA COLLEGE,** Mr. Donald E. Taylor, Chief Aviation Instructor, 7250 Mesa College Dr., San Diego, CA 92111, (619) 560-2729.

- **SAN JOAQUIN DELTA COLLEGE,** Mr. Doug Fritz, Division Chairman, Technical Arts Dept., 5151 Pacific Ave., Stockton, CA 95207, (209) 474-5151.

- **SAN JOSE STATE UNIVERSITY,** Dr. H. Gene Little, Professor & Chairman/Dept. of Aviation, One Washington Square, San Jose, CA 95192-0081, (408) 924-6580.

- **SANTA BARBARA CITY COLLEGE,** Mr. Tom Travis, Coordinator/Aviation Program, Aviation, 300 N. TurnPike, Santa Barbara, CA 93110, (805) 687-0812.

- **SANTA ROSA JUNIOR COLLEGE,** Mr. Dennis Ryan, Head of Aeronautics Dept., Aeronautics Dept., 1501 Mendocino Ave., Santa Rosa, CA 95401, (707) 527-4475.

- **SHASTA COLLEGE,** Mr. Ted Lord, Instructor, Aviation Dept., Box 496006, Redding, CA 96049, (916) 225-4677.

- **SKYLINE COLLEGE,** Mr. Donald Biederman, Director, Science/Math/ Technology Div., 3300 College Dr., San Bruno, CA 94015, (415) 355-7000.

- **SOLANO COMMUNITY COLLEGE,** Mr. Dave L. Wright, Director/School of Aviation, 4000 Suisun Valley Rd., Suisun City, CA 94585, (707) 864-7000.

- **SOUTHWESTERN COLLEGE,** Mr. Dayton L. Smith, Coordinator/Senior Flight Instructor, 900 Otay Lakes Rd., Chula Vista, CA 92010, (619) 421-6700.

- **UNIVERSITY OF CALIFORNIA - BERKELEY,** Dr. A.K. Kanafani, Director/ Inst. of Transportation, University of California-Berkeley, Berkeley, CA 94720, (415) 642-3585.

- **UNIVERSITY OF SOUTHERN CALIFORNIA,** Prof. Richard H. Wood, Director, Aviation Safety Programs, 3500 S. Figueroa St., Suite 202, Los Angeles, CA 90007, (213) 743-6523, FAX (213) 745-6769.

- **WEST LOS ANGELES COLLEGE,** Mr. Martin C. Wolf, Dept. Chairman, Airport/ Aviation Avionics, 9700 S. Sepulveda Blvd., Los Angeles, CA 90045, (213) 776-5264.

- **YUBA COLLEGE,** Mr. R. Webb, Instructor, Aeronautics Dept., 2088 N. Beale Rd., Marysville, CA 95901, (916) 741-6700.

COLORADO

- **AIMS COMMUNITY COLLEGE,** Mr. Marvin L. Bay, Chief Instructor, P.O. Box 69, Greeley, CO 80632, (303) 330-8008.

- **COLORADO AERO TECH,** Mr. Barry Scoles, Director of Admissions, 10851 West 120th Ave., Broomfield, CO 80021, (800) 888-3995 or (303) 466-1714.

- **COLORADO NORTHWESTERN COMMUNITY COLLEGE,** (303) 675-2261. Ray Mallett, Program Director/Aviation Flight Technology, 500 Kennedy Dr., Rangely, CO 81648, (303) 675-3284.

- **EMERY AVIATION COLLEGE,** Mr. Dennis H. Hennings, Director of Admissions, 1955 N. Union Blvd., Colorado Springs, CO 80909, (719) 632-8116.

- **METROPOLITAN STATE COLLEGE,** Prof. Robert K. Mock, Chairman/Aerospace Science Dept., 1006 11th St., Denver, CO 80204, (303) 556-2982.

- **MORGAN COMMUNITY COLLEGE,** Dr. Tom Henry, Dean of Instruction, 17800 County Rd. 20, Ft. Morgan, CO 80701, (303) 867-3081.

- **PIKES PEAK COMMUNITY COLLEGE,** Mr. Art Thompson, Instructor/Aviation, P.O. Box 13089, Ft. Carson, CO 80913, (719) 576-4783.

CONNECTICUT

- **THAMES VALLEY STATE TECHNICAL COLLEGE,** Mr. Bob Granato, College Counsel Student Services, 574 New London, Norwich, CT 06360, (203) 886-0177.

- **UNIVERSITY OF NEW HAVEN,** Mr. David P. Hunter, Director/Aviation Dept., 300 Orange Ave., W. Haven, CT 06516, (203) 932-7203.

DELAWARE

- **DELAWARE STATE COLLEGE,** Dr. Daniel E. Coons, Director/Airway Science Program, Delaware State College, Dover, DE 19901, (302) 736-3535.

- **WILMINGTON COLLEGE,** Mr. Mickey Turnbo, Chairman/Business Dept., 320 Dupont Hwy., New Castle, DE 19720, (302) 328-9401.

DISTRICT OF COLUMBIA

- **UNIVERSITY OF THE DISTRICT OF COLUMBIA,** 4200 Connecticut Ave, NW, Washington, DC 20008, (202) 282-3200. Aviation contact: Col. Ernest J. Davis, Jr., Chairperson/Dept. of Aerospace Technology, Hangar 10, Washington Nat'l Airport, Washington, DC 20001, (202) 282-7420.

FLORIDA

- **BROWARD COMMUNITY COLLEGE-SOUTHERN,** Ms. Ursula Davidson, Dept. Head/BCC-Aviation, 7200 Hollywood Blvd., Pembroke Pines, FL 33024, (305) 963-8910.

- **COLLEGE OF BOCA RATON,** Mr. E.K. Morice, Coordinator/Aviation Management, 3601 N. Military Trail, Boca Raton, FL 33431, (407) 994-0770.

- **DAYTONA BEACH COMMUNITY COLLEGE,** Ted Zoller, Coordinator/School of Technologies, Box 1111, Daytona Beach, FL 32015, (904) 255-8131.

- **EMBRY-RIDDLE AERONAUTICAL UNIVERSITY AT DAYTONA,** Mr. William A. Martin, Dean/College of Aviation Technology, Embry-Riddle Aeronautical University, Daytona Beach, FL 31014-3900, (904) 239-6821 or (904) 239-6000.

- **FLORIDA COMMUNITY COLLEGE,** Mr. Mel Carpenter, Prof. of Aviation, Kent Campus, 3939 Roosevelt Blvd., Jacksonville, FL 32205-8999, (904) 387-8166.

- **FLORIDA INSTITUTE OF TECHNOLOGY,** Mr. Gregory A. Johnson, Admissions Director/School of Aeronautics, 150 W. University Blvd., Melbourne, FL 32901-6988, (800) 352-8324 (out of state), (800) 348-4636 (in state).

- **FLORIDA INTERNATIONAL UNIVERSITY,** Dr. Milton Torres, Chairperson/Industrial Engineering, Industrial Engineering, VH211, Miami, FL 33199, (305) 554-2256.

- **FLORIDA MEMORIAL COLLEGE,** Mr. David L. Hosley, Director/Airway Science, 15800 NW 42nd Ave., Miami, FL 33054, (305) 623-4277.

- **GULF COAST COMMUNITY COLLEGE,** Mr. Robert E. Wright, Program Manager/ Aviation Technology, 5230 W. Hwy. 98, Panama City, FL 32401, (904) 769-1551.

- **JACKSONVILLE UNIVERSITY,** Mr. Curtis C. Truver, Director/Aeronautics Program, Jacksonville University, 2800 N. University Blvd., Jacksonville, FL 32211, (904) 744-3950.

- **LAKE-SUMTER COMMUNITY COLLEGE,** Mr. Jacob Kertz, Instructor, Business/Technical, Leesburg, FL 32788, (904) 787-3747.

- **MANATEE JUNIOR COLLEGE,** Ms. Gayle Davis, Coordinator/Aerospace Program, Dept. of Technology, P.O. Box 1849, Bradenton, FL 33507, (813) 755-1511.

- **MIAMI-DADE COMMUNITY COLLEGE - NORTH,** Dr. Gerard Pucci, Chairman/Aviation, 11011 SW 104 St., Miami, FL 33176, (305) 347-2572.

- **MIAMI-DADE COMMUNITY COLLEGE - SOUTH,** Dr. Gerard Pucci, Professor/Aviation, 11011 SW 104 St., Miami, FL 33176, (305) 347-2572.

- **PALM BEACH COMMUNITY COLLEGE,** 4200 S. Congress Ave., Lake Worth, FL 33461, (407) 439-8000.

- **PENSACOLA JUNIOR COLLEGE,** Ms. Jean Norman, Coordinator/Professional Development, 1000 College Blvd., Pensacola, FL 32504, (904) 484-1797.

- **ST. PETERSBURG JUNIOR COLLEGE,** Dr. David B. Fellows, Chief Ground Instructor and Prof., 2465 Drew St., Clearwater, FL 34625, (813) 791-2528.

GEORGIA

- **CLAYTON STATE COLLEGE,** Mr. Jack R. Moore, Dept. Head/Aviation Dept., 9013 Tara Blvd., P.O. Box 285, Morrow, GA 30260, (404) 961-3569.

- **GEORGIA STATE UNIVERSITY,** Dr. Marvin Weintraub, College of Public and Urban Affairs, Georgia State University, University Plaza, Atlanta, GA 30303, (404) 651-3519.

HAWAII

- **HONOLULU COMMUNITY COLLEGE,** Mr. Brian J. Isaacson, Head Instructor/ Aeronautics, 402 Aokea St., Honolulu, HI 96819, (808) 833-2977.

IDAHO

- **IDAHO STATE UNIVERSITY,** Mr. Richard Lighter, Head Instructor, 1427 W. 10th Ave. B, Pocatello, ID 83204, (208) 232-8485.

ILLINOIS

- **AERO-SPACE INSTITUTE,** Ms. Patricia L. Newton, Admissions Representative, 161 W. Harrison St., Chicago, IL 60605-1017, (312) 408-0101.

- **BELLEVILLE AREA COLLEGE,** Dr. Clarence L. Hall, Coordinator/Aviation Program, 10 Omega Dr., Sauget, IL 62206, (618) 398-0795.

- **CARL SANDBURG COLLEGE,** Darrell F. Clevidence, Chairman/Math-Science Div., 2232 S. Lake Storey Rd., Galesburg, IL 61401, (309) 344-2518.

- **DANVILLE AREA COMMUNITY COLLEGE,** Ms. Jan Bennett, Secretary/ Continuing Education Dept., 2000 E. Main, Danville, IL 61832, (217) 443-1811.

- **ELGIN COMMUNITY COLLEGE,** Mr. Jim Resser, Dean/Advanced Technology Dept., 1700 Spartan Dr., Elgin, IL 60123, (312) 697-1000.

- **JOHN WOOD COMMUNITY COLLEGE,** Gerry Carter, Dean/Community Services, 150 S. 48th Street, Quincy, IL 62301, (217) 224-6500.

- **JOLIET JUNIOR COLLEGE,** James King, Instructor/Technical, 1216 Houbolt, Joliet, IL 60436, (815) 729-9020.

- **KISHWAUKEE COLLEGE,** Mr. John Eakle, Instructor/Community Education, Alt. 38 & Malta Rd., Malta, IL 60150, (815) 825-2086.

- **LAKE LAND COLLEGE,** Mr. Ron Sanderson, Dean/Career Education, South Rt. 45, Mattoon, IL 61938, (217) 235-3131.

- **LEWIS UNIVERSITY,** Dr. Kathleen Owens, Dean/College of Arts & Sciences, Rte. 53, Romeoville, IL 60441-2298, (815) 838-0500.

- **LINCOLN LAND COMMUNITY COLLEGE,** Dr. Mark D. Harbaugh, Dean/ Occupational Programs, Shepherd Rd., Springfield, IL 62708, (217) 786-2270.

- **OAKTON COMMUNITY COLLEGE,** Mr. Eric Dryden, President/Aviation Club, 1600 E. Golf Rd., Des Plaines, IL 60016, (312) 635-1695.

- **PARKLAND COLLEGE,** Dr. John Leap, Dept. Chairman/Engineering Science & Technology, 2400 W. Bradley, Champaign, IL 61821, (217) 351-5726.

- **PARKS COLLEGE OF ST. LOUIS UNIVERSITY,** Dr. Paul A. Whelan, Vice President, Falling Springs Rd. & Hwy. 157, Cahokia, IL 62206, (618) 337-7500.

- **PRAIRIE STATE COLLEGE,** Dr. Don Kinzy, Dean/Div. of Business and Technology, Halsted & 197th St., Chicago Heights, IL 60411, (312) 709-3536.

- **ROCK VALLEY COLLEGE,** Mr. Charles Billman, Associate Professor, 3301 N. Mulford Rd., Rockford, IL 61101, (815) 397-6795.

- **SOUTH SUBURBAN COLLEGE,** Mr. Douglas Tweeten, Associate Dean/Physical Science & Math Dept., 15800 S. State St., S. Holland, IL 60473, (312) 596-2000.

- **SOUTHERN ILLINOIS UNIVERSITY,** Mr. Paul Harre, Associate Dean, Southern Illinois University-Carbondale, Carbondale, IL 62901, (618) 536-6682 or (618) 536-4405.

- **UNIVERSITY OF ILLINOIS - INSTITUTE OF AVIATION,** Mr. Tom W. Emanuel, Jr., Head of Academics/Institute of Aviation, One Airport Rd., Savoy, IL 61874, (217) 244-8671 or (217) 244-8601.

- **WAUBONSEE COMMUNITY COLLEGE,** Ms. Nancy Partch, Program Developer/Community Services, Rte. 47 at Harter Rd., Sugar Grove, IL 60554, (312) 466-4811.

- **WILLIAM RAINEY HARPER COLLEGE,** Ms. Nancy Domain, Continuing Education Dept., 1200 W. Algonquin, Palatine, IL 60067, (312) 397-3000.

INDIANA

- **BALL STATE UNIVERSITY,** Dr. Kenneth Poucher, Professor/Industrial and Technology, 131 Practical Arts, Muncie, IN 47304, (317) 285-5641.

- **INDIANA STATE UNIVERSITY,** Mr. James E. Crehan, Chairman/Aerospace Technology, Indiana State University, Terre Haute, IN 47809-2201, (812) 237-2641.

- **PURDUE UNIVERSITY,** Prof. William P. Duncan, Dept. Head/Aviation Technology Dept., Purdue University, W. Lafayette, IN 47906, (317) 743-3896.

- **VINCENNES UNIVERSITY,** Mr. Donald Marquez, Chairman/Aviation Flight, Vincennes University, 1002 N. First St., Vincennes, IN 47591-9986, (812) 885-4500 or (812) 885-4200.

IOWA

- **HAWKEYE INSTITUTE OF TECHNOLOGY,** Mr. Roger Beck, Dept. Head, 1501 E. Orange Rd., Waterloo, IA 50704, (319) 296-2320.

- **INDIAN HILLS COMMUNITY COLLEGE,** Dave Huebner, Dept. Head/Aviation Mechanic, Ottumwa Industrial Airport, Ottumwa, IA 52501, (515) 683-5215.

- **IOWA LAKES COMMUNITY COLLEGE,** 19 S. 7th St., Estherville, IA 51334. Aviation contact: Mr. Roy Powers, Dept. Chairman, 300 S. 18th St., Estherville, IA 51334, (712) 362-2604.

- **IOWA WESTERN COMMUNITY COLLEGE,** Mr. Earl Henriksen, Aviation Program Coordinator/Aviation, 2700 College Rd., Box 4C, Council Bluffs, IA 51502, (712) 325-3373.

- **KIRKWOOD COMMUNITY COLLEGE,** Mr. George Colbert, Program Coordinator/ Community Education, P.O. Box 2068, Cedar Rapids, IA 52406, (319) 398-5411.

- **NORTHWEST IOWA TECHNICAL COLLEGE,** Ms. Lynn Rolfsmeir, Coordinator/Business, Trade, & Industry Dept., Hwy. 18 W., Sheldon, IA 51201, (712) 324-5061.

- **UNIVERSITY OF DUBUQUE,** Mr. Edward S. Rebholz, Associate Professor and Chairman/Aviation Administration, 2000 University Ave., Dubuque, IA 52001, (319) 589-3179.

- **WESTERN IOWA TECHNICAL COMMUNITY COLLEGE,** 4647 Stone Ave., Box 265, Sioux City, IA 51102. Aviation contact: Mr. Dennis Krause, Adult and Continuing Education Division, 4647 Stone Ave., P.O. Box 265, Sioux City, IA 51106, (712) 274-6400.

KANSAS

- **BARTON COUNTY COMMUNITY COLLEGE,** Great Bend, KS 67830, (316) 792-2701.

- **CENTRAL COLLEGE,** Mr. Richard L. Mahnke, Aviation Coordinator, Central College, 1200 S. Main, McPherson, KS 67460, (316) 241-0723.

- **COLBY COMMUNITY COLLEGE,** Mr. Theron Johnson, Director of Admissions/ Admissions Dept., 1255 S. Range, Colby, KS 67701, (913) 462-3984.

- **FORT HAYS STATE UNIVERSITY,** Dr. Maurice H. Witten, Aviation Coordinator/ Dept. of Physics, Fort Hays State University, Hays, KS 67601-4099, (913) 628-4271.

- **FORT SCOTT COMMUNITY COLLEGE,** Mr. Dallas Foster, Coordinator of Aviation Programs, Airport, Rt. 4, Box 24, Ft. Scott, KS 66701, (316) 223-2700.

- **FRIENDS BIBLE COLLEGE,** Mr. Lonnie Choate, Admission Director, P.O. Box 288, Haviland, KS 67059, (316) 862-5252.

- **GARDEN CITY COMMUNITY COLLEGE,** Mr. Gale Seibert, Ground School Instructor, 801 Campus Dr., Garden City, KS 67846, (316) 276-7611.

- **HESSTON COLLEGE,** Mr. R. Wendell Sauder, Director of Aviation, Box 3000, Hesston, KS 67062, (316) 327-8325 or (800) 835-2026.

- **INDEPENDENCE COMMUNITY JUNIOR COLLEGE,** Mrs. Debra A. Warner, Director of Guidance, College Ave., Independence, KS 67301, (316) 331-4100.

- **JOHNSON COUNTY COMMUNITY COLLEGE,** Mr. Dave Lonborg, Dean/ Community Services Dept., 12345 College at Rivera, Overland Park, KS 66210, (913) 469-8500.

- **KANSAS COLLEGE OF TECHNOLOGY,** Mr. Kenneth W. Barnard, Dean/Aeronautics, 2409 Scanlan Ave., Salina, KS 67401, (913) 825-0275.

- **LABETTE COMMUNITY JUNIOR COLLEGE,** Mr. Gayle Huff, Instructor/ Aviation, Continuing Education Dept., 200 S. 14th St., Parsons, KS 67357, (316) 421-6700.

- **NEOSHO COUNTY COMMUNITY COLLEGE,** Dr. Gary Church, Dean/ Instruction Dept., 1000 S. Allen St., Chanute, KS 66720, (316) 431-6222.

- **PITTSBURG STATE UNIVERSITY,** Dr. C. Dale Lemons, Chairman/Dept. of Industrial Arts & Technology, Pittsburg State University, Pittsburg, KS 66762, (316) 231-7000.

- **SEWARD COUNTY COMMUNITY COLLEGE,** Mr. William G. Bolton, Aviation Dept., P.O. Box 1137, Liberal, KS 67901-1137, (316) 624-1951 or (316) 231-2000.

- **UNIVERSITY OF KANSAS,** Dr. David Downing, Chairman & Professor/Aerospace Engineering, 2004 Learned Hall, Lawrence, KS 66045, (914) 864-4267.

- **WICHITA STATE UNIVERSITY,** Brent D. Bowen, Director/Aviation Management Program, Campus Box 88, Wichita State University, Wichita, KS 67220, (316) 689-3367.

KENTUCKY

- **EASTERN KENTUCKY UNIVERSITY,** Dr. Wilma J. Walker, Coordinator and Professor/Aviation Programs, Eastern Kentucky University-Stratton 249, Richmond, KY 40475, (606) 622-1014.

- **NORTHERN KENTUCKY UNIVERSITY,** Dr. Thomas Edwards, Coordinator/Business

Administration, BEP 414, Highland Heights, KY 41076, (606) 572-5469.

- **SOMERSET COMMUNITY COLLEGE,** Mr. Ernest Crovan, Dean/Academic Affairs, 808 Monticello Rd., Somerset, KY 42501, (606) 679-8501.

LOUISIANA

- **DELGADO COMMUNITY COLLEGE,** Brian Satterlee, Division Chair/Engineering and Technology Division, 615 City Park Ave., New Orleans, LA 70119, (504) 483-4444.

- **LOUISIANA TECHNICAL UNIVERSITY,** Mr. Dale Sistrunk, Head/Dept. of Professional Aviation, P.O. Box 3181 T.S., Ruston, LA 71272, (318) 257-2691.

- **NICHOLLS STATE UNIVERSITY,** University Station, Thibodaux, LA 70118, (504)446-8111. Aviation contact: Mr. Dan G. Vincent, Director of Operations/Aero Science, P.O. Box 1222, Thibodaux, LA 70302, (504) 447-3386.

- **NORTHEAST LOUISIANA UNIVERSITY,** Mr. William T. Hemphill, Jr., Head/Dept. of Aviation, 700 University Ave., Monroe, LA 71209, (318) 342-2148.

- **NORTHWESTERN STATE UNIVERSITY OF LOUISIANA,** Mr. Larry Varnado, Coordinator/Division of Aviation Science, Northwestern State University, Natchitoches, LA 71457, (318) 357-5102.

MAINE

- **CENTRAL MAINE VOC-TECH INSTITUTE,** R. Serenbetz, Dean/Division of Continuing Education, 1250 Turner St., Auburn, ME 04210, (207) 784-2385.

MARYLAND

- **CATONSVILLE COMMUNITY COLLEGE,** Mr. Jeffrey B. Burbridge, Coordinator/Aviation Science, 800 S. Rolling Rd., Catonsville, MD 21228, (301) 455-4441.

- **ESSEX COMMUNITY COLLEGE,** Mrs. Broadwater, Air & Sea Community Programs, Essex Community College, 7201 Rossville, Baltimore Co., MD 21237, (301) 522-1754.

- **FREDERICK COMMUNITY COLLEGE,** Mr. Gerard L. Blake, Manager/ Aviation Maintenance Program, 7932 Opossumtown Pike, Frederick, MD 21701, (301) 694-1281.

- **HAGERSTOWN JUNIOR COLLEGE,** Ms. Virginia Young, Administrative Assistant/Continuing Education, 751 Robinwood Dr., Hagerstown, MD 21740, (301) 790-2800.

- **UNIVERSITY OF MARYLAND - EASTERN SHORE,** Mr. Abraham D. Spinak, Director/Airway Science Program, University of Maryland - Eastern Shore, Princess Anne, MD 21853, (301) 651-2200.

MASSACHUSETTS

- **BERKSHIRE COMMUNITY COLLEGE,** Woody Printz, Professor/ Engineering Technology, West Street, Pittsfield, MA 01201, (413) 499-4660.

- **BRIDGEWATER STATE COLLEGE,** (508)697-1200. Aviation contact: Mr. William L. Anneseley, Coordinator/Mgmt. and Aviation Science Dept., Bridgewater State College, Bridgewater, MA 02325, (508) 697-1395.

- **CAPE COD COMMUNITY COLLEGE,** Mr. Peter Birkel, Dean/Continuing

Education and Community Service, W.
Barnstable, MA 02668, (617) 362-2131.

- **NORTH SHORE COMMUNITY COLLEGE,** Dr. Robert S. Finkelstein, Prof./ Coordinator, Aviation Science Program, 3 Essex St., Beverly, MA 01915, (508) 922-6722.

- **SALEM STATE COLLEGE,** Ms. Valerie Bockman, Chairperson/Business Administration, Salem, MA 01970, (508) 741-6000.

- **SUFFOLK UNIVERSITY,** Dr. John L. Sullivan, Coordinator/Aviation Programs, 8 Ashburton Place, Boston, MA 02108, (617) 573-8488.

- **WENTWORTH INSTITUTE OF TECHNOLOGY,** W. Cassie, Dept. Head/ Aeronautical, 550 Huntington Ave., Boston, MA 02115, (617) 442-9010.

MICHIGAN

- **ANDREWS UNIVERSITY,** Dr. Raymond O. Swensen, Chairman/Dept. of Aviation Technology, Andrews University, Griggs Dr., Berrien Springs, MI 49104, (616) 471-1455 or (616) 471-7771.

- **CHARLES S. MOTT COMMUNITY COLLEGE,** Mr. Thomas Goetz, Coordinator/Flight Technology, 1401 E. Court St., Flint, MI 48502, (313) 762-0500.

- **DELTA COLLEGE,** Ms. Marilyn Gillett, Registrar, University Center, MI 48710, (517) 686-9000.

- **EASTERN MICHIGAN COLLEGE,** Mr. Timothy Doyle, Program Coordinator/ Interdisciplinary Technology, College of Technology, Ypsilanti, MI 48197, (313) 487-1161.

- **GOGEBIC COMMUNITY COLLEGE,** Dr. George Mihel, Dean of Instruction, Ironwood, MI 49938, (906) 932-4231.

- **HENRY FORD COMMUNITY COLLEGE,** Mr. Hicks, Instructor/Aviation, 22586 Anarbor Trail, Dearborn Heights, MI 48127, (313) 271-2750.

- **JACKSON COMMUNITY COLLEGE,** Mr. David A. Frazier, Director/Aviation Technology, 3610 Wildwood Ave., Jackson, MI 49202, (517) 787-7012.

- **KIRTLAND COMMUNITY COLLEGE,** Mr. George Maroney, Coordinator/Aviation Program, 10775 N. St. Helen Rd., Roscommon, MI 48653, (517) 275-5121.

- **LANSING COMMUNITY COLLEGE,** Mr. Gayland L. Tennis, Director/Aviation Center, 3428 W. Hangar Dr., Lansing, MI 48906, (517) 483-1406.

- **MACOMB COMMUNITY COLLEGE,** Mr. David A. Pilon, Associate Dean/ Mechanical Technology Dept., 14500 Twelve Mile Rd., Warren, MI 48093, (313) 445-7000.

- **NORTH CENTRAL MICHIGAN COLLEGE,** Mr. Harris Stevens, Continuing Education Dept., 1515 Howard St., Petoskey, MI 49770, (616) 347-3973.

- **NORTHERN MICHIGAN UNIVERSITY,** Dr. Elaine F. Alden, Dept. Head/Occupational Studies, Northern Michigan University, Marquette, MI 49855, (906) 227-2067.

- **NORTHWESTERN MICHIGAN COLLEGE,** Mr. Robert Buttleman, Director/Dept. of Aviation, 1701 E. Front St., Traverse City, MI 49684, (616) 922-1220.

- **ST. CLAIR COUNTY COMMUNITY COLLEGE,** Mr. Ivan Smith, Dept.

122   Airline Pilot

Chairman/Applied Power Technology, 323 Erie St., Port Huron, MI 48060, (313) 984-3881.

- **SCHOOLCRAFT COLLEGE,** Ms. Sherry Zylka, Coordinator/Continuing Education, 18600 Haggerty Rd., Livonia, MI 48152, (313) 591-6400.

- **SOUTHWESTERN MICHIGAN COLLEGE,** Dr. Norman C. Ashcraft, Dean/ School of Technology, 58900 Cherry Grove Rd., Dowagiac, MI 49047, (616) 782-5113.

- **WESTERN MICHIGAN UNIVERSITY,** Dr. Harley Behm, Chairman/Engineering Technology Dept., Western Michigan University, Kalamazoo, MI 49008, (616) 387-6515 or (616) 387-1000.

MINNESOTA

- **ANOKA TECHNICAL INSTITUTE,** Mr. Bob Anderson, Program Chairperson/Aviation Dept., 1355 W. Hwy. 10 Anoka T.I., Anoka, MN 55303, (612) 427-1880.

- **AUSTIN COMMUNITY COLLEGE,** Ms. Penny Reynen, Director of Admission, 1600 8th Ave. NW, Austin, MN 55912, (507) 433-0508.

- **INVER HILLS COMMUNITY COLLEGE,** Mr. Brian D. Addis, Program Coordinator, 8445 College Trail, Inver Grove Heights, MN 55075, (612) 450-8564 or (612) 450-8500.

- **ITASCA COMMUNITY COLLEGE,** Mr. David S. Henemier, Director of Aviation, 1851 E. Hwy. 169, Grand Rapids, MN 55744, (218) 327-4460.

- **MANKATO STATE UNIVERSITY,** Mr. John O. Roberts, Program Dir./Aviation Management, Box 14 MSU, Mankato, MN 56002, (507) 389-5430.

- **ST. CLOUD STATE UNIVERSITY,** 3rd Ave. S., St. Cloud, MN 56301, (612)255-0121. Aviation contact: Mr. Kenneth W. Raiber, Assistant Prof./Technology, Headley Hall 101 SCSU, St. Cloud, MN 56301, (612) 255-2108.

- **SOUTHWEST STATE UNIVERSITY,** Mr. M. Runholt, Engineering Technology, Marshall, MN 56258, (507) 537-7021.

- **THIEF RIVER FALLS TECHNICAL INSTITUTE,** Mr. Allen Mickelson, Aviation Director, Hwy. One E., Thief River Falls, MN 56701, (218) 681-5424.

- **UNIVERSITY OF MINNESOTA,** Mr. Larry W. Leake, Chairman/Aviation Dept., 355 South Bd., Crookston, MN 56716, (218) 281-6510.

- **UNIVERSITY OF MINNESOTA AT DULUTH,** LTC Douglas B. Robinson, Dept. Head/Aerospace Studies, 6219 E. Superior St., Duluth, MN 55804, (218) 726-8159.

- **VERMILION COMMUNITY COLLEGE,** Mr. David S. Henemier, Director/Aviation Dept., 1900 E. Camp St., Ely, MN 55731, (218) 365-3256.

- **WINONA STATE UNIVERSITY,** Dr. George Bolon, Director, Airway Science/ Aviation, Winona State University, Winona, MN 55987, (507) 457-5000.

MISSISSIPPI

- **DELTA STATE UNIVERSITY,** Mr. Robert H. Ryder, Chairman/Commercial Aviation Dept., Box 3203 DSU, Cleveland, MS 38733, (601) 846-4206 or (601) 846-4205.

- **EAST MISSISSIPPI COMMUNITY COLLEGE,** Mr. David N. Phillips,

Instructor, Dept. Head, P.O. Box 100, Mayhew, MS 39753, (601) 327-6322 or (601) 327-1112.

- **HINDS COMMUNITY COLLEGE,** Mr. Bill Elliott, Instructor/Aviation, Raymond, MS 39154, (601) 857-5261.

- **JACKSON STATE UNIVERSITY,** Dr. Raphel Lee, Chairman, Dept. of Technology/Industrial Arts, Jackson State University, Jackson, MS 39217, (601) 968-2466.

- **MERIDIAN COMMUNITY COLLEGE,** Ms. Nelda Kennedy, Director/Community Service, Community Service, 5500 Hwy. 19 N., Meridian, MS 39305, (601) 483-8241.

MISSOURI

- **CENTRAL MISSOURI STATE UNIVERSITY,** Dr. John W. Horine, Chairman/Dept. Power and Transportation, Broad & Maguire, Warrensburg, MO 64093, (816) 429-4975.

- **CROWDER COLLEGE,** Dr. Herbert C. Schade, Chairman/Physical Science and Technology, 601 Laclede, Neosho, MO 64850, (417) 451-4700.

- **MAPLE WOODS COMMUNITY COLLEGE,** Mr. Gary D. May, Aviation Dept. Coordinator, 2601 NE Barry Rd., Kansas City, MO 64156, (816) 436-6500.

- **MINERAL AREA COLLEGE,** Mr. A.C. Sullivan, Dean/Vocational Division, Flat River, MO 63601, (314) 431-4593.

- **ST. LOUIS COMMUNITY COLLEGE AT MERAMEC,** Mr. Frank Block, Program Director/Aviation Technology Dept., Kirkwood, MO 63122, (314) 863-7811.

- **THE SCHOOL OF THE OZARKS,** Mr. Jerry P. Allen, Chairman/Aviation Science Dept., The School of the Ozarks, Point Lookout, MO 65726, (417) 334-6411.

- **SOUTHWEST MISSOURI STATE UNIVERSITY,** Dr. House, Industrial Dept., 901 S. National, Springfield, MO 65804, (417) 836-5270.

- **STATE FAIR COMMUNITY COLLEGE,** Mr. Greg Bell, Dean of Community Service, 3201 W. 16th, Sedalia, MO 65301, (816) 826-7100.

MONTANA

- **FLATHEAD VALLEY COMMUNITY COLLEGE,** Dr. Howard Fryett, President, Number One First St. E., Kalispell, MT 59901, (406) 752-5222.

- **ROCKY MOUNTAIN COLLEGE,** Mr. Benjamin H. Diggs, Director/Aviation Studies, 1511 Poly Dr., Billings, MT 59102, (406) 657-1084.

NEBRASKA

- **CHADRON STATE COLLEGE,** Dr. Jack Swanson, Professor, Chadron State College, 10th & Main Sts., Chadron, NE 69337, (308) 432-6218 or (308) 432-6365.

- **KEARNEY STATE COLLEGE,** Dr. Dick Lebsack, Professor, Kearney State College, 25th St. and 9th Ave., Kearney, NE 68849, (308) 234-8515.

- **WESTERN NEBRASKA COMMUNITY COLLEGE,** Mr. James E. Joyce, Chairman/Aviation Dept., Western Nebraska Community College - Sidney, Sidney, NE 69162, (308) 254-5450.

NEVADA

- **WESTERN NEVADA COMMUNITY COLLEGE,** Ms. Sherry Hong, Director/

Community Service, 2201 W. Nye Ln., Carson City, NV 89701, (702) 887-3114.

NEW HAMPSHIRE

- **DANIEL WEBSTER COLLEGE,** Mr. Thomas L. Teller, Chairman/Aviation Division, 20 University Dr., Nashua, NH 03063, (603) 883-4991 or (603) 883-3556.

NEW JERSEY

- **ATLANTIC COMMUNITY COLLEGE,** Mr. Edmund J. Zorauski, Division Chairman, Atlantic Community College, Mays Landing, NJ 08330, (609) 343-5023 or (609) 343-5001.

- **CUMBERLAND COUNTY COLLEGE,** Dr. W. Edward Pollard, Dean/Education, P.O. Box 517, Vineland, NJ 08360, (609) 691-8600.

- **MERCER COUNTY COMMUNITY COLLEGE,** Mr. Joseph Blasenstein, Coordinator/Aviation Programs, 1200 Old Trenton Rd., Trenton, NJ 08690, (609) 586-4800.

- **THOMAS A. EDISON STATE COLLEGE,** Mr. Howard A. Bueschel, Senior Academic Program Advisor, 101 W. State St., CN 545, Trenton, NJ 08625, (609) 984-1158 or (609) 984-1100.

NEW MEXICO

- **EASTERN NEW MEXICO UNIVERSITY,** Box 6000, Roswell, NM 88201, (505) 624-7312.

- **NEW MEXICO JUNIOR COLLEGE,** Mr. Don Wilson, Division Chairperson/Business and Technology, Lovington Hwy., Hobbs, NM 88240, (505) 392-4510.

- **UNIVERSITY OF NEW MEXICO,** Mr. Don Gassoway, University College, Room 20, Albuquerque, NM 87106, (505) 277-0111.

NEW YORK

- **COLLEGE OF AERONAUTICS,** Dr. George Brush, Aeronautical Maintenance Div., LaGuardia Airport, Flushing, NY 11371, (718) 429-6600.

- **CORNING COMMUNITY COLLEGE,** Dr. Richard W. Vockroth, Prof. of Mechanical Technology and Aviation, Corning Community College, Spencer Hill, Corning, NY 14830, (607) 962-9243 or (607) 962-9011.

- **DOWLING COLLEGE,** Idle Hour Blvd., Oakdale, Long Island, NY 11772, (516) 589-6100. Aviation contact: Prof. Robert Smith, Dean/Aeronautics and Airway Science, Dowling College, Oakdale, NY 11769, (516) 244-3322.

- **JAMESTOWN COMMUNITY COLLEGE,** Mr. Joseph Minarovich, Aviation Instructor, Office of Continuing Education, 525 Falconer St., Jamestown, NY 14701, (716) 665-5220.

- **NIAGARA UNIVERSITY,** Rev. Daniel O'Leary, Dean/Continuing Studies, Niagara Falls, NY 14109, (716) 285-1212.

- **ST. FRANCIS COLLEGE,** Prof. Emmett N. O'Hare, Chairman/Aviation Dept., 180 Remsen St., Brooklyn Heights, NY 11201, (718) 522-2300.

- **STATE UNIVERSITY OF NEW YORK - FARMINGDALE,** Mr. Paul K. Baumann, Chairman/Aerospace Technology, Melville Road, Farmingdale, NY 11735, (516) 420-2314.

- **SYRACUSE UNIVERSITY,** Dr. John E. LaGraff, Director/Aerospace Engineering, 141 Link Hall, Syracuse, NY 13244, (315) 443-4366.

- **WESTCHESTER COMMUNITY COLLEGE,** Mr. George Albrecht, Institutional Research, 75 Grasslands Rd., Valhalla, NY 10595, (914) 285-6854.

NORTH CAROLINA

- **BLADEN TECHNICAL INSTITUTE,** Mr. Charles Moore, Director/Continuing Education, Continuing Education Dept., P.O. Box 266, Dublin, NC 28332, (919) 862-2164.

- **CATAWBA VALLEY TECHNICAL INSTITUTE,** Ms. Sue Asp, Highway 64-70, Hickory, NC 28601, (704) 327-9124.

- **COLLEGE OF ALBERMARLE,** Mr. Floyd Horton, Associate Dean/Continuing Education, Riverside Ave., Elizabeth City, NC 27909, (919) 335-0821.

- **DURHAM TECHNICAL COMMUNITY COLLEGE,** Ms. Mary Ann Freedman, Program Director/Continuing Education, 1637 Lawson St., Durham, NC 27703, (919) 598-9222.

- **ELIZABETH CITY STATE UNIVERSITY,** Dr. Edward A. Ianni, Assistant Vice Chancellor/Academic Affairs, 1001 Parkview Dr., Elizabeth City, NC 27909, (919) 335-3316.

- **GASTON COLLEGE,** Mr. John Merritt, Coordinator of Aviation Programs/Aviation Dept., 201 Hwy. 321 S., Dallas, NC 28034, (704) 922-8041.

- **GUILFORD TECH COMMUNITY COLLEGE,** (919)334-4822 Mr. Thomas W. Freeman, Aviation Dept. Chairman, P.O. Box 309, Jamestown, NC 27282, (919) 334-1126.

- **LENOIR COMMUNITY COLLEGE,** Mr. Paul A. Craig, Aviation Dept. Head/ Director, Center for Aviation Education, P.O. Box 188, Kinston, NC 28502, (919) 522-1735.

- **MITCHELL COMMUNITY COLLEGE,** Mr. Dan Ballard, Extention Director/ Continuing Education, W. Broad St., Statesville, NC 28677, (704) 878-3220.

- **NASH TECHNICAL INSTITUTE,** Ms. Pam Drum, Occupational Extension Coordinator, P.O. Box 7488, Rocky Mount, NC 27804, (919) 443-4011.

- **NORTH CAROLINA STATE UNIVERSITY,** Dr. John N. Perkins, Mechanical & Aerospace Engineering, Box 7910, Raleigh, NC 27650, (919) 737-2365.

- **PIEDMONT BIBLE COLLEGE,** George F. Dougherty, Director/Aerospace Ed., Aerospace Education, Sugar Valley Airport, Mocksville, NC 27028, (919) 998-3971.

- **SAMSON TECHNICAL COLLEGE,** Mr. Jimmy Naylor, Instructor, Continuing Education, Clinton, NC 28328, (919) 592-8081.

- **SANDHILLS COMMUNITY COLLEGE,** Mr. Harlen McCaskill, Dean/ Continuing Education, 2200 Airport Rd., Pinehurst, NC 28374, (919) 692-6185.

- **SOUTHEASTERN COMMUNITY COLLEGE,** Mr. Harry Foley, Continuing Education, P.O. Box 151, Whiteville, NC 28472, (919) 642-7141.

- **STANLY TECHNICAL COLLEGE,** Mr. Lonnie Swanner, Dean/Continuing Education, Rt. 4, Box 55, Albermarle, NC 28001, (704) 982-0121.

- **TRI-COUNTY COMMUNITY COLLEGE,** Mr. Harry Jarrett, Dean/ Continuing Education, P.O. Box 40, Murphy, NC 28906, (704) 837-6810.

- **WAKE TECHNICAL COMMUNITY COLLEGE,** Dr. Larry Robertson, Dean/ Evening Division, 9101 Fayetteville Rd., Raleigh, NC 27603, (919) 772-0551.

- **WAYNE COMMUNITY COLLEGE,** Mr. Harry W. Blanchard, Chairman/Aviation Maintenance Technology Dept., Caller Box 8002, Goldsboro, NC 27530, (919) 735-5151.

NORTH DAKOTA

- **NORTH DAKOTA STATE SCHOOL OF SCIENCE,** Mr. Robert Gette, Dean of Business Division, 800 N. 6th St., Wahpeton, ND 58075, (701) 671-1130.

- **NORTH DAKOTA STATE UNIVERSITY,** Mr. George Wallman, Director of Admissions, University Station, Box 5596, Fargo, ND 58105, (713) 591-3500.

- **UNIVERSITY OF NORTH DAKOTA,** Mr. William F. Shea, Chairman/Aviation Dept., P.O. Box 8216, University Station, Grand Forks, ND 58202, (701) 777-2791.

OHIO

- **BOWLING GREEN STATE UNIVERSITY,** Mr. David A. Lombardo, Assistant Prof./Dept. of Technology, Bowling Green State University, Bowling Green, OH 43403-0302, (419) 372-2439.

- **CINCINNATI TECHNICAL COLLEGE,** Mr. Jim Schmid, Chairman/Engineering Technology, 3520 Central Pkwy., Cincinnati, OH 45223, (513) 569-1751.

- **COLUMBUS STATE COMMUNITY COLLEGE,** Mr. Clifton T. Marr, Chairman/ Aviation Maintenance Technology, 5355 Alkire Rd., Columbus, OH 43228, (614) 878-1038.

- **CUYAHOGA COMMUNITY COLLEGE,** Mr. Robert Kekelik, Coordinator/Aviation Technology, 11000 Pleasant Valley Rd., Parma, OH 44130, (216) 987-5287.

- **DAVIS COLLEGE,** Kevin Lambert, Senior Vice President/Aviation, 4747 Monroe St., Toledo, OH 43623, (419) 473-2700.

- **HEIDELBERG COLLEGE,** Dr. Leon Wise, Professor/Psychology, 310 E. Machet St., Tiffin, OH 44883, (419) 448-2309.

- **KENT STATE UNIVERSITY,** Dr. Eugene G. Ripple, Director, Kent State University Airport, 4020 Kent Rd., Stow, OH 44224, (216) 672-2640 or (216) 672-2444.

- **MIAMI UNIVERSITY,** Mr. Tom Schroeder, Chief Flight Instructor, Miami University Airport, Oxford, OH 45056, (513) 529-2735.

- **MUSKINGUM TECHNICAL COLLEGE,** Robert Kuhn, Associate Professor/Business, 1555 Newark Rd., Cambridge, OH 43725, (614) 454-2501.

- **THE OHIO STATE UNIVERSITY,** Mr. William E. Pippin, Program Manager/Dept. of Aviation, Box 3022, Columbus, OH 43210-0022, (614) 292-5460.

- **OHIO UNIVERSITY,** Ms. Joan E. Mace, Chairman, Ohio University Airport, Athens, OH 45701, (614) 698-4114 or (614) 593-1000.

- **OHIO UNIVERSITY - SOUTHERN CAMPUS,** Dan Hieronomous, Faculty/ Aviation, 1804 Liberty Ave., Ironton, OH 45638, (614) 533-4600.

- **SINCLAIR COMMUNITY COLLEGE,** Mr. Gary S. Clark, Aviation Administration Program Coordinator/Dept. of Marketing, 444 W. Third St., Dayton, OH 45402, (513) 226-2927 or (513) 226-2963.

- **UNIVERSITY OF TOLEDO,** Ms. De Schroder, Continuing Education, 2801 W. Bancroft, Toledo, OH 43606, (419) 537-4242.

- **WILBERFORCE UNIVERSITY,** Wilberforce, OH 45384, (513) 376-2911.

- **WRIGHT STATE UNIVERSITY,** Lt. Col. Michael Jackson, Commander & Prof./ Aerospace Studies, Air Force, 232 Frederick A. White Center, Dayton, OH 45435, (513) 873-2600.

OKLAHOMA

- **NORTHEASTERN OKLAHOMA A&M,** Mr. Robert M. Anderson, Instructor, Station 1, Box 15, Miami, OK 74354, (918) 542-8441.

- **NORTHEASTERN STATE UNIVERSITY,** Dr. Vernon H. Isom, Chairman/Division of Technology, Tahlequah, OK 74464, (918) 456-6375 or (918) 456-5511.

- **NORTHERN OKLAHOMA COLLEGE,** Dr. E. D. Mang, Instructor/Aviation, 1220 E. Grand Ave., Tonkawa, OK 74653, (405) 628-2581.

- **OKLAHOMA CHRISTIAN COLLEGE,** Dr. Stafford North, Executive Vice President, P.O. Box 11000, 2501 E. Memorial, Oklahoma City, OK 73136, (405) 425-5180 or (405) 425-5000.

- **OKLAHOMA CITY COMMUNITY COLLEGE,** Mr. Robert Allen, Institute Manager/Science and Manufacturing, 7777 S. May, Oklahoma City, OK 73159, (405) 682-7457.

- **OKLAHOMA STATE UNIVERSITY,** Mr. Glen E. Nemecek, Coordinator/Aviation Education, 300 N. Cordell, Stillwater, OK 74078-0422, (405) 744-5856.

- **PHILLIPS UNIVERSITY,** Mr. Richard T. Anderson, Registrar, University Station, Enid, OK 73701, (405) 237-4433.

- **ROGERS STATE COLLEGE,** Bob Willis, Coordinator/Applied Science Division, Will Rogers and College Hill, Claremore, OK 74017, (918) 341-7510.

- **ROSE STATE COLLEGE,** Ms. Sharland G. Kirkpatrick, Aviation Program Manager, 6420 S.E. 15th St., Midwest City, OK 73110, (405) 733-7378 or (405) 733-7450.

- **SOUTHEASTERN OKLAHOMA STATE UNIVERSITY,** Bill Edwards, Chairman/ Aerospace, Station A, Box 4136, Durant, OK 74701, (405) 924-6886.

- **SOUTHWESTERN OKLAHOMA STATE UNIVERSITY,** Mr. Don McMillon, Instructor/Industrial Education, P.O. Box 262, Weatherford, OK 73096, (405) 772-6143.

- **SPARTAN SCHOOL OF AERONAUTICS,** (918)838-3966. Ms. Pauline Belew, Director of Admissions, 8820 E. Pine St., P.O. Box 582833, Tulsa, OK 74158-2833, (918) 836-6886.

- **UNIVERSITY OF OKLAHOMA,** (405)329-2789. Aviation contact: Director/ Dept. of Aviation, 1700 Lexington, Rm. 124, Norman, OK 73069, (405) 325-7231.

- **WESTERN OKLAHOMA STATE COLLEGE,** Mr. Henry F. Hartsell, Director/ Technology Education, Coordinator/Aviation, 2801 N. Main, Altus, OK 73521, (405) 477-2005 or (405) 477-2000.

OREGON

- **LANE COMMUNITY COLLEGE,** Mr. Terry L. Hagberg, Chairman/Flight Technology Dept., 28715 Airport Rd., Eugene, OR 97405, (503) 689-2021.

- **MT. HOOD COMMUNITY COLLEGE,** Mr. Charles Darland, Aviation Coordinator, 26000 S.E. Stark St., Gresham, OR 97030, (503) 667-7230.

- **PORTLAND COMMUNITY COLLEGE,** Mr. Harry Day, Aviation Coordinator, Aviation Box 19000, Portland, OR 97219, (503) 244-6111.

- **TREASURE VALLEY COMMUNITY COLLEGE,** Mr. Don Green, Director/ Occupational Education, 650 College Place, Ontario, OR 97914, (503) 889-6493.

PENNSYLVANIA

- **CENTRAL PENNSYLVANIA BUSINESS SCHOOL,** Mr. Anthony K. Psyck, Chairman/ Travel Division, College Hill Rd., Summerdale, PA 17093, (717) 732-0702.

- **COMMUNITY COLLEGE OF ALLEGHENY COUNTY,** Prof. Ted Staub, Chief Ground School Instructor/Aviation, 808 Ridge Ave., 513 Milton Hall, Pittsburgh, PA 15212, (412) 237-2506.

- **COMMUNITY COLLEGE OF BEAVER COUNTY,** Mr. James M. Johnson, Coordinator/Aviation Dept., Beaver County Airport, Beaver Falls, PA 15010, (412) 843-9202.

- **EAST STROUDSBURG UNIVERSITY OF PENNSYLVANIA,** Dr. Paul N. Houle, Professor/Physics, E. Stroudsburg, PA 18301, (717) 424-3350.

- **LEHIGH COUNTY COMMUNITY COLLEGE,** Dr. Charlotte Mastellar, Dean of Business, Science & Technology, 2370 Main St., Schnecksville, PA 18078, (215) 799-1101.

- **PENNSYLVANIA COLLEGE OF TECHNOLOGY,** Mr. C.W. Williamson, Assistant Dir./Transportation Technology, 1005 W. Third St., Williamsport, PA 17701, (717) 326-3761.

- **PENNSYLVANIA STATE UNIVERSITY,** Dr. Hubert C. Smith, Dir. of Undergraduate Studies, Aerospace Engineering, 233 Hammond Building, University Park, PA 16802, (814) 238-7035.

- **PENNSYLVANIA STATE UNIVERSITY - BERKS CAMPUS,** Mr. Walter Fullan, Director/Continuing Education, Tulpehocken Rd., P.O. Box 7009, Reading, PA 19610, (215) 320-4800.

- **UNITED WESLEYAN COLLEGE,** Dr. Paul Faulkenberry, Academic Dean, Academic Office, 1414 Cedar St., Allentown, PA 18103, (215) 439-8709.

- **WESTMORELAND COUNTY COMMUNITY COLLEGE,** Mr. Paul J. Salonick, Instructor/Science & Technology Division, Westmoreland County Community College, Armbrust Rd., Youngwood, PA 15697-1895, (412) 925-4161 or (412) 925-4062.

- **WILLIAMSPORT AREA COMMUNITY COLLEGE,** Mr. C.W. Williamson, Assistant Dir./Transportation Technology, 1005 W. Third St., Williamsport, PA 17701, (717) 326-3761.

PUERTO RICO

- **INTERNATIONAL AMERICAN UNIVERSITY OF PUERTO RICO,** P.R. Rd. #1, Corner of Sein St., Rio Piedras, PR 00919. Aviation contact: Mr. Eleazar D. Lamboy, Coordinator/Airway Science Program, P.O. Box 1293, Hato Rey, PR 00919, (809) 758-8000.

SOUTH CAROLINA

- **ANDERSON COLLEGE,** Dr. Mark L. Hopkins, President, Administration, 316 Boulevard, Anderson, SC 29621, (803) 231-2100.

- **BOB JONES UNIVERSITY,** Mr. Philip D. Smith, Provost, Greenville, SC 29614, (803) 242-5100.

- **MIDLANDS TECHNICAL COLLEGE,** Mr. Richard McConnell, Coordinator of Aviation Programs/Continuing Education Dept., P.O. Box 2408, Columbia, SC 29202, (803) 822-8080.

- **TRIDENT TECHNICAL COLLEGE - BERKELEY,** Mr. David H. Guerin, Aircraft Maintenance Technology Program Coordinator, P.O. Box 10367, Charleston, SC 29411, (803) 792-8812.

SOUTH DAKOTA

- **AUGUSTANA COLLEGE,** Dr. V.R. Nelson, Head/Aviation Dept., FAA Examiner C66A, 29th and Summit, Sioux Falls, SD 57197, (605) 336-4910 or (605) 336-0770.

- **SOUTH DAKOTA STATE UNIVERSITY,** Mr. Jim Benkem, Aviation Education, University Station, Box 2201, Brookings, SD 57007, (605) 688-6319.

TENNESSEE

- **CHATTANOOGA STATE TECHNICAL COLLEGE,** Mr. Ben W. Carr, Jr., Associate Prof. of Aerospace, 4501 Amnicola Hwy., Chattanooga, TN 37406, (615) 697-4441.

- **CLEVELAND STATE COMMUNITY COLLEGE,** Dr. Frank C. McKenzie, Assistant Dean/Business & Technology, P.O. Box 3570, Cleveland, TN 37311, (615) 472-7141.

- **HIWASSEE COLLEGE,** Mr. Jack Miller, Division Head/Math & Science Division, Madisonville, TN 37354, (615) 442-2001.

- **MIDDLE TENNESSEE STATE UNIVERSITY,** Dr. Wallace R. Maples, Chairman/Prof., Aerospace Dept., MTSU, Box 67, Murfreesboro, TN 37132, (615) 898-2788.

- **MOODY BIBLE INSTITUTE,** Mr. Kenneth Simmelink, Director, Moody Aviation, P.O. Box 429, Elizabethton, TN 37643, (615) 629-8900.

- **TENNESSEE STATE UNIVERSITY,** Mr. Ted Ledwith, Coordinator/Technical Aeronautics, Tennessee State University, 3500 John A. Merritt Blvd., Nashville, TN 37209-1561, (615) 320-3275 or (615) 320-3287.

- **UNIVERSITY OF TENNESSEE AT MARTIN,** Dr. R.L. Perry, Dean/ Engineering Technology, EPS 113, UTM, Martin, TN 38238, (901) 587-7380.

- **UNIVERSITY OF TENNESSEE SPACE INSTITUTE,** Mr. Fred Watts, Professor/ Aviation System, UTSI Rd., Tullahoma, TN 37388, (615) 455-0631.

- **VOLUNTEER STATE COMMUNITY COLLEGE,** Mr. Roland Whitsell, Chairman/Business Division, Nashville Pike, Gallatin, TN 37066, (615) 452-8600.

- **WALTERS STATE COMMUNITY COLLEGE,** Dean Locke, Morristown, TN 37814, (615) 581-2121.

TEXAS

- **AMERICAN TECHNICAL UNIVERSITY,** Mr. Roy F. Bonnett, Chairperson/Division of Technological Studies, U.S. Hwy. 190 W., Killeen, TX 76540, (817) 526-1423.

- **CENTRAL TEXAS COLLEGE,** Mr. Curtis R. Gibson, Dept. Chairman/Career Aviation Dept., P.O. Box 1800, Killeen, TX 76540-9990, (817) 526-1241.

- **LEE COLLEGE,** Dr. Howard Duhon, Manager/Business & Industrial Development Center, 511 S. Whiting, Baytown, TX 77520, (713) 425-6539.

- **LETOURNEAU COLLEGE,** Mr. Lauren Bitikofer, Chairman/Division of Aviation, 2100 S. Mobberly, Longview, TX 75602, (214) 753-0231.

- **MOUNTAIN VIEW COLLEGE,** Mr. Daniel M. Salter, Chief Flight Instructor, 4949 W. Illinois Ave., Dallas, TX 75211-6599, (214) 333-8700.

- **NAVARRO COLLEGE,** Ms. Jo C. Jones, Director/Career Pilot, 3200 W. 7th, Corsicana, TX 75110, (214) 874-7849.

- **NORTH TEXAS STATE UNIVERSITY,** Ms. Patricia Warde, Associate Director, CCE & CM, P.O. Box 5344, Denton, TX 76203, (817) 565-2000.

- **PALO ALTO COLLEGE,** Mr. Bruce D. Hoover, Dept. Head/Aviation Technology, 1400 W. Villaret, San Antonio, TX 78224, (512) 921-5000.

- **ST. PHILLIPS COLLEGE,** 2111 Nevada, San Antonio, TX 78203. Aviation contact: Mr. Wayne E. Eades, Chairman/Dept. of Welding, Aviation, 800 Quintana Rd., San Antonio, TX 78211, (512) 921-4634.

- **SAM HOUSTON STATE UNIVERSITY,** Dr. Nedom C. Muns, Dept. Chairman/ Industrial Technology, Box 2266, SHSU, Huntsville, TX 77341, (409) 294-1190.

- **SAN JACINTO COLLEGE,** Mr. Larry D. Tucker, Dept. Chairman/Aero. Technology, 8060 Spencer Hwy., Pasadena, TX 77505, (713) 476-1501.

- **SOUTHWEST TEXAS JUNIOR COLLEGE,** Uvalde, TX 78801, (512) 278-4401.

- **TARRANT COUNTY JUNIOR COLLEGE,** Mr. Gary Marszen, Chairman/ Aeronautical Technology, 4801 Marine Creek Pkwy., Ft. Worth, TX 76179, (817) 625-8855.

- **TEXARKANA COLLEGE,** Prof. Larry F. Gordon, Chief Flight Instructor, 2500 N. Robinson Rd., Texarkana, TX 75501, (501) 774-6261 or (214) 838-4541.

- **TEXAS AERO TECH,** Mr. Randy Long, Director of Admissions, 7326 Aviation Place, Dallas, TX 75235, (800) 527-3563.

- **TEXAS SOUTHERN UNIVERSITY,** Dr. Naomi W. Lede, Dir./Dean, Center for Transportation, 3100 Cleburne Ave., Houston, TX 77004, (713) 527-7283 or (713) 639-1847.

- **TEXAS STATE TECHNICAL INSTITUTE - AMARILLO,** Mr. Jerry E. Lester, Program Chairman/Aviation Maintenance, P.O. Box 11035, Amarillo, TX 79111, (806) 335-2316.

- **TEXAS STATE TECHNICAL INSTITUTE - WACO,** Mr. Raymond P. Sancton, Jr., Program Chairman, TSTI-Waco, Waco, TX 76705, (817) 799-3611, ext. 2600.

UTAH

- **DIXIE COLLEGE,** Mr. V. Lowell Hansen, Aviation Programs Coordinator, 255 S. 700 E. St., St. George, UT 84770, (801) 673-4811.

- **UNIVERSITY OF UTAH - SALT LAKE CITY,** Ms. Betty Ward, Administrative Assistant/Continuing Education, Annex Bldg., Rm. 2202, Salt Lake City, UT 84112, (801) 581-8086.

- **UTAH STATE UNIVERSITY,** Dr. Maurice Thomas, Dept. Head, Logan, UT 84322-6000, (801) 750-1795.

- **WESTMINSTER COLLEGE,** Mr. Dan Taylor, Director/Aerospace Studies, 1840 S. 1300 East, Salt Lake City, UT 84105, (801) 484-7651.

VIRGINIA

- **AVERETT COLLEGE,** Mr. David R. Ruev, Assistant Prof. of Aviation, 420 W. Main St., Danville, VA 24541, (804) 791-5600.

- **BLUE RIDGE COMMUNITY COLLEGE,** Dr. Frank William, Coordinator of Aviation Programs, Science, Math, & Engineering Technology, P.O. Box 80, Weyers Cave, VA 24486, (703) 234-9261.

- **HAMPTON UNIVERSITY,** Mr. Herbert B. Armstrong, Coordinator/Airway Science Program, Hampton University, Hampton, VA 23668, (804) 727-5418 or (804) 727-5417.

- **J. SARGEANT REYNOLDS COMMUNITY COLLEGE,** Mr. Victor Linscomb, Hanover Industrial Park, 124 Hopson Rd., Ashland, VA 23005, (804) 371-3000.

- **LIBERTY UNIVERSITY,** Mr. John Heath, Chief Flight Instructor, Box 2000, Lynchburg, VA 24506, (804) 582-4011.

- **NEW RIVER COMMUNITY COLLEGE,** Ms. Chris Simpkins, Continuing Education Dept., Drawer 1127, Dublin, VA 24084, (703) 674-3600.

- **NORTHERN VIRGINIA COMMUNITY COLLEGE,** Mr. Robert W. Harmon, Aviation Program Head, 6901 Sudley Rd., Manassas, VA 22110, (703) 368-0184.

- **PIEDMONT VIRGINIA COMMUNITY COLLEGE,** Coordinator of Aviation Programs, Admissions Office, Rt. 6, Box 1A, Charlottesville, VA 22901, (804) 977-3900.

WASHINGTON

- **BIG BEND COMMUNITY COLLEGE,** Mrs. Mary Anne Allard, Secretary/Aviation Admissions, 28th & Chanute, Moses Lake, WA 98837, (509) 762-5351.

- **CENTRAL WASHINGTON UNIVERSITY,** Dr. Robert M. Envick, Chairman/Industrial & Engineering Technology, Central Washington University, Ellensburg, WA 98926, (509) 962-3691.

- **COMMUNITY COLLEGE OF SPOKANE,** Mr. August A. Lake, Dept. Chairman, N. 1810 Greene St., Spokane, WA 99207, (509) 536-7320.

- **EVERETT COMMUNITY COLLEGE,** Mr. Harry R. Moore, Instructor and Coordinator, Bldg. C-80, Paine Field, Everett, WA 98204, (206) 259-7151.

- **GREEN RIVER COMMUNITY COLLEGE,** Mr. John R. Dinnis, Instructor, 12401 S.E. 320th St., Auburn, WA 98002, (206) 833-9111.

- **SOUTH SEATTLE COMMUNITY COLLEGE,** Mr. Theodore Rigoni, Chairman/Aviation Maintenance Technology, 6000 16th Ave. SW, Seattle, WA 98106, (206) 764-5373.

- **WALLA WALLA COLLEGE,** Mr. Tom R. Graham, Director of Aviation Education, 204 S. College Ave., College Place, WA 99324-1198, (509) 527-2712.

- **YAKIMA VALLEY COMMUNITY COLLEGE,** Mr. Leland Ash, Instructor/ Aviation, P.O. Box 1647, Yakima, WA 98902, (509) 575-2373.

WEST VIRGINIA

- **SALEM COLLEGE,** Mr. Gary S. McAllister, Director of Aviation, Salem College, Salem, WV 26426, (304)782-5332 or (304) 782-5011.

WISCONSIN

- **BLACKHAWK TECHNICAL COLLEGE,** Gregg Bosak, Administrator/Community Information, 6004 Prairie Rd., P.O. Box 5009, Janesville, WI 53545.

- **CONCORDIA COLLEGE WISCONSIN,** Dr. Philip J. Arnholt, Chairman/Dept. of Science, 12800 N. Lake Shore Dr., Mequon, WI 53092, (414) 243-5700.

- **GATEWAY TECHNICAL INSTITUTE,** Mr. McGuire, 3520 30th Ave., Kenosha, WI 53140, (414) 656-6976.

- **MADISON AREA TECHNICAL COLLEGE,** Dr. Louise Yeazel, Instructor/ Technical & Industrial, 3550 Anderson St., Madison, WI 53703, (608) 233-6002.

- **MILWAUKEE AREA TECH COLLEGE,** Mr. Ken Mischka, Instructor/Aviation Dept., 422 E. College Ave., Milwaukee, WI 53207, (414) 762-2500.

- **NORTH CENTRAL TECHNICAL INSTITUTE,** Mr. Clyde Owens, Coordinator/ Technical Industrial Dept., 1000 Campus Dr., Wausau, WI 54401, (715) 675-3331.

- **NORTHEAST WISCONSIN TECHNICAL INSTITUTE,** Mr. John Pogorele, Coordinator/Industrial Trade Dept., 2740 W. Mason St., Green Bay, WI 54307, (414) 498-5400.

WYOMING

- **LARAMIE COUNTY COMMUNITY COLLEGE,** Mr. Dick All, Director/ Agriculture & Mechanical Trade Dept., 1400 E. College Dr., Cheyenne, WY 82007, (307) 634-5853.

Chapter 10
WHAT IT TAKES: RATINGS, BACKGROUND

The average new-hire major or national airline pilot has a four-year college degree, an Airline Transport Pilot Certificate and Flight Engineer written exam, approximately 3,000 hours of flying experience, and over 1,200 hours of turboprop or jet time.

The minimum licensing requirement to get an airline flying job is a Commercial Pilot Certificate with instrument and multi-engine ratings. Some airlines, especially smaller regional carriers that start pilots out right away as first officers, prefer the Airline Transport Pilot Certificate (ATP) as a matter of company policy. You must have the ATP to become an airline captain.

A few airlines have a flight engineer corps separate from the pilot corps, and they recruit only those flight engineers who have earned not only a Flight Engineer (FE)

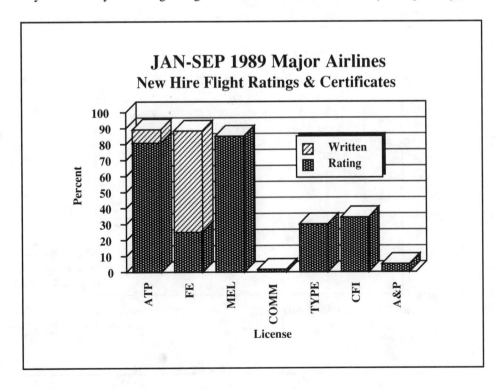

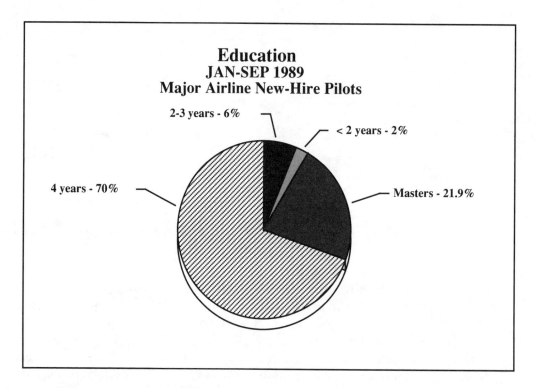

Certificate but a mechanic license, which is called an Airframe and Powerplant (A&P) Certificate. In other words, they hire Professional Flight Engineers (PFEs). PFEs, as opposed to FEs, do not upgrade to the pilot seats, and they have their own esprit de corps and own unions.

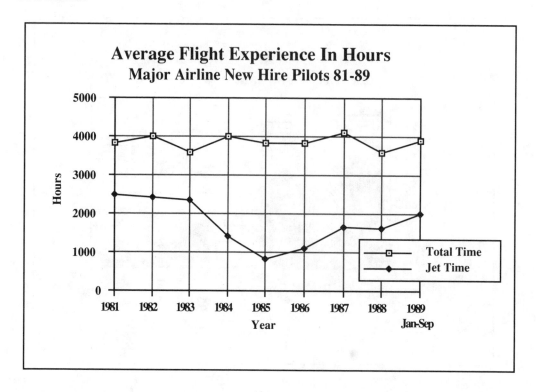

In the past, the military aviator has had a tremendous advantage over most civilian pilots in the amount of knowledge, training and experience that he or she was able to bring to the major airline job search. The civilian pilot need not suffer any shortfall of credentials, however, because today opportunities exist for parity with the military pilot.

A civilian pilot's chances can be improved by having any of the following:

- *A Flight Engineer Certificate.* This involves formal schooling, and the student must go deeply into aircraft systems and principles of operation.

- *A Formal Checkout Program in a High-Performance Aircraft.* This step will involve attending a school that includes extensive classroom training in systems and performance data, not just enough training to get your type rating.

- *An Associate or Bachelor's Degree in Aviation.* This kind of curriculum includes courses in aircraft systems, theories of flight, meteorology, aerodynamics, performance data, etc.

- *An Airframe and Powerplant Mechanic's License.* The A&P carries more weight if it is received from a nationally recognized school than if it is obtained from on-the-job experience or self-study. Again, acquiring the A&P entails formal training in systems and theory. Some carriers require the license. The A&P license also provides an edge in flying jobs other than airline piloting, e.g., many smaller corporations looking for pilot-mechanics. These pilots often will start out in the right seat and work on the plane when not flying. As they move to the left seat, their mechanic duties may or may not be dropped.

Home study courses or books on the previously mentioned subjects also can be helpful as an add-on to the formal training.

The schooling is far more important than many pilots realize. So are ratings and other factors. Too many pilots overstress the importance of total time as they compete for jobs. Usually, once a pilot has between 2,000 and 3,000 hours, competitiveness is not greatly increased by adding flight time. The most important factors then become additional ratings, inside contacts, education, the kind of equipment flown, and the time spent in the job search.

The other thing to remember about flight time is the value of the right kind of flying experience. The best experience background you can have is to fly equipment comparable to that flown by the airline at which you are applying, and over a wide route structure. While it is not essential, experience carrying passengers is preferred by passenger airlines. The closer your background is to the actual airline operation, the better your chances of being hired.

Initially, however, building flight time is critical: Among time builders are working and flying as a flight instructor; flying for pipeline and power line patrols, for small freight companies, or for FBOs in forestry duty or other contract work; ferrying aircraft, banner towing, charter flying and crop dusting; and corporate piloting or co-piloting.

The suggested minimum licenses, ratings and flight experience to work as a regional airline or corporate pilot are (1) Commercial Pilot License with multi-engine land rating and instrument rating; (2) Class II medical certificate (Class I preferred); (3) 1,500 hours of total flight time (more or less, varying with pilot demand) with 250

Airlines Currently Hiring PFEs   1/89

Company	Aircraft
AIRBORNE EXPRESS	DC-8
AMERICAN TRANS AIR	B-727, L-1011
BUFFALO	B-707
EVERGREEN	B-727, DC-8, B-747
GULF AIR	B-727
KALITTA	B-727
KEY	B-727
ORION	B-727, DC-8, B-747
REEVE ALEUTIAN	L-188, B-727
RICH	DC-8
ROSENBALM	DC-8
SOUTHERN AIR TRANSPORT	B-707, L-382
TPI	L-188
TOWER	B-747
TRANS AIR LINK	DC-6
TRANS CONTINENTAL	DC-6
TRANS GLOBAL	DC-8, B-737
UPS	DC-8, B-727, B-747

POSSIBLY HIRING: CHALLENGE, FIVE STAR, MARKAIR, TOWER, ZANTOP

Minimum qualifications for PFEs include FE turbojet rating and an A&P license. Most PFEs are not allowed to upgrade to captain or copilot.

hours of multi-engine flight time (500 hours preferred) and as much turbine time, jet or turboprop, as you can obtain.

The average recent qualifications of major airline new-hire pilots are excellent health and physical condition, with height in proportion to weight; vision correctable to 20/20 and not worse than 20/200 uncorrected (around 80 percent of the pilots have 20/20 uncorrected vision); a four-year degree, although about 20 percent have fewer than four years of college; 30 to 35 years of age (the requirement is 21 years old and up), with a few new-hires being over 50.

The technical and experience qualifications are the ATP certificate, the FE turbojet written exam, and flight time proportional to age, to wit: 1,200 hours if you are 21; 3,000 hours at 31; 5,000 hours at 41; and 8,000 hours at 51.

Below are flight time requirements for the various licenses as set forth under Part 61 of the Federal Aviation Regulations (FARs). Many schools base their curricula not on Part 61, but on Part 141. Others train under both sets of regulations. In most cases, Part 141 schools use a more sharply defined flight curriculum and more comprehensive ground school program than do strictly Part 61 schools. As a result, the FAA allows students to obtain licenses with less flight time at Part 141-approved schools. Thus, training at one of these schools may be less expensive than at a Part 61 school, but not necessarily: Many students fail to complete their ratings, especially their private license, in the minimum flight time, and, if the school is charging by the hour for flight time, the additional hours necessary for achieving ratings can run the bill up to equal what you would pay at a Part 61 school. Most full university programs in aviation operate under both Part 141 and Part 61, and flight time often is included under basic matriculation charges.

Where costs are concerned, consider the course length, travel expenses, lodging, meals, local transportation, and the charges for books/manuals, check rides, additional ground/flight training, and written exams needed to complete the course.

Obtaining the needed licenses in the order listed below will prevent you from wasting time and money pursuing unnecessary qualifications.

Pre-Solo (Student Pilot)

Your instructor, generally called a Certified Flight Instructor (CFI), will brief you on the components of the aircraft and the events that will occur on your first training flight. All flying at this stage is usually done in a light, single-engine trainer aircraft, such as a Cessna 152 (CE-152), Piper Cherokee (PA-28), or Beech Sundowner (BE-23).

> NOTE WELL: This flight and all subsequent flights will be recorded in your pilot logbook. Your pilot's log must accompany you throughout your aviation career. In your log, you will record each flight you make along with the type of aircraft, tail number, date, point of takeoff and landing, duration of flight, flight conditions, and training received (if any).

I. PRE-SOLO (STUDENT PILOT)
a. Minimum age, none.
b. Medical certificate, none.
c. Written test, none.

Recreational Pilot License

In August 1989 the FAA instituted a new pilot certificate with reduced minimum flying time requirements of 30 hours. Operations under this certificate are limited to daytime hours within 50 nautical miles of your home field and in airspace where no communications with air traffic control is required. Aircraft restrictions include a single engine of 180 horsepower or less, fixed landing gear and a maximum of four seats. Because of these operating limitations this license would be of limited utility to a person planning an aviation career and is not recommended.

Solo Student Pilot Requirements

The medical certificate serves as your Student Pilot license. It must be endorsed by a flight instructor when you have met the flight time and skill requirements specified for solo flight. NOTE WELL: You may not carry passengers at this point. While working toward your Private Pilot license, you do all of your flying either solo (alone) or dual (with an instructor).

COST COMPARISON CHART – LICENSES, RATINGS AND CERTIFICATES

LICENSES CERTIFICATES RATINGS	FARs—Part 141—SCHOOLS				FARs—Part 61—SCHOOLS		
	Minimum Flight Hour Requirements	Minimum Ground School Requirements	Approx. Cost	Completion Time	Minimum Flight Hour Requirements	Minimum Ground School Requirements	Approx. Cost
Student Pilot & 3rd. Class medical Cert. To Solo	Approx. 15 hrs. to Solo	Pre-Solo Written Exam	$1,000	1-2 weeks	Approx. 15 hrs. to solo (no minimum)	FAR—Part 91	$1,000
Private Pilot License	35 hrs. total	35 hrs.	$3,000	6 weeks	40 hrs. total	Home Study and Instructor Endorsement	$2,300
Separate Instrument Rating	125 hrs. total 35 hrs. Instruct	35 hrs.	$3,200	6 weeks	125 hrs. total 40 hrs. Instr. 15 hrs. Instruct	Same as above	$5,600
Combined Commercial License with Instrument Rating	190 hrs. total	65 hrs.	$11,000	5 months	250 hrs. total	Same as above	$11,000
Multi-Engine Rating	10 hrs. this rating	6 hrs.	$2,000	1 week	10-12 hrs. minimum)	None required	$1,750
Total for Comm. Instrument Multi-Engine	200 hrs.	106 hrs.	$16,000	7 months	250 hrs. total	Same as above	$14,500-$16,800 above
CFI Certified Flight Instructor -Airplane	20 hrs. this rating	40 hrs.	$2,500	2 weeks	Approx. 3 hrs. This rating (no minimum)	Approx. 10 hrs. Home Study and Instructor Endorsement	$500
CFII Flt. Instructor Instrument	20 hrs. this rating	20 hrs.	$2,500	3 weeks	Approx. 3 hrs. this rating (no minimum)	Same as above	$1,000
CFI-ME Flt. Instructor Multi-Engine	20 hrs. this rating	20 hrs.	$4,200	3 weeks	Approx. 7 hrs. this rating (no minimum)	None required	$1,000
Grnd. Instructor Basic					N/A	3 days	$250
Grnd. Instructor Advanced					N/A	3 days	$250
Grnd. Instructor Instrument					N/A	3 days	$250
ATP Airline Transport Pilot License	10 hrs. this rating	13 hrs.	$2,200	2 weeks	1500 hrs. total	Authorized by FAA	$1,000
FE Flight Engineer License Turbo-Jet					10 hrs. A/C or 15 hrs. CPT & 10 hrs. sim.	160-235 hrs.	$5,000-$7,000
Medical Certificates 3rd Class	N/A	N/A	$45	1 hour	N/A	N/A	$45
2nd Class	N/A	N/A	$45	1 hour	N/A	N/A	$45
1st Class	N/A	N/A	$45	1 hour	N/A	N/A	$45
Written Tests	ATP-1500 hrs.	See requirements above	$30	2-6 hrs.	ATP-1500 hrs.	See requirements above	$30
Practical Tests	See requirements above	See requirements above	$130-$170	2-4 hrs.	See requirements above	See requirements above	$130-$170
Type Ratings							
Citation	5 Sim, 5 A/C	24 hrs.	$3,500	5-7 hrs.	4 hrs.	24 hrs.	$3,500
Lear	5 Sim, 5 A/C	40 hrs.	$7,000	5-8 hrs.	5 Sim, 5 A/C	40 hrs.	$7,000
DC-9					14 Sim, 2 A/C	110 hrs.	$11,000
B-737					14 Sim, 2 A/C	110 hrs.	$11,000
B-727					14 Sim, 2.5 A/C	120 hrs.	$12,000
B-747					14 Sim, 2 A/C	150 hrs.	$14,000

	Completion Time	Prerequisites	Duration	Currency Requirements	Remarks
	1-2 weeks	16 years of age 3rd Class medical	2 years	30-day Instructor Endorsement	Read, speak & understand the English language, 1st stage of pvt pilot license
	4-6 months	17 years of age 3rd Class medical	Indefinite with AFR/BFR 3rd Class med.	3 take-offs & landings in 90 days	Night requirements: 3 hrs. and 10 take-offs and landings
	4-6 months	Must hold Private Pilot license or better	Same as above	6 hrs. in previous 6 months & 6 approaches	Normally obtained in combination with the commercial license at a cost savings
	1-2 years	18 yrs of age, 2nd Class medical Commercial & Instr. written	Indefinite with BFR 2nd Class med.	3 take-offs and landings within 90 days	Need instrument rating or must remain within 25 NM when flying for hire
	1 week (no	Medical certificate	Same as above	Same as above	Prior to carrying passengers
	1-2 years	Medical certificate	Same as above	Same as above	Package prices for flight training may lower cost per rating
	2 weeks	2nd Class medical Commercial License 2 Writtens (FOI & CFI-A)	2 years	Must be renewed	Must be renewed each 24-month period by attending flight instructor seminar or practical test or 10 students preceding 24 months.
	2 weeks	2nd Class medical (CFI-I) Written	Same as above	Same as above	SAME AS ABOVE
	1 week	2nd Class medical	Same as above	Same as above	Same as above
	3 days	No medical required	Same as above	None	Rating not needed if you hold a flight instructor certificate
	3 days	No medical required	Same as above	None	Same as above
	3 days	No medical required	Same as above	None	Same as above
	1-2 weeks	23 years of age 1st Class medical ATP Written	Indefinite with BFR 1st Class	3 take-offs & landings	FAA Authorization
	4-6 weeks	Commercial-Inst. Pilot & FE Written Exam[B]	Same as above	50 hrs. in last 6 months	FE license requirements governed by FAR Part 63
	1 hour	None	2 years	Issued in previous 24 months	Required for private pilot and non-commercial operations
	1 hour	None	1 year	Issued in previous 12 months	Required for commercial operations
	1 hour	None	6 months	Issued in previous 6 months	Required for ATP operations
	2-6 hrs.	Instructor endorsement	2 years	Expires at end of 24 mo. period	Ground School or Home Study
	2-4 hrs.	Instructor endorsement written passed	See requirements above	See requirements above	Includes oral and FLT tests
	5-7 days 5-8 days 30 days 30 days 30 days 30 days	Oral exams Practical test A/C and/or simulator	Indefinite with BFR & medical certificate	3 take-offs & landings in 90 days	Includes checkride. Flight time requirements apply: Approx. 1500 hrs. - ATP w/ written exam. Approximately 500 hrs. ME w/ turbine.

Legend

AFR	=	Annual Flight Review
ATP/W	=	ATP Written Exam
A/C or ARCFT	=	Aircraft
BFR	=	Biannual Flight Review
CERT	=	Certificate
CFI-A	=	Flight Instructor —Airplane
CFI-I	=	Instrument Flying for Instructors
Complx	=	Complex Aircraft
CPT	=	Cockpit Procedural Trainer
FAA	=	Federal Aviation Administration
FAR	=	Federal Aviation Regulations
FLT	=	Flight
FOI	=	Fundamentals of Instructions
HRS.	=	Hours
INSTR	=	Instrument
INSTRUCT	=	Instructor
LDG	=	Landing
LIC	=	License
MO	=	Month
NM	=	Nautical miles
PIC	=	Pilot in Command
PVT	=	Private
SIM	=	Simulator
TO	=	Take-off
Tot'l	=	Total
W/	=	With
YR	=	Year
X/C	=	Cross Country

B - See FAR Part 63 for additional ways to meet the experience requirements for the FE Certificate.

II. SOLO STUDENT PILOT REQUIREMENTS

a. **Minimum age, 16.**

b. **Medical certificate, Third Class. This medical certificate is obtained from an aviation medical examiner (AME), i.e., a doctor designated by the FAA.**

c. **Written test, none.**

Private Pilot Requirements

All of these flight time requirements are bare minimums. Acquiring the Private Pilot license generally takes several hours beyond the minimums, usually 45 to 60 hours.

The written examination administered by the FAA (the Private Pilot Written Examination) will be handled by a Designated Flight Examiner, i.e., a pilot authorized by the FAA to administer the Private Pilot flight test. You must obtain the written endorsement of your instructor prior to taking your flight check. Your flight check will consist of a review of your logbook for proper endorsements and flight time; an inspection of your medical certificate and written exam results; and an oral examination on aerodynamics, on the aircraft you are using (including its equipment), and on your duties and responsibilities as a pilot. You will plan a cross-country flight and conduct a pre-flight inspection of the aircraft. Once in the air, you will perform the maneuvers required by the FARs; you must demonstrate the level of skill required by these regulations.

III. PRIVATE PILOT REQUIREMENTS

a. **Minimum age, 17.**

b. **Medical certificate, Third Class.**

c. **Written test, Private Pilot written exam.**

d. **Flight time, 40 hours minimum, consisting of the following:**
   - **20 hours dual, 20 hours solo.**
   - **Dual check-out in cross-country flying and 10 hours solo cross-country flying.**
   - **Three hours of night flying instruction including 10 takeoffs and landings.**
   - **Flight under simulated instrument conditions.**

e. **Oral exam and practical test (private pilot flight test).**

Instrument Rating Requirements

All of your instrument flight training will be done with a vision-limiting device (hood), on a flight simulator, or in actual "instrument" conditions (weather conditions that prevent outside reference to the natural horizon, i.e., in the clouds). After you meet the requirements, you are recommended for your check ride by your instructor. The Instrument flight test will determine your ability to control the airplane safely under instrument meteorological conditions (IMC) and under the direction of air traffic control (ATC).The Instrument rating may be obtained prior to the Commercial Pilot flight test because the flight time requirements for the Instrument rating are slightly less than those for the Commercial license.

IV. INSTRUMENT RATING REQUIREMENTS
a. **Minimum age, 17.**
b. **Medical requirements, Third Class.**
c. **Written test, Instrument written exam.**
d. **Flight time requirements are as follows:**
- **125 hours total time.**
- **50 hours of cross-country as a Pilot in Command (PIC).**
- **40 hours of simulated or actual instrument time, not more than 20 of which may be in an instrument ground trainer (flight simulator).**
- **15 hours of instrument instruction, at least five of which must be in an airplane.**

e. **Oral exam and practical test (Instrument Rating flight test).**

Commercial Pilot License Requirements (Part 61)

You must have an instrument rating. If you do not have an instrument rating, you may not fly beyond 25 miles from the airport of departure or at night while carrying passengers for hire. If you wish, you may obtain your instrument rating during the Commercial Pilot flight test. You also must have completed the flight time and training requirements and be recommended by your instructor.

As a commercial pilot, you will now have the qualifications to earn a living as a professional pilot in single-engine aircraft, but the jobs for single-engine-only pilots are limited.

NOTE WELL: It is recommended that you obtain your Flight Instructor - Single Engine Land first, then start working toward your multi-engine rating. You can work and earn money while pursuing the other ratings, and you may get a discount on your flight training. An alternate method is to fly the required 10 hours of complex time in the Commercial Course in a multi-engine aircraft. You must then use both single and multi-engine aircraft in the checkride in order to obtain both single and multi-engine commercial privileges.

V. COMMERCIAL PILOT LICENSE REQUIREMENTS (PART 61)

a. **Minimum age, 18.**

b. **Medical certificate, Second Class — somewhat more restrictive than the certificate required for a private pilot, because you will now be able to carry passengers for hire.**

c. **Written test, Commercial Pilot written exam.**

d. **Total flight time, 250 hours (no more than 50 in a simulator), including the following:**
   - **50 hours of instruction.**
   - **10 hours of instruction in a "complex" airplane, i.e., one which has more than 200 horsepower or which has a retractable landing gear, controllable pitch propeller, and flaps.**
   - **5 hours of nighttime flying with at least 10 takeoffs and landings.**
   - **50 hours of cross-country flight, with one flight of at least 250 miles in length (150 in Hawaii).**
   - **100 hours of Pilot in Command (PIC) time.**

e. **Oral exam and practical test (Commercial Pilot flight test).**

Certified Flight Instructor Rating (CFI) Requirements

You must take two written tests for a basic instructor's rating (CFI-Airplane), Fundamentals of Instruction and Flight Instructor Airplane (and dynamics) exams. A third test is required to become an instrument instructor (CFI-Instruments). In order to instruct in single-engine aircraft, you must take your flight test in a single-engine aircraft. To instruct in a multi-engine aircraft, you must take another flight test in multi-engine aircraft. Before you can instruct in a multi-engine aircraft, you must have 15 hours of multi-engine flight time. In other words, you need three separate instructor endorsements and two written tests for the categories in which you wish to instruct (aircraft instructor and instrument instructor).

VI.   CERTIFIED FLIGHT INSTRUCTOR RATING (CFI) REQUIREMENTS

a. **Minimum age, 18.**
b. **Medical certificate, Second Class.**
c. **Written test:**
   - **Fundamentals of Instruction.**
   - **Flight Instructor, Airplane (aerodynamics).**
   - **Flight Instructor, Instruments (to become an Instrument instructor).**
d. **Commercial Pilot license, Instrument rating.**
e. **Oral exam and practical test (Flight Instructor flight test).**

Multi-Engine Rating Requirements

Notice that, while the apparent requirements for this rating are minimal, you must obtain the endorsement of your instructor certifying your competence; then you must pass the flight test. Multi-engine flying calls for a higher degree of skill than your previous ratings required, so your training must be thorough. Although multi-engine training can be expensive, you must have it to qualify for higher-paying jobs. Most multi-engine qualification courses require five to 10 hours of flying.

You must now obtain as much flight time in multi-engine turbine-powered aircraft as you can get while working toward your Airline Transport Pilot license, with a multi-engine land rating. Today, this license is virtually a "must" for anyone seeking an airline career. In any case, fly whatever you can to build time. You also will be more competitive if you take the written tests for the various ground instructor ratings and the Flight Engineer-Turbojet written examination.

VII. THE MULTI-ENGINE RATING REQUIREMENTS

a. **Minimum age, as required for license held.**
b. **Medical certificate, as required for license held.**
c. **Written test, none.**
d. **Oral exam and practical test.**

Flight Engineer (FE)-Turbojet Written Exam Requirements

If you do not complete your full FE rating, *these are the only test scores a prospective employer will ever see*. All others, for every other rating, are collected by your examiner when you get your license or rating. You must pass the FE in order to be considered for major airline employment. A few corporations operate large jet equipment that requires a flight engineer, and if you want to fly these aircraft for them, you will need the FE. This examination will test both your knowledge of large aircraft systems and your fluency in normal and emergency procedures for operating the systems.

VIII. FLIGHT ENGINEER (FE)-TURBOJET WRITTEN EXAM REQUIREMENTS

a. **Minimum age, 21.**
b. **Commercial Pilot license with Instrument rating.**
c. **Written test: Flight Engineer Basic (FE) and Turbojet (FEJ).**

Flight Engineer Requirements

Flight Engineer license requirements call for a brief explanation. There are essentially three separate Flight Engineer ratings. Many large aircraft built during and after World War II mandated a third crew member, not to fly the plane, but to operate the aircraft systems. The technology available at the time did not allow a two-pilot crew to operate aircraft systems and fly the aircraft at the same time, hence the need for a "flight engineer." As powerplants evolved from reciprocating to turboprop and then to turbojet or turbofan, separate categories of the Flight Engineer license were established.

Currently, the most common turboprop aircraft using flight engineers are the civilian versions of the C-130 and the Lockheed Electra. The Boeing B-707, B-727, B-747, Douglas DC-8, DC-10 and some versions of the Airbus A-300 series are turbojet aircraft using flight engineers. Flight engineers are seldom used today in reciprocating aircraft, and we do not recommend that you pursue the reciprocating aircraft FE rating.

An aviation mechanic also may get a Flight Engineer rating. The only difference between a mechanic's and a pilot's obtaining an FE rating is that the mechanic must obtain a minimum of five hours of instruction in the actual airplane (rather than a simulator) at the flight engineer's station. Turbojet aircraft cost $2,000-$6,000 per hour to rent, so getting the required training on your own is very expensive.

There are a few corporate jobs available for flight engineers. Most of these jobs require the flight engineer to have an Airframe and Powerplant (A&P) license. Since most corporations have no maintenance department, the flight engineer-mechanic serves as an alternative to the expensive investment required for complete in-house maintenance capability.

Most flight engineer positions available today are offered by the major airlines. FE is a new-hire pilot position with these carriers; you eventually will move into the pilots' seats. A few airlines and air freight companies (turboprop and turbojet) have professional (non-pilot) flight engineers.

A few airlines require the full Flight Engineer rating; most require only the writtens. Some other airlines have no aircraft utilizing flight engineers; in fact, the trend in the aircraft industry is to build airplanes for two-man crews. By the year 2000, the number of aircraft still flying that utilize flight engineers will have decreased dramatically.The full FE rating is expensive (see chart on pages 140-141). Therefore, you should target the portion of the aviation industry that you wish to pursue and then decide if the full rating is for you. If you decide to obtain the full rating, get the Flight Engineer-Turbojet. The B-727 is the most common airline aircraft that requires a flight engineer.

IX.   FLIGHT ENGINEER REQUIREMENTS*
   a. Minimum age, 21.
   b. Medical certificate, First or Second class. Written tests:
      1. Flight Engineer, Basic.
      2. Flight Engineer
         a. Propeller
         b Turbo-propeller
         c. Turbojet
   c. Required licenses:
      1. Commercial Pilot license with an Instrument rating or
      2. Airframe and Powerplant (mechanic's) license.
   d. Oral examination, simulator check ride, and aircraft check ride.

   * See FAR Part 63 for additional ways to meet the experience requirements for the FE Certificate.

The Airline Transport Pilot License Requirements

It is recommended that you obtain this license in a light multi-engine aircraft. A single-engine Airline Transport Pilot rating is good only to prevent your written exams from expiring (two years from exam date) because very few companies transport passengers in single-engine aircraft.

Once you have obtained the Airline Transport Pilot license, your marketability in the aviation industry will be greatly enhanced. There is no higher rating.

X. THE AIRLINE TRANSPORT PILOT LICENSE REQUIREMENTS

a. **Minimum age, 23 (you may take the written and flight test at 21 if you possess the flight time requirements, but until you turn 23, you will receive a letter in lieu of a license).**

b. **Medical certificate, First Class.**

c. **Written test, Airline Transport Pilot.**

d. **Flight time requirements are as follows:**
   - **1,500 hours total flight time, including:**
   - **500 hours cross-country.**
   - **100 hours of night flight time.**
   - **75 hours of instrument or simulated instrument time, at least 50 hours of which were in actual flight.**
   - **150 hours of PIC time.**

e. **Oral exam and practical test.**

Type Rating Requirements

The FAA requires an endorsement on your pilot license to act as pilot in command of an airplane that is turbojet-powered (jet) or has a takeoff gross weight above 12,500 pounds (large or heavy aircraft). The complexity of this type of airplane requires special training for safe operation. Many corporations and regional airlines, and all major airlines, operate equipment of this type.

Type ratings should not be added to your licenses below the level of ATP. Type rating training is expensive.

XI. TYPE RATING REQUIREMENTS
a. Medical certificate: corresponds to your pilot license (e.g., Commercial, Second Class; ATP, First Class).
b. Written test, none.
c. Flight time requirements: Instructor's recommendation or approved school's course requirements.
d. Oral exam and practical test.

Airline Aircraft Fleet

At one given time, these were the aircraft fleets for major and national airlines.
These are subject to change frequently and should only be used for general knowledge and not for specific information.

Majors	A-300	A-310	B-727	B-737	B-747	B-757	B-767	BAC-111	BAe-146	CV-580	CV-640	DC-8	DC-9	DC-10	DHC-7	F-27	F-28	L-188	L-1011	MD-80	SD3-60	YS-11	Total
American			164			33							60	35						123			382
Continental	12		106	99								46	15	8						66			352
Delta			132	83	33	24					10	36	9						35	12			374
Eastern	28		122		25							84							23				284
Fed Ex			58											20									78
Flying Tigers			11	21							6												38
Northwest			77	40	28				13			129	21							8			316
Pan Am	12	13	56	7	38																		126
Piedmont			34	99		4										45							182
TWA			76	18		11					29		46						33	29			213
United			154	92	31	19	6					46	55						6				386
USAir			10	63		20						70											163
Totals	52	13	1000	443	158	86	91	20	13		45	411	182			45		20	97	238			2894

Nationals	A-300	A-310	B-727	B-737	B-747	B-757	B-767	BAC-111	BAe-146	CV-580	CV-640	DC-8	DC-9	DC-10	DHC-7	F-27	F-28	L-188	L-1011	MD-80	SD3-60	YS-11	Total
Airborne											13	19										12	44
Air Wisconsin															14						6		60
Alaska			23	6																9			38
Aloha			12	12																			12
Amer. Trans Air			8																10				18
America West				69	7						5			3									79
Arrow												5											5
Braniff			25																				25
DHL			12																				12
Evergreen			20								13	2					2						37
Hawaiian											6	12		8				5					33
Midway			12	12							42	27											39
UPS			36																				87
Southwest			75	75																			75
World													4										4
Zantop										9	7						21						37
Total	124	174			10		10		13	9	86	60	4	11	14		23	15		11	6	12	575
Grand Totals	52	13	1124	617	164	96	91	20	10	13	9	131	471	186	11	14	45	23	112	249	6	12	3469

Chapter 11
MILITARY PILOTS: HOW TO LAUNCH A CIVIL FLYING CAREER

Qualifications

Military pilots must convert their military experience to a commercial license with an instrument rating. If you are on active flying status, getting the required license and ratings is relatively easy. You can take your military training records to the local FAA office and be given a pilot competency written exam. A passing score will earn a commercial instrument pilot's license.

If you have a commercial license with a restriction, you must have the restriction removed by taking a military or civilian check ride on an unrestricted aircraft. (An example of a restriction would be centerline thrust. If you are restricted to single-engine aircraft and to those few multi-engine aircraft with centerline thrust, you will not be allowed to fly the great majority of multi-engine aircraft since, if an engine goes out on these aircraft, you must know how to deal with asymmetrical thrust. When an engine is lost on an aircraft with asymmetrical thrust, one side of the aircraft becomes dead weight that the good engine has to carry from its position out on a wing. Piloting the aircraft then becomes a difficult job.) If you have taken your check ride on a military aircraft, then you must present flight records or orders to the FAA office proving that you have checked out on an unrestricted aircraft before the FAA will issue you a new license without the restriction.

If you have not been on active flying status within the previous 12 months, the procedure for obtaining the commercial license and instrument rating will take more time and money. You must:

- Hold an FAA medical certificate appropriate to the pilot certificate you seek.

- Show documentation that you were a rated military pilot before the beginning of the 12 months before the month in which you are applying for the license.

- Have an endorsement from a flight instructor 60 days before application.

- Pass the appropriate flight test.

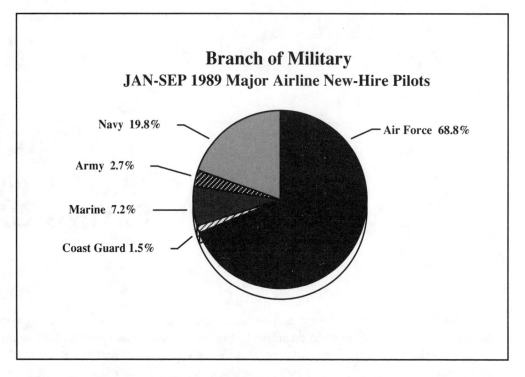

If you have a commercial instrument license but are not current, you must get current (applies to all situations). To be current, you must have:

• Had a biennial flight review in the last two years (required every two years).

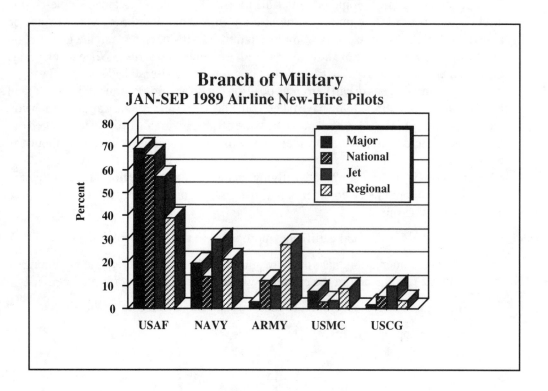

• Completed three takeoffs and landings to a full stop within the last 90 days.

• Completed six hours of instrument flying and six instrument approaches within the last six months, or have received an instrument competency sign-off by an instructor. It is recommended that you also get some actual flying time, preferably in a multi-engine aircraft or simulator.

Once you have received the commercial license and instrument rating and are current, you should complete the Flight Engineer written exam or rating. Ninety-four percent of all pilots hired by the major airlines in 1988 had the flight engineer written exam or rating.

If you are considering taking the written exam, there are two types. The "FEX" is a combined comprehensive exam consisting of 80 questions. The second type consists of two individual exams, a separate exam for the aircraft portion (turbojet/turboprop/reciprocating) and a separate exam for the basic portion. The exams contain 40 and 60 questions, respectively. It is recommended that you complete either the combined FEX exam or the two separate exams (basic and turbojet). You also should complete the ATP written exam and rating if you meet the requirements for the license. Seventy-seven percent of all pilots hired by major airlines in 1988 had the ATP rating. Minimum qualifications for the Airline Transport Pilot (ATP) license are as follows: 23 years old; 1,500 hours total time; 500 hours cross-country; 100 hours night; 75 hours total instrument, of which 50 must be actual instrument time; and FAA Class I medical.

To get the ATP license, you must take the required FAA written exam, oral exam and practical test. You can prepare for the written exam through a cram course (two to three days), audio/video program, or text course; or you can complete a ground school. The oral exam and flight test are very comprehensive and demanding. Completing a ground school program will better prepare the pilot for the oral exam and practical test.

When To Start Applying to the Airlines

Military pilots should start applying to the airlines at least one year before separation, retirement or terminal leave date. Some companies have been interviewing and offering class dates to pilots still on active duty or terminal leave. In 1989, airlines following this practice included American and Northwest, both offering class dates six months in advance of separation, and Braniff, offering class dates nine months in advance of separation.

Once you have separated or retired from the military, a short period of time when you are not employed is accepted. However, long periods on the ground (two months or longer) are considered a negative factor. Ideally, you should get a flying job, any flying job, and apply to the airlines while you are working. Options to be considered are corporate aviation, regional or commuter airlines, flight instruction, or reserve flying. The most important requirement for your career is to maintain flying currency. If you accept temporary work in a non-aviation environment, you can keep current by flying for fun or part time.

Military Pay Rates

ACTIVE DUTY: COMMISSIONED OFFICERS
MONTHLY BASIC PAY RATES*

Pay Grade	2nd year and Under	4th year	10th year	20th year
O-10	5710.80	5911.80	6291.60	6291.60
O-9	5061.30	5304.30	5439.30	6291.60
O-8	4584.30	4833.60	5193.90	6291.60
O-7	3809.10	4068.80	4496.70	5551.20
O-6	2823.30	3305.10	3305.10	4250.40
O-5	2257.80	2834.70	2920.50	3845.10
O-4	1903.50	2472.30	2808.60	3327.60
O-3	1768.80	2339.10	2676.30	2877.90
O-2	1542.30	2091.60	2135.40	2135.40
O-1	1338.90	1684.50	1684.50	1684.50
ACIP**	125.00	206.00	400.00	340.00

* Take home pay includes housing, subsistence and other allowances
and aviation career incentive pay in addition to the listed basic pay rate.
** Aviation Career Incentive Pay (Flight Pay).

RESERVIST DUTY: COMMISSIONED OFFICERS
4 PAY PERIOD, 2-DAY WEEKEND DRILL PAY***

Pay Grade	2nd year and Under	4th year	10th year	20th year
O-8	611.24	644.48	691.19	838.88
O-7	507.88	542.51	599.56	740.16
O-6	376.44	440.68	440.68	566.72
O-5	301.04	377.96	389.40	512.68
O-4	253.80	329.64	374.44	443.68
O-3	235.84	311.88	356.84	383.72
O-2	205.64	278.88	284.72	284.72
O-1	178.52	224.60	224.60	224.60
ACIP**	16.67	27.47	53.33	45.33

** Aviation Career Incentive Pay (Flight Pay).
*** 1 pay period is 4 hours in length.

Flight Time Considerations

When you are interviewing, your military flight records will be reviewed to verify the flight times on your employment application. In evaluations of flight time, consideration is given for the type of flying, e.g., fighter pilots get less time than transport pilots but have to handle an aircraft under more trying circumstances.

Some companies will allow military pilots to present flight time with a conversion factor, while others will not. The only way to use the conversion factor accurately and legally is to keep a separate civilian logbook and log each flight block-to-block (includes taxi time). The most commonly used conversion factors are .2 to .3 hours per flight.

Just as airlines vary in their willingness to allow military pilots to use conversion factors, some airlines will let the pilot add flight engineer and simulator time to the total, while others will not. Most flight times asked for on the application are specific and straightforward, e.g., multi-engine, single-engine, jet, etc. However, the following guidelines will be of help in calculating other flight time categories that may not be clear to some.

Pilot-in-Command (PIC): While to the FAA, PIC time is any flying time accumulated while the pilot is in command of the aircraft, some airlines will not accept as PIC time any hours spent as an evaluator or in any position that merely involves observing another pilot's flying. If both pilots are PIC-qualified, only one can log PIC time for the flight. PIC time is the same as First Pilot or Aircraft Commander time. Go ahead and list as PIC time all hours logged as first pilot or aircraft commander. In airline interviews, your total time then will be probed to see how it was compiled.

Actual Instruments: This is the same as weather flying.

Heavy Jet: By definition, a heavy jet is any aircraft weighing 300,000 pounds or more. Aircraft in this category are the DC-8, DC-10, B-707, B-767, B-747, A-300, KC-135, C-5, B-l and B-52.

Large Transport Aircraft: Any aircraft weighing 12,500 to 299,999 pounds. Examples are the B-727, B-737, DC-9, P-3 and C-130 aircraft.

Turbine: Turbine is a total of fixed-wing jet, turboprop, and turbine helicopter time.

Terminology

Whenever possible, a military pilot applying for a commercial flying job should use civilian aircraft designations and crew position titles.

Your initial contact with most companies will be with a personnel representative. These professionals usually do not have a military background and may not be familiar with the terms used or with military aircraft designators. So you must use designations which they will recognize. For example, the CT-39 is a Sabreliner, the E-4 is a B-747. Instead of using "patrol plane commander," you should say "pilot-in-command." You should not use Aircraft Commander to convey that 100 percent of your flying time was as pilot-in-command at the controls of the airplane. It would be better to show PIC time and total aircraft commander time separately.

In some cases, you will not be able to provide a civilian designation for a military aircraft. In that case, you should give a brief description of the aircraft, e.g., OV-1 (large single-pilot ME turboprop).

Applying for the Job

As a pilot candidate, your task is to market yourself and play by the current rules. The time to apply for a pilot's position is now. Today, there are more job opportunities for pilots than ever before. Nobody knows how long these opportunities will last.

Seniority is based on date of hire and will govern your entire career. This fact makes it imperative that you land your preferred career job as soon as possible. All airlines base promotions and pay increases on a seniority system. Thus, your chance to upgrade to captain will be determined by your seniority number alone and not by your individual accomplishments. The most senior pilots choose the best trips, vacation dates and time off, make the most money, and become the last to be furloughed.

Timing is very important. A decision must be made at the earliest age possible concerning career pilot employment. As a pilot gets older, job opportunities decrease, especially at major airlines. The average age of new-hire pilots with major and national airlines is 33 to 38, and the maximum age is in the low 50s.

As mentioned, aviation hiring is very cyclical. To take advantage of the varying demand for pilots, you must obtain the necessary education, qualifications and experience. You should exert a maximum effort to get the job desired during times when hiring is at a peak and work on improving your qualifications during periods when hiring is slow.

Pilot supply and demand will cause minimum and average qualifications to vary. Therefore, you should continuously improve your qualifications and experience until hired by a career-goal company or airline.

Chapter 12
GETTING STARTED:
APPLYING, INTERVIEWING,
EVALUATING JOB OFFERS

You should launch your job search with a positive attitude and be well informed. Being fully prepared will require a lot of mental and physical work on your part. How much effort you decide to expend will determine how successful you are, or how long it takes you to reach your career goal.

The Basics

If you are a pilot seeking airline or other commercial employment, you should:

- Develop and produce a quality resume and cover-letter package and send a resume every time you correspond with a company.

- Update your logbook. Regardless of how much flying time you have, your logbook will be checked at the interview. This is standard in an interview; no exceptions are made. If you have many logbooks, or the entries in your logbooks are a little messy, you should use a summary page. However, the summary page should not be used in lieu of the logbook; it may be presented along with the logbook(s).

- Keep a detailed work history. The airlines will want to know and be able to verify that history. It will take time to compile this information, especially if you have to list employment from 20 years ago. You will need dates, names of employers, addresses with zip codes and phone numbers. In the case of companies that have gone out of business, you can use tax records and pay stubs to verify employment. If you are required to list the names and phone numbers of former supervisors and the task proves impossible, you should use as a contact someone who at least can verify that you were employed at that particular company (a co-worker, for example). The airline representatives are aware that these situations exist. However, their job is to verify work history, and no matter how difficult the data may be to assemble, they will require that you provide them with this information.

You should never assume that they will understand and sympathize with you about long-ago flying jobs; they won't.

- Acquire your college transcripts. You should call the school from which you graduated and request that your transcript(s) be sent to you. Usually there is a fee per transcript. Since acquisition of transcripts may take four to six weeks, you should make your request as soon as possible. A wise precaution is to have a few to hand out, or make a copy of the original and show the original at the interview. (You should be sure to ask the interviewer if he will accept a copy of the original transcript).

- Keep copies of all training records in order to verify flight qualifications and training. Copies of records should be acquired right after training has been completed since the records are hard to come by if the company folds or you leave the company.

- Provide any medical records or tests to document that any previous medical problem (e.g., a broken arm) has been corrected. It is a good idea to get a complete physical before the interview or even sooner if you have never had one. More on this topic will be discussed in "The Flying Career Needs a Backup," a sidebar to Chapter 21.

Know Who Is Hiring and Who Will Hire You

First, as a pilot candidate, you should find out who is hiring. In its monthly *Job Report* newsletters, FAPA provides information to its members on hiring activity throughout the aviation industry. Another source of information, if you know how to use it, is the aviation press, i.e., such publications as *Aviation Daily*, *Air Transport World*, *Aviation Week & Space Technology*, *Career Pilot Magazine*, *Flight Crew*, *Air Line Pilot* (published by ALPA), *Airline Executive*, *Commuter Air*, etc. The clever pilot can often deduce from seemingly minor reports in such publications that a particular carrier is about to go on a hiring binge. If you are lucky enough to have this kind of "future sight," you will have an edge on other applicants because you will be able to get your application in early, along with a brief cover letter in which you reveal your knowledgeability by referring to the press reports that first tipped you off about the carrier's hiring needs.

Even without future sight, simply being well informed will enable you to launch a more effective job search. Take note: According to FAPA, its members consistently are among the first in the newly hired training classes.

Second, you should become fully informed with regard to both the minimum and the average requirements of the airlines that are hiring. You can waste time, money and energy applying to airlines that are not hiring or that require qualifications you do not have; you can even waste time if the pool of applicants includes a large number of pilots better qualified than you because in such a case, you may fall too far below the airline's average profile. (One precautionary measure you can take is to compare your qualifications with each airline's average pilot candidate profile as published in the feature articles and new-hire class surveys of FAPA's *Career Pilot Magazine*.).

Remember that airline pilot candidate standards change continually, moving up and down with the supply of and demand for qualified applicants. Of the companies that are hiring, you should determine who *currently* is a potential employer, given your qualifications and experience. FAPA's *Directory of Employers* provides an annually updated listing of minimum qualifications, starting salaries, equipment, domiciles and more. Being realistic about your qualifications, you should apply first to those companies for which you are eligible to work (apply with 10 to 20 companies, more if possible).

A third step you should take is to list those companies for which you would like to work. Many people become discouraged because they set goals that are unreachable, but there are also those who set their aim below their potential. You cannot be accepted if you do not apply. Your strategy should be to apply as soon as you are minimally qualified, then keep periodically updating your file with the airline as you improve your qualifications.

Acquire an Accurate Address List and the Right Contact Names

Once you know who is hiring and where you want to apply, you will need current addresses. The annual FAPA *Directory of Employers* includes current addresses and recommended contact names. Address changes and new employment information are published in the monthly *Job Report* newsletter.

There are other sources for obtaining the appropriate company addresses, many of which can be found at the local library. The *World Aviation Directory* (WAD) is the most comprehensive manual; it includes addresses and general information for specific companies. However, the contact names listed in the WAD are not necessarily the ones to use as contacts on employment correspondence sent to the companies.

The National Business Aircraft Association (corporate) has a listing of corporations with flight departments. This publication can be found in the local library; it includes addresses, contact names and aircraft types in the fleet.

There is nothing to keep you from calling the company and talking with the switchboard operator. Whenever possible, you should ask for a contact name and the title of the person actually responsible for recruitment, along with the address. Without fail, the spelling of the person's name should be verified.

Set Up a Filing System

An organized filing system will allow you to keep records of your job search. A separate folder should be created for each company so that clippings and articles about the companies which interest you can be collected and stored for future reference. When correspondence is received from a company, it should be placed in that company's folder.

You may want to place copies of your resume and cover letter with the file for each company. This practice is a simplified method of keeping track of which version of your resume and cover letter you last sent to each company. Your resume, especially, will evolve continually toward an increasingly more fully airline-qualified profile. You want to be sure you know which version each airline has on file, and having that version in the file will serve as a double-check of your other method(s) of keeping up with which applications need updating.

These company files should include photocopies of completed employment applications, since the file will be used for quick reference. All pertinent information should be filed under each company's name. A typical file would include news articles, a list of minimum qualifications, copies of completed employment applications, records of updates and revisions, telephone contacts, letters of recommendation, etc.

You should record every action you take, through the mail, on the phone or in person, including the dates and names of contacts, phone numbers and any other information. Also, you should record the dates of correspondence or any other contact made by the company.

Once you have established a good filing system, updating and recordkeeping will be easy. Good files are the only way you will be able to track your job-search progress.

Obtain Employment Applications

You should request applications from a broad range of airlines and companies. The initial contact with any company should be to request an application and to place a resume on file. You should apply to as many hiring companies as time and money will allow: FAPA recommends applying with at least 10 to 20 companies initially.

It is unrealistic to make all of your efforts with a single company. Statistics show that only one of every 100 applicants is granted an interview. It is not uncommon for only one of every 10 applicants interviewed by the major airlines to be offered employment. Your expectations and those of the company may not be the same, leading to a less-than-desirable interview. Besides, your chances of doing well at an interview are determined largely by how much interviewing experience you have. *Your very first interview should not be with your first choice of career employer.* You need a couple of interviews under your belt before interviewing for the "dream" job. However, if the dream job is the first offer for an interview, YOU MUST GO. You may never be offered that opportunity again.

When deciding on the companies with which you will apply, you should not limit your choice of employers based on the present standing of the company, its size or its area of operation. The company's growth potential should be considered. In the present economic environment, many companies are expanding. They are constantly adding new equipment and routes. Many previously domestic companies now fly international routes. You should not evaluate a prospective employer until after an interview. CREATE A CHOICE. Until a job offer is made, you do not have a choice.

You also should prepare individual application request packages for the specific companies to which you are applying. You should include a current resume, cover letter, self-addressed, stamped envelope, and copies of your medical certificate, licenses, and DD-214 forms (military). Where appropriate, you should include documentation of current Part 121 qualification with copies of training records.

Occasionally, a pilot's resume will be returned with a date stamped on it, or the employment application he or she receives may have a date stamped on it with instructions to complete and return it within a specified time. The pilot should re-submit the stamped resume along with a completed employment application. The fine print on the application should be read carefully. It may request that you return a resume with the completed application. If no correspondence is received from a company within a month, a follow-up is recommended. You should not assume that your application request package has been received.

Do not be alarmed by the different responses from specific companies. Each airline has its own procedures.

Remember always to keep track of the responses received. By being well-organized, you can determine the exact information that you have on file at the companies to which you have applied. You should update your files every few months, or any time you have a change in qualifications or address and telephone number. You ought to re-apply every six months to a year with a new application and resume, more frequently if possible.

You should network with friends. This approach involves making contacts or asking friends if they know someone who is connected to aviation and who could offer employment in a flying position. Networking works well in the general aviation community. Many of the flying positions available are advertised word-of-mouth and are given to those individuals who know the right people or who are in the right place at the right time. Even though these jobs may not be the most desirable, many aspiring pilots have gotten their first real chance to fly and to build valuable flight time by networking.

A pilot should call and visit prospective employers regularly. Many applicants make personal visits or call the employment offices of the companies of their choice. This method may not always be effective because the chance of talking to the right person often is remote. Normally, a pilot will need an appointment to talk to any company official, and receptionists and switchboard operators are expert at protecting their bosses from intrusions by applicants without appointments. However, a pilot sometimes may receive a warm welcome and be directed or connected immediately to the person in charge of recruitment. This may happen more often with smaller companies than with large ones.

You should never be a nuisance. Politeness is a must. The person with whom you are talking may be busy but pleasant in order not to offend. You should ask the person if he or she has a few minutes to spare before beginning to ask questions about the company. If the official cannot talk at the moment, you should try to set up an appointment for a later date. The pilot who does not show appreciation for the valuable time an official has granted is making a potentially serious blunder; again, a pilot should always leave a resume with the receptionist in a walk-in situation. A good impression in person is as necessary as a good one over the telephone.

Chapter 13
THE RESUME

The resume is the most important document in your quest for a satisfying aviation career. It is a synopsis of your qualifications and experience and should be tailored to meet your objectives.

The average time spent reading a resume is 20 seconds; therefore, a one-page resume is best. If a two-page format is used, the pilot's address and phone number should be on every page since multiple pages may get separated.

The pilot's resume should:

• Be easy to read. The eye should be able to focus on the major topics at a glance.

• Not be repetitive; most important, it should be specific and consistent.

• Be well organized. Major topics should be listed in order of importance.

• Follow a when, where and what format similar to that of employment applications.

How To Use the Resume

The resume is used by airlines as a preliminary screening device prior to distributing applications. It will be scored: A high score can produce an interview opportunity, and some companies grant interviews from resumes only.

You should bring a current resume to the interview since you may be asked for one at that time. You should have extra copies of your resume to help you complete or update applications during the interview.

You should use your resume as a calling card when visiting employment offices without a formal interview appointment and take extra copies of the resume with you to distribute whenever you make airline contacts.

Resumes given to friends and acquaintances make it easier for those who know you to recommend you.

How To Write an Effective Resume

To compose an effective resume, you should:

- Organize your materials before beginning. You should outline your personal biography, writing down every detail. At this stage, you should not be constrained by what you judge to be important.

- Use the when, where, what format of employment applications. This is the format with which most recruiters are familiar. It is easy to read because it is well organized.

The Heading

The heading should include your full name (first, middle, last), a current mailing address, and a permanent or alternate address (that of a relative or friend). There should be two phone contacts, and the phone must be answered 24 hours a day. You may wish to invest in an answering machine, answering service or a beeper in order to give a potential employer every opportunity to make contact.

Objective

A short, specific statement is recommended. Saying "career pilot employment" is all that is needed.

Certificates and Ratings

All ratings and certificates should be listed, including the medical certificate; you should refer to your certificates and licenses for the proper wording. You also should indicate any written exams you have completed without obtaining a full rating. Military pilots must have civilian licenses and ratings. (Review Chapter 10 on how to obtain the necessary certificates.)

Work Experience

Work history is one of the most important sections of the resume. It will generate the most points on most airline numerical scoring systems.

As stated, you should use a when (date), where (name of employer/address), what (job description) format similar to that of employment applications. You will be required to show employment history since college graduation. If you do not have a degree, you should show your employment history since the last date you attended school.

Employment history should be listed in reverse chronological order, starting with the current or most recent employment. The pilot should show three employers if possible. The work history should be continuous, with no gaps to reflect instability. Military personnel can effectively give employment history in terms of base assignments or tours of duty (usually two years in duration). They should combine any tours in which

WILL U. HIREME   RESUME OF QUALIFICATIONS

Present address: 1122 Home Avenue, Las Vegas, Nevada 89100 Phone (702) 555-1212
Permanent address: P.O. Box 11202, Las Vegas, Nevada 89119 Phone (702) 555-8376

JOB OBJECTIVE PILOT OR FLIGHT CREW POSITION

FLIGHT TIME

Total time	4200	Turboprop	4000
Pilot in Command	2000	Multi-Engine	4000
Second in Command	1400	Simulator	200
Instructor	1550	Instrument	550

CERTIFICATES Airline Transport Pilot (L-188 type)
Flight Engineer Certificate (B-727)
Flight Engineer — Turboprop — Written
FAA Class I Medical

EDUCATION Orange High School, Orange, New Jersey, June 1968

Bachelor of Arts in Geology, Chemistry/Physics Minor, University of Arizona, Tucson, Arizona, 1972

U.S. Naval Air Training, 1972, Pensacola, Florida — Corpus Christi, Texas

Patrol Squadron 31, P-3 Pilot Training, 1977
NAS: Moffett Field, California

PREVIOUS

November 1979 to Present: United States Naval Reserves, VP-2919, Naval Air Reserve Detachment, Moffett Field, California
Pilot in Command of a 12 man P-3 Electra Anti-Submarine Warfare crew; Pilot and Flight Engineer Training Officer for 22 pilots and 3. Flight Engineers.

January 1979 to October 1979: United States Naval Reserves; NARDET, NAS Moffett Field, California. Administrative Officer; Assistant Program Manager of a reserve unit of 100 flight crewmembers and 150 ground support and maintenance personnel.

November 1976 to January 1979 Patrol Squadron Nine, NAS Moffett Field.
Patrol Plane Commander (P-3B). Aircraft Division Officer —July 1978 to January 1979. The duties of Aircraft Division Officer include control of power plants, airframes, corrosion control, aviation equipment and Phase Maintenance shops. Supervised 5 Officers and 70 maintenance crew specialists which kept 9 aircraft mission-ready.

OPERATIONAL EXPERIENCE My pilot experience has progressed from Co-pilot to Patrol Plane Commander to Flight Instructor for Familiarization, Advanced and Instrument phases of instruction and Maintenance Check Pilot in the P-3 Electra.

My Pilot in Command experience includes domestic and international all-weather experience which ranges from extended flights from Iran and Thailand to winter operations is Misawa, Japan and Northeastern United States and includes high density domestic aircraft experience in the San Francisco area.

PERSONAL DATA

Date of Birth:	June 24, 1950
Weight:	140 lbs.
Height:	5'9"
Marital Status:	Single
Health:	Excellent/Non-Smoker
Security Clearance:	Top Secret
Hobbies:	Photography, Skiing, Hiking, Auto Mechanic

Available immediately.
Will relocate.
References available upon request.

<u>Resume of</u>

WILL U. HIREME

<u>**PRESENT ADDRESS**</u>
1122 Home Avenue
Las Vegas, Nevada 89100
Phone: (702) 555-1212

<u>**PERMANENT ADDRESS**</u>
P.O. Box 11202
Las Vegas, Nevada 89001
Phone: (702) 555-8376

<u>**JOB OBJECTIVE**</u>
FLIGHT OFFICER

<u>**CERTIFICATES AND EDUCATION**</u>
Airline Transport Pilot
ATP Type Rating in B-737, DC-3
Flight Engineer — B-727
B.S. Degree — History
FAA Class I Medical

<u>**AIRCRAFT FLOWN**</u>
B-737

DC-3

Light Aircraft

<u>**FLIGHT TIME**</u>
3000 Total
2000 Jet
1000 PIC (Jet)
2500 Cross-Country
2750 Multi-engine
635 Instrument

<u>**OPERATIONAL EXPERIENCE**</u>

AIRLINE — January 1976 to January 1980 — Captain and First Officer in B-737 with airline in Middle East. Operation includes flights over scheduled routes transporting passengers and cargo throughout several major cities in Western Europe and the Middle East. Operations requires flights in all types of adverse weather and airfields ranging from major international aerodromes with high density traffic to small, isolated airports with limited navigational aids. Three years total experience accumulating over 2000 flight hours.

January 1974 to January 1976 — Captain and First Officer in DC-3 with company in California. Operation included flights into several airports throughout California transporting passengers and cargo. Two years experience totaling over 600 flight hours.

FLIGHT INSTRUCTOR — April 1973 to January 1974 — Instructed student pilots in various MEL and SEL light aircraft. Managed and administered ground training for our flight school. Total experience eight months.

<u>**SPECIAL DUTIES AND ACHIEVEMENTS**</u>
• Graduated in top 10% of college class
• Obtained all FAA ratings at minimum age.
• Financed entire college education and flight training through part-time employment.
• Promoted to assistant chief pilot for airline in Middle East in less than two years.
• Evacuated forest fire victims in Northern California.
• Airlifted foreign dignitaries.
• Assist chief pilot in managing flight operations for airline in Middle East,

<u>**PERSONAL INFORMATION**</u>
Date of Birth: Dec. 15, 1950
Height: 6'0"   Weight: 165 lbs.
Health: Excellent/Non-smoker
Marital Status: Married, no children
Hobbies: Jogging and tennis

Available Immediately
Will Relocate.
References Available on Request

PRESENT OCCUPATION: Captain on B-737 in Middle East.

their duties were the same, or combine base assignments they may have had more than once but at different times.

When listing employers who are no longer in business, you still should show the employment period, using the former company's name and address.

If your employment history is lengthy, you should use a summary paragraph (two to three lines maximum) to account for positions held prior to the last employment shown on the resume.

Formal Education

Formal education should be listed in reverse chronological order, using the when, where, what format (the same as in the work experience section).

The education description should begin with the highest degree obtained or the highest level of school completed. If you have a two-year degree or higher, you should not list your high school experience. If you do not have a degree, you should list any college time completed in terms of years or credit hours earned. If you have more than one degree, you ought to show only that which is related to aviation or is technical in nature. You should include performance and participation in extracurricular activities while in school since these matters will give insight into career and personal interests.

Special Aviation Training

Training other than formal education is beneficial if it pertains to the position sought. Training received at factory schools and reputable training facilities (FlightSafety, Garrett Engine, Bell Helicopter, etc.) should be listed, as well as any initial, upgrade, transition, instructor, civil and military training.

Personal Data

This section is designed to reveal avocational and recreational pursuits and will round out a pilot's self-portrait. The applicant should follow any available published guidelines, including FAPA's *Directory of Employers*, to avoid showing any personal information that may hurt his or her chances in the screening process.

Many companies have filing systems using the Social Security number. Therefore, it is recommended to either show your Social Security number in the heading with your name and address (space permitting) or include it as part of the personal data section.

Also, if you hold a security clearance of any kind, you should show it in the personal data section.

If you are a minority (woman, black, Hispanic, etc.), this information can be included on your resume, but at your own discretion.

Availability

Being flexible and available are requirements of the job; however, you should not give the impression that you would leave your present employer without proper notice. Two weeks' notice is the common and acceptable response. If you are in the military or in school, you should state your separation, retirement or graduation date.

References

References should not be included as part of the resume. They should be listed on a separate sheet of paper, including complete addresses and phone numbers, and submitted when requested at the interview. You should use personal and professional references that you have known for at least five years.

Resume Formatting

The careful applicant will edit his or her resume many times before it is finished. The results of these efforts will be a high-scoring, one-page, easy-to-read and professional-looking resume.

In the resume, you should use action words in short, clearly written phrases. You should be brief and concise, avoid wordiness, and use one-word qualifiers to convey the message. All prepositions that do not change the meaning of entries should be eliminated.

Individual categories should be marked clearly with easy-to-find headings. A combination of underlining, bold type and capitalization may be used to make major headings stand out.

The resume should be drafted a few times before you complete the final product.

The Cover Letter

A professional, well-constructed cover letter will interest the reader and make him or her want to read a resume. The cover letter will give the reader that all-important first impression. It will introduce you and highlight your qualifications and experience.

How To Use the Cover Letter

Every resume should be accompanied by a cover letter. A cover letter allows you to personalize your job search.

The cover letter may be used to request an employment application and/or interview, to accompany completed applications, and to update your file with the company.

Addressing the cover letter to a specific person will distinguish it from general correspondence. FAPA's resume department has a list of approved contact names for most of the companies. FAPA's *Directory of Employers* lists contact names. The WAD, found at most libraries, will list company officers. A pilot also can call the airline's switchboard and ask the operator for the name and spelling of the person in charge of

CORRESPONDENCE SAMPLES

REQUEST LETTER

Will U. Hireme
P.O. Box 11202
Las Vegas, NV 89727

February 15, 19___

Director of Employment
Acme Airways, Inc.
747 Ronald Drive
McDonaldland Park, MD 54321

Dear Sir:

May I have a pilot employment application for Acme Airways? I am enclosing a self-addressed, stamped envelope and my resume for your consideration.

Thank you for your assistance.

Yours Truly,

Will U. Hireme
Will U. Hireme

COVER LETTER

March 16, 19___

Will U. Hireme
P.O. Box 11202
Las Vegas, NV 89727

Mr. Person L. Manager
Director - Pilot Recruitment
Acme Airways, Inc.
747 Ronald Drive
McDonaldland Park, MD 54321

Dear Mr. Manager:

Enclosed are my pilot employment application and resume. Please note that I hold a full ATP certificate. I expect to take the FE written exams in the near future.

I am presently a Metroliner First Officer with Crowded Airlines, a leading commuter carrier in my area. I will soon upgrade to Captain.

Acme Airways is a growing company, and I would appreciate an opportunity to work hard and contribute to Acme's expansion. I can be available to interview any time. Thank you for considering my application.

Sincerely,

Will U. Hireme
Will U. Hireme

UPDATE LETTER

Will U. Hireme
580 Willy Makit Road
Bettiwill, PA 12345

March 16, 19___

Mr. Person L. Manager
Director - Pilot Recruitment
Acme Airways, Inc.
747 Ronald Drive
McDonaldland Park, MD 54321

Dear Mr. Manager:

I wish to update my pilot application and resume of March 1. I have changed my address, increased my flying time, and passed the FE written exam.

My previous address was P.O. Box 11202, Las Vegas, . My new address is listed above. My new telephone number (702) 555-1212.

I have flown an additional 100 hours in the Metroliner which brings my total flight time to 2100 hours. I have upgraded to Captain and expect to be adding more fli

My scores on the FE basic and turbojet written e 100% and 97% respectively. I took the exams on

I am doing everything I can to make myself a for employment with your company. I would ap consideration you want to give me.

Sincerely,

Will U. Hireme
Will U. Hireme

PERSUASIVE LETTER

Will U. Hireme
P.O. Box 11202
Las Vegas, NV 89727

March 16, 19___

Mr. Person L. Manager
Director - Pilot Recruitment
Acme Airways, Inc.
747 Ronald Drive
McDonaldland Park, MD 54321

Dear Mr. Manager:

According to what I have been reading in numerous industry publications, Acme Airways is planning an expansion program. I am extremely interested in flying for your company, and if you would give me an interview, I could come to Los Angeles immediately.

I have both the ATP and FE certificates, 2100 hours total flying time with 900 hours in the Metroliner, including experience as a Captain. I have flown regularly into several of our nation's major, high-density airports as well as many small, isolated ones with limited navigational aids--often in adverse weather.

I would like to put my experience to work for Acme. Thank you for your time and your consideration.

Sincerely,

Will U. Hireme
Will U. Hireme

recruitment. Care should be taken in choosing contact names. It is inappropriate to send correspondence to the wrong person.

Writing an Effective Cover Letter

The Heading. The heading consists of your current address and phone number, the date (upper right corner), company address, and salutation (flush with left margin). This is one of the format styles used for standard business correspondence, but there are other variations that are acceptable (e.g., the block format where the applicant's address, date, company address, salutation and signature block is flush with the left margin).

The Opening and Body. You should state your objective in the opening paragraph, then highlight your qualifications and experience.

The Close. Say something about yourself as an individual, ask for an employment application or an interview, and express your appreciation to the reader for giving you a few moments of his or her time.

The reader should be able to absorb the letter quickly. Long paragraphs lose the reader's attention and should be broken into two to three short ones.

The signature is the most personal aspect of the letter. Sign all correspondence with a friendly, contrasting color, such as blue. A felt-tip fine-point marker is recommended.

Editing and Proofreading

Abbreviations are acceptable when necessary to save space. On either your cover letter or resume, you should use only standard abbreviations found in the dictionary.

Your most important qualifications and experience should be highlighted. You should cover all minimum requirements and focus on specific information pertaining to your experience. Avoid extraneous information. Action words should be used at the beginning of each sentence. Your writing style on both cover letter and resume should reflect your message. Ask yourself: Will my cover letter/resume make an employer want to read my resume/interview me?

When proofreading, you should be organized. A ruler can be used to proofread individual lines. Words should be read one at a time. Another precaution is to read the resume and cover letter from end to beginning (that is, bottom to top): Misspelled words will stand out. You should carefully review a list of commonly misspelled words before proofreading. It may help to read the resume out loud, and you should use a brightly colored pen to mark errors.

When typing draft copies, you should double-space text for easy reading and proofing and compare the revised copy with the corrected copy.

Envelopes

The envelopes should be of the same stationery, with the same ink color and typeface, as the cover letter and resume. Appearance of the package can be improved through the use of a picture or commemorative stamp.

The envelope should be personalized, using the same address and contact name as on the cover letter. The lower left-hand corner should be used to describe the contents/ purpose of the letter (pilot application, resume, etc.).

Verification Postcards

Verification cards are used to let job candidates know that their resumes or applications have been received. You should send a self-addressed verification card whenever you send an employment application and/or an updated resume.

The U.S. Postal Service requires a "business card" weight, 10-pound or heavier paper, cut 3.5" x 5" or larger. The card should be addressed in the format of a self-addressed envelope, with the appropriate message on the back. A contrasting stationery color will be more noticeable.

Production

When you are ready to produce the resume and cover letter, you must decide whether to use a professional typing service; a typesetter and printer; or your own typing skills.

A typing service or word processing center is recommended. Word processing services may provide electronic text storage for the cover letter and resume, making short-notice access and updating simple. Address-merging capability also makes printing a large order of personalized cover letters possible. Many word processors also have spell-check capabilities.

Typesetting provides a clean, error-free copy of the resume and cover letter. It will produce the highest print quality, but it is only cost-effective when large quantities are printed and used at one time. One drawback to typesetting is that it is not flexible if frequent changes are required. Also, typesetting makes personalizing one's cover letters virtually impossible.

Typing multiple copies of the resume and cover letter is not recommended because of the time involved and the increased risk of making mistakes. If you choose this method, a quality correctable typewriter is a must.

Copying

Modern plain paper or bond copying machines produce high-quality copies. You should use a professional printer's copy machine.

The original should be printed in black ink on plain white copy bond or reproduction paper. Copies from copies are to be avoided. Use an original to make your copies, and always keep it in a safe place.

You should never give up the last copy of your resume! You may need it to make additional copies.

Paper, ribbon and typeface should be considered also when you are producing the resume and cover letter.

Paper

Stationery for resumes and cover letters should be at least 22- to 24-pound weight. Many textures, such as cotton, linen, or laid finish, are available.

A printer or business supply store can advise you on the best paper to use for printing and typing requirements. You should avoid very rough and textured surfaces since they will affect print quality. You should ask to see printed samples of the paper if possible

Pastel colors are recommended and are professional in appearance (blue, gray, natural white, ivory, etc.).

Ribbon

Although you should be conservative when using colored ink or ribbon, blue or brown ink or ribbon can give a resume a distinctive look.

You should ask to see samples. Ink colors may not look the same when printed on colored paper.

Typeface

You should choose a typeface that is easy to read and pleasing to the eye. The typeface of the resume and cover letter should be the same, or a close match. Italic and script type styles are not appropriate for business correspondence.

Assembling the Airline Packages

A complete airline package consists of a resume, cover letter, copies of licenses and medical records, and the appropriate envelopes and verification cards.

The resume and cover letter should be folded together in a standard accordion fold. Ideally, the opening statement of the cover letter should be visible to the reader as the letter is taken out of the envelope.

Before sealing the envelopes, you should make sure that:

- All cover letters are signed.

- Stamps are placed on all self-addressed envelopes and verification cards.

- The envelopes and verification cards match the addresses on the cover letters.

- A copy of your resume is enclosed.

- Copies of licenses and medical certificate are enclosed.

- The entire package is placed in the appropriate regular addressed envelope.

Only when the packages have been double-checked should you seal the envelopes and mail them.

Special Letters

Letters of recommendation may have great impact on potential employers. The smaller the company, the greater the impact of the letter. Some companies have files especially for recommended applicants, and these are pulled first when screening begins.

You should never submit a personal letter of recommendation without a resume.

The ideal person to recommend you is a senior employee of the company with which you are applying (line pilot, station agent, flight attendant, etc.), but you must make sure this person is in good standing with the company.

Third-party recommendations (a friend of a friend) also can be effective, as well as political contacts outside the company.

A contact, no matter how well-intentioned, may procrastinate in writing the recommendation letter, so you should ask several people in order to make sure at least one comes through for you. In the case of people who do not work for the company with which you are applying, or who are domiciled away from the company's employment and testing center, you should offer to pay for the mailing. In some instances (e.g., your contact may be willing to write but unable to find the time), you may be within the bounds of courtesy to write the letter yourself, with, of course, your contact's approval and signature. If your contact works at the company and is conveniently located with respect to the employment office, find out if he or she would mind hand-delivering the letter of recommendation and your resume.

Letters of recommendation and resume packages should be forwarded as soon as possible. You should consider express mail service (again, you are offering to bear the costs), but if that is not feasible, packages should be sent by certified mail, receipt requested. Because of the cost, special mailing is not recommended for regular resume packages.

Interview Follow-Up Letters

Letters of thanks should be written and mailed the day after an interview. The longer you wait, the less impact they will have. Many pilots have made a practice of writing and mailing the letter of thanks immediately upon returning from their interviews to their hotel rooms. For greatest impact, you should handwrite the letter, highlighting some aspect of the interview.

You should make sure you know the name and correct spelling of the interviewer. You should be prepared and carry appropriate stationery with you on all trips as long as you are job hunting. Hotel stationery is to be avoided.

Chapter 14
EMPLOYMENT APPLICATIONS

Employment applications are graded on content, completeness and appearance and are given a numerical score by the airlines. Individual categories, such as work history and experience, will be scrutinized.

Applications are legal documents, and all information contained in them is considered to be true. Any false information discovered after you are hired, depending on the situation, can lead to immediate dismissal. The application will include a set of instructions, either on the front page, a separate page, or before each major section. You should follow the instructions carefully.

Never attach a resume in lieu of completing the employment application; send both.

Read the entire application before you begin drafting. The instructions will specify whether you must type or may print the application.

Typing the Application

A typed application is easier to read. The overall appearance is more professional.

Typing applications requires practice and good typing skills; a professional typing service is recommended.

Make at least two copies of the original. Use one for the original draft and one or more to practice typing in the given spaces. The original application should be kept in a safe place.

Make additional copies of pages with difficult sections and practice until you feel confident before typing the original. With experience, you may be able to avoid draft-typing the entire application and may just zero in on the difficult sections.

Keep your entries brief and edit accordingly.

Handwritten Applications

Follow the same guidelines as when typing an application. Handwritten applications should be neatly printed in ink.

Completing the Original

Once you have transferred the text to the original, you should:

• Proofread the application carefully.

• Let someone else read it as well. Another eye may pick up an error that you have missed.

• Check for typos, spelling mistakes and areas not completed. If an error is found, do your best to correct it.

• Be sure to sign the application.

• Before mailing the application, make a photocopy for your files.

• Mail applications with a copy of your resume and licenses.

Special Considerations

Applications vary in their complexity. Following are sections of the application that require special attention.

• *Prior conviction of a felony or misdemeanor.* Being convicted of a felony is hard to hide. Avoid a lengthy explanation until the interview.

• *Traffic violations.* Before listing any minor traffic violations, you should find out if you have any on record.

• *Minimum salary.* Most companies pay pilots based on a contractual rate. Simply state: "current contract."

• *Nepotism.* Some corporations have strict rules prohibiting relatives from working in the same company or division. If you are not sure if this applies to you, simply call the company and ask.

• *Desired location.* You should list one or a few of the bases you prefer, or say "no preference."

• *Work experience.* The full name, address and phone number of current and previous employers will be required. To verify employment from 20 years ago or from a business that has folded, use old pay stubs, tax records, company correspondence, etc. When required to list previous supervisors, use the supervisor's name if this person can be contacted. If not, you may use the name and phone number of a person who can verify your employment, e.g., a former co-worker or perhaps even a high executive who will be sure to remember you (and, of course, will speak well of you).

• *Length of employment.* This is important; the longer the employment, the better. The employment sequence should be continuous, with no gaps. If your employment history is lengthy, you might make copies of this section of the employment application and use the copies to complete this section. Then attach the extra pages to the application.

- *Reason for leaving current employer*. When asked for a reason for leaving your current employment, never be negative. The answer could be career advancement, pursuit of a technical career, departmental transfer, furlough, bankruptcy, moving away, a personal matter, or "To be discussed."

- *Asked to resign*. Be discreet and avoid being negative. It is always better to discuss such matters face-to-face with the interviewer. You should find out if an incident is on record before disclosing any information.

- *Medical problems*. To determine if you have a problem, you should be aware of the company requirements. If you do have medical problems (such as high blood pressure, color blindness, back injury, arthritis, etc.), state on the application, "To be discussed." You also should bring to the interview any medical documentation that will show how this problem has been corrected or controlled.

- *Essay questions*. These questions require time and thought. Do not be concerned about right or wrong answers. Most companies are looking for the ability to communicate, in the service of which correct spelling, neat penmanship, and good grammar and punctuation are useful; however, these niceties are insufficient in themselves if your thinking is muddy.

- *Special interests and hobbies*. You can use this section to note any volunteer work experience and any special achievements and awards. Avoid mentioning political, religious or controversial groups by name or identifying features.

- *Photographs*. If a photograph is required, a good snapshot (Polaroid) will do. Dress for the picture as if going to an interview. Submit a picture only if required; however, if you are in a minority group (woman, black, Hispanic, etc.), sending a picture with all applications and resumes may be to your advantage.

- *Certificates and ratings*. You should list all of your current certificates. Where appropriate, specify the class and category of each certificate, e.g, Airplane, MEL. If you are uncertain how to word entries, refer to your certificates for the proper wording.

- *Flight time break-out*. Flight times should be listed as total times using the flight times documented in your logbook. It is important that the flight times on the application correspond to those in your logbook/military flight records. If necessary, you should attach your own supplement sheet. If you have used a conversion factor from military flight time, you should note this on the application.

- *Addresses*. Use a three-line address, including zip code, for employment history listings. Some applications will require phone numbers with area codes. You can refer to the post office and the phone book to find this information. Be brief and to the point when giving a job description. Your resume can help in completing this section.

Update your applications as needed by sending a new resume. The airlines keep most applications on active status for only six months to a year, so applications should be updated regularly. Before the end of one year, you may be required to complete a new employment application.

Use any valid reason to update. You should update immediately when you have moved, changed telephone numbers, obtained additional education or received additional ratings.

Chapter 15
THE INTERVIEW: PLAYING THE GAME

The hiring process is becoming increasingly structured. Evaluation techniques include:

- Interviews with personnel department representatives, chief pilots and/or a board of pilots.

- Talks with psychologists.

- Up to eight hours of achievement/personality tests.

- Simulator checks graded by computer or a check pilot.

- Extensive physical exam, including stress EKG, blood work, height/weight check.

A pilot candidate must be both mentally and physically prepared for the interview process.

Mental Preparation

Attitude is paramount. It can make or break the interview.

Every pilot who is interviewed is qualified for the job. Therefore, you must display a positive attitude to succeed. It helps to remember that you have to deal with the personnel department only to get the job. The rest of your career will be in the environment to which you are accustomed: pilots dealing with pilots.

Furloughed or older applicants have a lower level of enthusiasm than pilots getting their first airline job. The older pilot must get excited in order to be competitive.

Each interviewee must concentrate on selling himself/herself. It will not pay to become preoccupied with what you think the interviewer wants to hear. Instead, you must compete using your achievements and communication skills.

Both mental and physical preparation are important. The more you know about the company you are interviewing with, the more comfortable you will feel during the entire process. There are various methods of gathering information.

The local library will have various publications with financial information (*Dun and Bradstreet*; *Standard & Poors Register of Corporations, Directors and Executives*).

Also, the pilot should read the daily stock market reports to obtain information on the financial stability of the company. For general information, The *World Aviation Directory*, *Aviation Daily* newsletter, and *Aviation Week & Space Technology* magazine are good sources.

A pilot should make sure to be up-to-date on current events. You may be asked to comment on certain topics, such as domestic or world events. Reading the local newspaper and/or watching television news will help.

While at the airport, pick up a current flight schedule. Most of these schedules include a map tracing the company route structure and outlining its operating fleet.

If you are flying to your interview, read the company's complimentary in-flight magazine. At this point, if you still do not know who the company president is, you can try looking for it by reading the foreword. Many times, this essay is written by the president. If it is not, then as a last resort you can ask a crew member the president's name.

You should talk to employees of the company. They will be able to tell you about the company's scheduling, salaries, benefits and training. Most employees are helpful and will be happy to talk. However, while en route to an interview on the company's plane, you should not interfere with the working crew's duties. At the beginning of the flight, you can let crew members know that you have an interview and would like to talk with them at their convenience.

FAPA's telephone information center offers career counseling to all pilot full-service members. This service includes extensive interview preparation and will provide the pilot with information about the interview screening process of specific companies.

FAPA's counselors are qualified airline pilots. They will give you a complete rundown on your upcoming interview, including company history, salaries, benefits, fleet, interview questions, written exams, physicals and simulator checks. Additionally, they will provide you with the typical "new hire" qualifications, enabling you to evaluate how you compare to the competition.

An automated interview briefing service called JET-LINE also is available for full-service FAPA members 24 hours a day from any touch-tone phone nationwide. It provides helpful interview details.

Physical Preparation

Most companies will provide a pilot with transportation to and from the interview, but hotel accommodations are usually at the pilot's own expense. If the pilot is staying overnight, he or she will need to make reservations early. When interviews are being conducted, many hotels near the interview site may be full. During phone conversations with the company or with hotels, the interviewing pilot should ask about hotel locations and transportation to the interview: Many hotels accommodating interviewees will provide transportation to the interview site at no extra charge.

If you have not been provided with transportation, you should make your own arrangements either by plane, train, bus or car. In addition, you can avoid a lot of pain and embarrassment if you:

• Plan your trip carefully.

• Allow extra time for delays and unforeseen emergencies.

• Always have a backup plan.

• Try to travel on the day or night before the interview. You will feel rested and relaxed during the interview if you arrive the night before. If you schedule your flight for the same day as your interview, your flight will have to be a quite early one in order for you to be on time for an afternoon appointment.

• Organize your packing the night before. You should lay out what you plan to wear and all of the materials that you will take with you to the interview.

• Make sure not to pack logbooks and other important documents (college transcripts, birth certificates, etc.) in your suitcase. These should be carried separately. If the suitcase is lost and your logbook(s) is in it, chances are you will not have your logbook for the interview.

• Bring along, without fail, all of your interview paperwork, which includes current copies of your resume, a copy of the employment application, a copy of references, and the interview invitation.

• Get a good night's sleep. If you cannot sleep, you should try only natural remedies to induce sleep. You should avoid any medication, no matter how mild. Sleep aids may make you groggy next morning and affect both your appearance and your performance during the interview. Also, you may be asked to take a physical examination. Any recent drug use will show up in the blood/urine tests.

• Arrive at the interview site at least 15 minutes early. If you are staying at a hotel, you should ask the desk clerk or concierge about departure times to and from the interview site. Also, you should inquire as to how long it will take to get there. Getting to the interview early allows time to relax and freshen up. (Note: An interviewee should use the restroom before the interview only if not scheduled for a physical that requires a urine test.)

• Maintain a conservative appearance. A quick glance at the advertising and promotional brochures of the airlines reveals that they prefer pilots with short hair, sharp-looking clothes, and a slim and trim physique. This does not mean they have not hired or will not hire pilots with none of the above, but it does indicate that in order to improve your chances, you should look as much like their "image" as possible.

    FAPA gives the following advice on grooming: "If you have a moustache, we generally recommend that you neatly shave and groom yourself. From the feedback we have received, the moustache is, at best, neutral. You must remember, most companies still look for a conservative image.

    "Dress conservatively. The recommended dress for men is a gray or blue two-piece suit, a white shirt and a conservative tie. You should wear dark socks with black shoes and be sure your shoes are nicely polished.

    "For women, we recommend a dress suit for the personnel and pilot board interview, but a pantsuit for the simulator check ride." FAPA recommends that the interviewing pilot read *Dress for Success*, by John T. Molloy, Warner Books, Inc., 666 Fifth Avenue, New York, NY 10103.

Basic Interview Preparation

As you prepare for your interview, rehearsing in front of a mirror will help. This will give you a chance to see your own facial expressions. Better yet, you can ask a friend to conduct a mock interview. This way, you will not be able to see, and therefore control, your facial expressions, and your friend can help make you aware of negative behavior. Keep in mind, however, that while practice is recommended, you should not sound as if you have rehearsed for a part in a play. Being prepared simply means knowing what to expect. This preparation will make you feel more comfortable and at ease. Trying to play a part will defeat this purpose. In fact, trying to remember lines will make you nervous. The interviewers want to observe a potential employee as he or she is. They are looking for spontaneity.

Seek out every possible interview opportunity. If the situation can be avoided, your first interview should not be for your dream job; a botched first interview is all too common. The more practice you have at interviewing, the better prepared you will be for your next interview.

After the interview, be sure to get the name of the interviewer and follow up with a thank-you letter. The letter should highlight one or two items discussed during the interview. Interviewing is very strenuous on the interviewers as well the interviewee, and the interviewers appreciate the applicant who takes the time afterwards to send a letter of appreciation. In many cases, this has made the difference in getting a job. Additionally, the after-interview letter gives you one more opportunity to sell yourself (but be brief).

In general, be sure that you:

- Review the application and correspondence with the carrier that has called you offering an interview.

- Brush up on current events.

- Read about the company.

- Take along some extra resumes.

- Stay in a hotel that offers a courtesy car to and from the interview, if this service is available.

- Get a good night's sleep.

- Are clean-cut, neat, conservative in appearance.

- When called for the interview, introduce yourself if you are not introduced and shake hands with the individuals if possible. Your handshake should be firm, but not a "bone crusher."

- Smile and be pleasant, even if the interviewer is not. Some tend to be intentionally unfriendly to see the applicant's reaction. Never get into an argument with an interviewer. You can only lose.

- Carry a freshen-up kit (toothbrush, breath mints, etc.) in case you have to wait several hours to be interviewed.

- Arrive 15 minutes early.

- Have some questions ready to ask the interviewers.

- Use good eye contact and good posture and speak with confidence. (Good eye contact is about a 75/25 split. No one can stand to be stared at all the time.)

- Are not distracted by things the interviewer does. Some will write while an interviewee is talking, and others may look out the window, seeming not to pay attention to the job seeker. Others may seem extremely bored. You should not be fooled or let such behavior shake you. The interviewers are listening to every word.

- Are professional.

- Are positive and confident without being cocky.

- Are not too solemn. Let a little personality show and reveal your enthusiasm.

- Are polite.

Recommended Reading

- FAPA's *Directory of Employers*

- *Career Pilot Job Report* newsletter

- *Piloting Careers* Magazine and Pilot Salary Survey.

- *Out-Interviewing the Interviewer*, by Stephen K. Mermar and John F. Maclaughlin, Prentice Hall, Inc., Englewood Cliffs, NJ 07632

- *The Evaluation Interview*, by Richard Fear, McGraw-Hill Book Company, New York, NY 10020

- *Sweaty Palms—The Neglected Art of Being Interviewed*, by H. Anthony Medley, Ten Speed Press, Box 7123, Berkeley, CA 94707. (Book most read by pilots hired by major airlines. This book can be ordered through FAPA. Call 1-800 JET JOBS.)

- *Airline Pilot Interviews: How You Can Succeed in Getting Hired*, by Irv Jasinski, Career Advancement Publications, P. O. Box 271409, Escondido, CA 92027. (Also available via FAPA.)

Types of Interviews

Personnel Interview/One-on-One Interview (a screening interview). The personnel interview tends to be personal and is conducted by a personnel representative. You can expect a "one-on-one" or "two-on-one" type of interview in which you are the only interviewee. At this point, your employment application will be reviewed. This also will be your chance to update any information as needed. Interview paperwork will be checked at this time (employment application/resume, flight records, transcripts).

All questions during this interview will be specific and will be used to extract information about you as an individual. The duration of the interview varies and depends on how well the pilot interacts with the interviewers.

Group Interview/Personnel Briefing. This type of interview is not a common technique used at pilot interviews. Group interviews consist of five to 20 applicants and one or two company officials addressing the group. A formal introduction of the company takes place.

Each applicant may be asked to stand and introduce himself (one to two minutes), giving a synopsis of his background. There also may be an informal question-and-answer session to give the applicants an opportunity to ask questions about the topics discussed by the company officials. This may also come in the form of a company briefing. You should make sure you are prepared to ask the company at least one question. If not, the company will ask you a question.

Pilot Board Interview/Panel Interview. This interview is a three-on-one interview in which you are required to address a panel rather than an individual. This panel will usually consist of management as well as line pilots. At this phase, your level of stress rises and your reaction to a battery of questions will be observed closely. A panel interview is intimidating because of the number of interviewers. More people will judge and evaluate your presentation and appearance. The interviewers will take turns asking you technical questions, primarily about your flying experience and knowledge.

You should answer questions one at a time. Never "lose your cool"; instead, remain calm and ask the interviewer to repeat questions, if necessary.

When answering questions, consider the following (extracted from *Sweaty Palms: The Neglected Art of Being Interviewed*, by H. Anthony Medley):

"The most important aspect that an interviewer gets out of an interview is a subjective feeling about the interviewee. You must enhance that feeling. Listen to the questions. If a question is ambiguous, you should either interpret it in your own way and say what puts you in the best light or ask for a clarification. Use ploys to get thinking time: Ask for a clarification or use a bridge. Don't worry about stopping to think for a few seconds before you answer. Act naturally."

Below are some tips by Medley on answering questions:

• Assume that every question is asked for a purpose.

• Be ready for the blockbuster question.

• Handle the offensive question firmly, but tactfully.

• Prepare good answers for questions that may probe skeletons in your closet.

• Accept responsibility for personality conflicts.

• Don't put the interviewer in the middle of the battle.

• Don't talk against a former employer. If you must discuss a bad situation with a former employer, do so dispassionately.

• Answer specific questions specifically.

• Don't respond to a serious question with a flip joke. If you joke, don't make the interviewer the butt of it.

• Recognize dual-purpose questions and answer them decisively.

Commonly Asked Interview Questions

What do you think of labor unions?

Have you interviewed with other companies?

Are you sorry you left the military?

Why do you want to work for our company?

What is a good pilot?

What do you think of "egos"?

What is your philosophy of life?

What is a good friend?

What would you change in your life?

What was the last book you read and why?

How did you decide what college to attend?

Tell us about your grades in college.

Does your family mind moving?

What makes a good parent?

Why do you feel you are a good candidate for this position?

How do you feel about male or female pilot insubordination?

What is your definition of professionalism?

Tell us what you know about this company.

What does your wife or husband think of you?

What are your outside interests?

What would you do if you lost your medical certificate?

What do/did you dislike about the military?

What do you think of the people you work with?

How did you arrange time for this interview?

What are your plans for your piloting career?

How would you deal with a downgrade from captain to first officer?

Use three adjectives to describe yourself.

Can you live on a starting salary?

What do you have to offer besides flying?

What are your career and personal goals five years from now?

Chapter 16
THE COMPANY PHYSICAL

Included in the basic physical exam are the review of the medical records of the applicant, completing the family tree or the medical history form, and an interview by the doctor. The medical history form is the most important part of the evaluation. You will be required to complete one of these forms at most airlines. If you apply at American Airlines, be prepared to fill out a family tree.

Although most commuters and corporations will require only that you have a current medical, a major airline will usually give a candidate a thorough physical.

You should start preparing weeks in advance, even months, with a physical exercise program. If you fail to do so, however, you definitely should not start a couple of days before the physical. Any sudden change could adversely affect the results. In addition, you should not change your diet unless it is a prescribed diet sent to you by the company to prepare you for the physical. A change in diet also could adversely affect the results.

How To Prepare for a Medical Evaluation (General Guidelines)

You should:

- Follow your usual diet/exercise program.

- Avoid excess (smoking and caffeine).

- Not drink alcohol for two to three days before the interview.

- Not exercise strenuously for 24 hours prior to the interview.

- Be well rested.

- Be well hydrated.

- Avoid noise for two to three days before the interview (by using ear plugs).

- Think positively; let go.

- Have an "executive type" medical evaluation on your own, reviewed by a Flight Surgeon.

- Be prepared to explain abnormalities/variations.

• Do not deceive, but also not tell more than you are asked.

• Follow the company's instructions.

• Have realistic expectations about results.

You can easily be rejected by:

• Not knowing your true health.

• Having no documentation of abnormalities.

• Being in poor control of the risk factors.

• "Cramming for the exam" (avoid extremes).

• Being tired, dehydrated, noise fatigued, nutritionally deficient.

• Not taking the medical evaluation seriously.

Urinalysis

The urinalysis tests performed include:

• Routine check.

• Drug screening.

Urinalysis tests the pH content of urine. A sample is taken and checked with litmus paper to determine if the urine is alkaline or acid. The sugar/carbohydrate level in your body also may be checked. Urine also is tested for drug use, especially illegal drugs. Keep in mind that prescription and over-the-counter medication can give a false positive indication of illegal drugs. Be prepared to document the effects of any legitimate medication which you take routinely on doctor's advice. A note from your physician explaining the need for such medication would be in order, too.

Blood Pressure

Blood pressure is checked for the following:

• High/low/normal pressure

• Hypertension (abnormal)

The airlines will always check blood pressure, which is expressed by two numbers (for example: 120/80). The first number is called systolic (pressure during heartbeat), the second, diastolic (pressure between heartbeats). The normal maximums are 140/90.

When checking blood pressure, the airlines are trying to determine that a pilot falls within the normal ranges. Hypertension is a frequent/constant state of elevated blood pressure, and this condition is abnormal. It can, however, be controlled by diet and regular exercise. You may want to consider purchasing a home monitoring unit so that you can check your own blood pressure regularly.

Hearing

The hearing tests usually include:

• Eardrum flexibility (by audiogram and tympanometry).

• Audiogram and hearing loss check. (Wearing ear plugs and avoiding high-level noise a few days before the test can improve the results.)

Hearing tests are given on an audiometer, which measures hearing loss in decibels throughout the effective speech and radio ranges. The range varies from airline to airline, but normally hearing is measured between 500 and 8,000 cycles per second. Each airline has its own hearing loss standard.

The audiometer (an instrument for measuring hearing thresholds for pure tones of normally audible frequencies) measures the weakest audible signal that one can hear at different frequencies. In other words, if a pilot has a hearing deficiency, the signal needs to be made louder by increasing the number of decibels. In addition to testing the middle-frequency voice range, the audiogram also can uncover high-frequency hearing loss, an important finding, as it is the first warning of potential permanent damage.

By far the most common cause of hearing loss to pilots is noise. Noise damage affects the high-frequency range first, long before it alters the voice range. Therefore, if you already have a high-frequency hearing loss, you can anticipate that with continued noise exposure (without adequate protection) the voice range eventually will suffer. It is important to note that noise factors other than those that are created by aircraft can cause the same degree of damage to hearing.

The FAA is concerned primarily with the frequencies of the voice range, i.e., 500, 1,000, and 2,000 cycles per second. If a hearing loss, one tested by audiogram, is in excess of 25 decibels (considered a severe loss) in either ear, this would then call for a more extensive evaluation.

A frequently asked question about hearing is, "If I have a waiver from the FAA for hearing loss, will a company give me a second thought?" The answer depends entirely upon the severity of the loss, plus the competition for the job you are seeking. Consider this, however: At the time of each exam, the FAA is only concerned about your flying ability, medically speaking, for the next six to 12 months. As an economical investment, however, a pilot's worth to a company must be evaluated for "20-plus years" from the date of employment. If you have a severe high-frequency hearing loss and are com- peting against an applicant who does not have any hearing impediment, you, as the hearing- impaired pilot, may lose out because the airline evaluators will expect you to have the greater risk of being medically grounded in the future.

Blood Tests

Blood tests are performed to determine:

• Anemia and blood cell disease.

• Blood fats (cholesterol, HDL, LDL, triglycerides).

Overview by an Expert

[The following article was written by Dr. Robert Anderson, formerly in charge of the TWA New-Hire Pilot Program.]

Many airline pilot applicants go all the way through the various airline selection programs and are not selected. And often, they have little indication why.

Traditionally, applicants exhaustively prepare themselves so they score high in the areas of flying skills and aviation knowledge. But few prepare themselves to pass the most selective aspect of the process: the medical evaluation.

Most pilots are unaware of the weak areas in their overall physical condition and/or medical history. Some of these deficiencies — if known to the pilot — are subject to improvement, or can be corrected if the proper action is taken. By addressing these issues prior to an airline medical examination, the applicant will substantially improve his chances of selection.

Medical Evaluation Limitations

A medical selection process consisting of one or two steps is the policy followed by most of the airlines. For reasons of economy and efficiency, some employ screening tests to "weed out" those pilots whose preliminary test results indicate that they may not pass a more comprehensive evaluation.

Medical testing results (both screening and comprehensive) generally fall into three broad areas of interpretation: normal, borderline or equivocal, and abnormal. Selection is usually made from only that group whose medical tests prove normal.

Airlines are reluctant to ask for follow-up tests on borderline cases for fear that the applicant, who may subsequently be rejected for some other reason, will single out the area

requiring follow-up as the item which led to non-selection. As a result, most airlines will not follow up on borderline or ambiguous data, but will instead simply pass over that individual and pick the next qualified applicant. The outcome of this process is that many pilot applicants who might test normally upon follow-up evaluation may lose their chance for employment because of unverified borderline or equivocal test results.

What is the answer? Every pilot applicant should carry with him to the airline medical evaluation a copy of a complete, authentic medical evaluation. This privately obtained, detailed pre-application evaluation can serve two important purposes. First, it helps the applicant in career planning. When fully briefed about his medical limitations, he can more intelligently choose a specific airline whose selection criteria are close to his set of circumstances. For some applicants, the pre-application evaluation may aid the individual in deciding whether to even consider a career as an airline pilot. Secondly, the privately obtained evaluation might serve as valuable ammunition should the individual be a borderline applicant. Here's an example: An applicant being examined by a major airline was found to have a significant hearing loss in one ear, for which he would have been disqualified. Coincidentally, the pilot had brought with him a recent detailed medical evaluation, including an audiogram entirely within normal limits. Investigation revealed an intermittent equipment malfunction in the airline's audiometer. The pilot was hired.

The pre-application medical evaluation should be complete and include all tests and studies reasonably expected at any major airline. The results, including raw data, should be made available in a complete report. It is suggested that the evaluation should be more comprehensive than any single airline evaluation, as different airlines have different testing protocols with varying degrees of thoroughness. Pilots faced with medical problems may want to direct their efforts toward companies that check Class I medical certificates but do not conduct a medical exam.

Testing Facility

Evaluations should be conducted by a medical facility with an established reputation in the airline medical community, one known for its professionalism, objectivity, and completeness (Mayo Clinic, Johns Hopkins, etc.). Choose a facility that has all the equipment and personnel necessary for a thorough evaluation. This will help you avoid the problems that occur when you attempt to have various facilities and practitioners contribute to a single comprehensive report, including loss of continuity, delays in report generation back to the pilot, and a much higher cost for the total evaluation.

Evaluating the Physician

Make sure you select a physician who is knowledgeable in the criteria used by airlines. As with the selection of the facility, the physician who signs the pilot medical evaluation report should be known and trusted by the airline medical community. Stay clear of overly favorable or deliberately biased reports. This will not fool the airline and might just jeopardize the overall credibility of the data in the report. Ask the examining physician to "tell it like it is" in his report. If the report is unfavorable, simply don't present it to the airline and just take your chances in their medical selection exam.

Raw Data

Your report should contain all copies or raw data, such as electrocardiograms, laboratory reports, etc. Interpretation of the data used by the examining physician may be sufficient for airline medical department needs. Interpretation of some test data varies in the medical community, so be sure to include all the raw data.

Suggested Testing Protocol

No single airline performs all of the various medical tests, measurements, and examination that would constitute a complete medical evaluation for a pilot. However, the pilot needs to be aware that a quite wide variety of procedures are being performed in various combinations at major airlines. The private examination, therefore, should be as comprehensive as possible.

Upon request by the pilot, the medical testing facility should forward a copy of the results directly to a prospective airline medical department, with cover letter attesting to the authenticity of the report.

Cost

A comprehensive medical evaluation may cost from $350 to $500, depending on the facility, types of individual tests, and location in the country. As the final report document is quite lengthy, most facilities will probably charge for extra copies of the report.

Conclusion

Don't take your physical condition for granted; be prepared and know where you stand before going in for an airline-sponsored "in-house" physical evaluation. Your medical presentation is part of the total package, and you want that package wrapped neatly and securely — and so do the airlines.

(Editor's Note: While the authors agree with the premise of Dr. Anderson's report, we also feel that many airlines would not require such an extensive or costly pre-application medical evaluation. Work within the confines of your budget or available medical facilities, but at least have a prior basic physical examination.)

GLUCOSE TOLERANCE DIET

In order for the Glucose Tolerance Test to be valid, adequate carbohydrates must be included in the diet for three days before the test. All of the starred(*) foods must be eaten. Additional foods may be eaten if desired.

No alcoholic beverages should be taken at or before the dinner meal on the third day. No beverages or food should be taken after midnight of the third day except water. Breakfast should not be eaten before the test is completed. Drink one glass of water in the morning before arriving at the office.

BREAKFAST
* 8 oz. fruit juice
* 1/2 cup cooked cereal or 3/4 cup dry cereal with 2 teaspoons sugar
* 1 egg
* 2 slices toast
Butter
* 1 Tbsp. jelly
* 8 oz. milk
Beverage with * 2 teaspoons sugar
Cream as desired.

LUNCH
3 oz. meat or fish, etc.
* 1/2 cup potatoes, rice or pasta
1/2 cup vegetable
* 1/2 cup canned fruit with syrup
* 1 slice bread or substitute
Butter
* 8 oz. milk
Beverage with * 2 teaspoons sugar
Cream as desired.

SNACK
Slice bread or 4 saltines
* 1 sweet dessert

DINNER
3 oz. meat
* 1/2 cup potatoes, rice or pasta
1/2 cup vegetable
* 1 slice bread or substitute
Butter
* Sweet Dessert
8 oz. milk
Beverage with * 2 teaspoons sugar

SNACK
1/2 C. fruit with syrup
* 1 slice bread or 4 crackers

P.S. This seems like a lot of food, and it is. But the diet is important as it will give you the best chance for a normal glucose tolerance test.

- Blood sugar.

- Glucose tolerance.

- Profiles (kidney, liver and cardiac).

- AIDS.

This could be the most comprehensive testing available in evaluating internal disorders in the human body. No one test can tell a doctor more about a person's physical well-being than the blood testing can tell. There are many items that blood can be checked for, and only a trained medical professional can explain the various items and interpret them. When having your blood checked privately, you can specify that it be evaluated for 12, 24 and possibly 30 elements, more commonly known as a blood test profile 12, 24 or 30. The larger the number, the more elements being tested.

Glucose Tolerance

This is a test that compares blood sugar levels before and after a gross sugar ingestion. The pilot will be asked to fast for a period of time and then to drink a glucose solution. At a given interval(s), blood samples will be taken to determine the ability of the pilot's body to neutralize the glucose by producing insulin.

The three-hour glucose tolerance test is used to detect the present status of (or a tendency toward) diabetes. Tests for sugar content in the blood and urine are measured first during fasting state, then at intervals of one, two, and three hours after ingestion of a high-carbohydrate liquid. Based on the resulting data from that specific testing period, the physician interprets whether or not the applicant's sugar content is completely normal or is suggestive of a diabetic condition. Since the results of the glucose tolerance test can vary from day to day for the same individual, the test is highly controversial. Some doctors even feel the glucose tolerance test over-diagnoses; that is, there are many people who have been diagnosed, strictly from the glucose tolerance test, as having a tendency toward diabetes, but who have not, in fact, developed the disease.

The test is not valid without following a 300-mg carbohydrate loading diet for three days immediately preceding the test. This diet ensures that the pancreas (the gland producing insulin, which is taken up by the bloodstream) is not in a dormant state from too little previous carbohydrate intake.

Although controversial, the test still is used by the FAA for determining the presence of diabetes. There are currently no alternative examinations to measure blood sugars. Diabetes that requires medication is a mandatory disqualification by the FAA; therefore, the detection of potential diabetes is extremely important in all pre-employment evaluations. For that reason, many airlines incorporate a glucose tolerance test (or a variation) in their pre-employment screening. In terms of the applicant, there are three possible outcomes: First, if the test proves completely normal, the applicant will pass; second, if the test shows gross abnormalities, the applicant will fail and will, without a doubt, be rejected for employment; lastly, the test may yield an equivocal result, which, depending on who does the interpreting, may or may not be significant. It is during the unfolding of this last scenario that the applicant's career may rest upon the mercy of the evaluator.

No one wants to ignore the factual presence of diabetes. However, with a career at stake, an equivocal reading often places the pilot applicant in quite a dilemma. There is little that the applicant can do to second-guess the suspicious or abnormal glucose tolerance test once it has been evaluated.

From a purely business standpoint, which is obviously the only sensible airline vantage point, if there are 10 applicants competing for one seat in a training class, and one of those applicants labors under a suspicion of potential diabetes, the potential diabetic will most certainly be the first one eliminated from the pack (unless one of the others has an even more disqualifying condition).

A common-sense regimen of keeping your weight down and decreasing total sugar intake is the best bet in preparing for a glucose tolerance test — and that goes for maintaining your general well-being also. More specifically, three days prior to the actual testing date, you should use the loading diet mentioned above. If such information is not provided by the employer, you can learn more about it from your family doctor. In fact, if you know you have had borderline test results in the past, you would be well advised to have a thorough evaluation by your own doctor. The results should then be documented for future use.

Heart/Physical Condition

Types of test to determine heart and overall physical condition include:

- Resting EKG.

- Exercise EKG (stress test), which also determines physical condition.

- Vital/lung capacity/spirometry/pulmonary function.

- EEG.

Most airlines check physical condition using the stress EKG.

This is the recording made by an electrocardiograph. The machine is used to diagnose disorders of the heart. It detects and then records the electric impulses that develop in the heart and spread through its muscles with each beat. These impulses make records of specific size and shape. If there is an abnormality, there will be a change in this pattern. Among the things that can be detected by an electrocardiogram are a diseased heart muscle, thinning of the walls of the heart chamber, and an irregular heartbeat.

EEG (Electroencephalogram)

An EEG measures and records the voltages, or electrical impulses, generated by the nerve cells in the brain. The test requires that sensors be attached to one's scalp. The recordings are called electroencephalograms or tracings. This test is used to locate brain tumors and in tracranial lesions and to distinguish between diffuse and focal brain lesions in epilepsy.

How's the Eyesight?

Early detection of any vision problem is especially important for a future career pilot. If you have never done so, it is imperative that you subject yourself to the most demanding visual acuity tests possible, and you should do so early in your job search. (Military flight surgeons may not be able to provide such tests.)

The eye exam may include:

- Acuity (near and far), especially for older pilots.

- Color-blindness.

- Glaucoma.

- Correction of acuity. If you wear glasses, you must know your uncorrected vision and must have your glasses with you.

- Contact lenses OK if not "extended wear" or tinted.

- Myopia (nearsighted); farsightedness.

- Ortho-K (not easily detectable) and Radial-K.

A pilot may be required to sign a statement about Ortho-K and Radial-K asking if he has had either treatment. (Both of these procedures, Ortho-K and Radial-K, are rejected by the airlines. If an applicant can be shown to have used one or the other, he will be disqualified for employment).

Several different areas are checked during a vision test. One is visual acuity or sharpness of vision. Many airlines use a machine instead of an eye chart. If you can read letters of a size that is "normal" for a person standing 20 feet away, your vision is expressed as 20/20. If you must be within 20 feet to read letters that a normal eye can see at 40 feet, you have 20/40 vision; and so on. You also may be checked for astigmatism, color-blindness, and glaucoma. Of the major airlines, the only one requiring 20/20 vision uncorrected is Delta Air Lines. Northwest requires 20/40 uncorrected; Continental, 20/200; and other major carriers, 20/70. Standards may change in the future, but for now, you may have to accept fact that if your vision is less than 20/40 uncorrected, you cannot qualify for Northwest or Delta. You should concentrate on other companies.

There are methods available to improve vision. Among those are Orthokeratology (Ortho-K), Radial Keratotomy (a surgical procedure) and visual therapy.

Ortho-K involves the use of corrective contact lenses to change the shape of the cornea and may leave the pilot with temporary 20/20 vision even after the lenses are removed.

Radial Keratotomy is an operation on the cornea to change its shape in order to achieve a certain visual acuity.

Neither Ortho-K nor Radial Keratotomy is accepted by the airlines.

Visual therapy is a series of exercises that strengthen the muscles that regulate the cornea, thus improving visual acuity. It has the advantage of not subjecting the eye to any foreign objects or trauma.

Height and Weight (Overweight vs. Overfat)

There can be few things more disappointing than to have passed every other phase of an interview and be rejected because of a couple of pounds too many. The chart below is representative of the height and weight standards many companies use. Many airlines will make no exceptions for applicants who exceed their weight standards.

You should make sure that your weight is in proportion to your height (this one element can and will eliminate a pilot candidate). Published height and weight scales are a significant parameter for all top companies, but are clinically evaluated.

If a pilot is grossly overweight, he or she has no chance.

Many companies have minimum and maximum height requirements. The trend is toward removing these restrictions. Pilots who do not meet the minimum height requirements for a certain company should go ahead and get an application on file since the requirements may change. Naturally, however, the bulk of such a pilot's time and money should be put into pursuit of companies that have a more lenient height requirement.

TYPICAL AIRLINE HEIGHT/WEIGHT SCALE

Height Up To:	Men	Women
5'2"	141	132
5'3"	145	135
5'4"	149	139
5'5"	153	142
5'6"	157	146
5'7"	161	150
5'8"	165	154
5'9"	170	159
5'10"	174	164
5'11"	179	169
6'0"	183	173
6'1"	188	178
6'2"	193	183
6'3"	199	*
6'4"	207	*
6'5"	216	*
6'6"	225	*
6'7"		*

Chapter 17
WHERE TO GO FOR CERTIFICATION HELP

As a professional pilot, you should understand any process so vital to your career as ongoing FAA medical certification and the periodic airline verification that you are healthy. And since you are not yet flying for your career goal airline employer, you have an even greater need to understand the process and know how best to utilize it in the interests of your career.

FAA regulations require only Part 121 airline captains to hold a Class I medical certificate, which must be renewed every six months. However, most airlines want even their most junior applicants to have a first-class medical certificate.

In your quest to know as much as possible about your health status, as well as to remain certified even if doing so requires an FAA waiver, you need a knowledgeable doctor with a reputation for helping overcome problems rather than for hiding them or for flunking the pilots. The doctor you consult should be, of course, an aviation medical examiner (AME).

Finding an AME

The FAA has designated certain doctors as AMEs. Of this group, only those who are designated "Senior AMEs" can give Class I medical exams.

Local FAA flight services offices have a directory of AMEs, coded to show which doctors are senior AMEs. For each physician, the directory lists name, address, phone number, and specialty. You might ask someone in your FAA flight services office for the name of a senior AME with a reputation for fair, honest, helpful conduct.

You also might try calling one or two of the airlines with domiciles or corporate offices closest to your home and asking for the name of a senior AME used by their pilots.

County medical societies and hospital physician referral services often can tell you which local physicians specialize in aviation medicine.

ALPA's Aeromedical Office can help a member find an FAA examiner with excellent medical qualifications, concern for pilots, and a clear understanding of his or her authority, according to Captain Dick Stone, ALPA executive chairman for aeromedical resources and a Delta pilot.

Giving Yourself a Physical Edge
By Richard O. Reinhart, M.D.

A pilot needs to follow a practical regimen going into a physical examination, whether the exam is for FAA Class I certification or for an airline's pre-employment screening.

Although the FAA does not require anyone but a Part 121 airline captain to hold a first-class medical certificate, virtually all airlines (some spurred by their insurance carriers) require first and second officers to pass a Class I medical at least once a year. This policy severely limits career opportunities for pilots who cannot pass a Class I medical exam. Airlines want pilots who can move into the left seat. They want to determine whether or not you are currently a safe and predictably productive pilot. The airline wants to know if you have a medical problem (of which you may be unaware) that could compromise flight safety or future FAA certification.

It also wants to ensure that you will remain a safe and productive pilot during the term of your employment and that you will be able to continue working to age 60. What the company is looking for is an individual who does not show a significant risk of developing problems in the next 10 to 20 years.

In other words, pre-employment criteria at most airlines are higher than FAA Class I medical standards. Some airlines do not even hire smokers, preferring to avoid possible problems down the road.

Other health-related causes of rejection by airlines include:

1. *Not knowing your true health.* Feeling OK can yield a false sense of your medical status. The only way you can know your true status is to have a good physical comparable to that which you can expect to undergo at a company.

2. *No documentation of "abnormals."* A doc-tor's statement simply alleging that your condition is no problem and that the company is overreacting will not satisfy company requirements.

If you know you have an abnormality, you must undergo advance testing and document the results.

3. *Poor control of risk factors.* If you are a smoker or chew tobacco, are overweight, are not following an adequate diet, or are avoiding an exercise program, these are situations that you are failing to control. These failures are an indication to a company of your poor judgment and lack of motivation. A company is not interested in anybody who takes health so lightly.

4. *Cramming for the physical.* "Crash" diet or exercise programs begun just a few days before the examination can cause problems. For example, a crash diet can affect your blood pressure, EKG, or urine dipstick tests. You know what you have to do to present yourself in excellent health and condition. If you have not been doing these things, however, or have too recently begun doing them, it will be far better to abstain from crash programs and go as you are to the exam.

5. *Presenting yourself tired, dehydrated and fatigued.* We are talking common sense. For instance, a pilot with eyestrain from studying all night for a check ride may not be able to see 20/20. Fatigue (or even a cold) can raise blood pressure. Review the various causes of fatigue, which in clude lack of sleep, poor nutrition, excessive coffee, previous alcohol intake, too much noise, and so on. Then act accordingly.

6. *Most important, not taking the physical seriously.* This is an indication of a poor attitude; the company does not want pilots who

are not taking good care of themselves. An example of behavior that might suggest a cavalier attitude: coming straight from a long, noisy flight to undergo your physical exam. A pilot who does not wear ear plugs on the flight or fails to leave enough time between the flight and the exam may not pass the audiogram test.

The ideal way to prepare for the Class I or the company physical is to stay in good shape by consistently eating a balanced diet, sticking with an aerobic exercise regimen, getting adequate sleep, not smoking, and not drinking alcohol excessively.

Focus on your overall health, well-being, and longevity. This sensible behavior will help you not only with an upcoming physical exam, but also with continuing to get Class I FAA certification.

Following is a list of things you can do to prepare for a physical exam:

1. *Follow your usual diet and exercise program.* Do nothing extreme just before the exam.
2. *Avoid excesses.* If you already are a smoker and drink a lot of coffee, then back off a little. Sudden withdrawal may cause "abnormals."
3. *Do no strenuous exercise for 24 hours prior to the exam.* If you regularly exercise a lot, taper off a little. Any strenuous exercise just before an exam can throw off blood and urine tests.
4. *Be well rested.* Ensure that you get a good night's sleep for several nights prior to the exam.
5. *Be well hydrated.* Even though some companies will require you to fast, you must still drink plenty of fluids.
6. *Avoid noise for two or three days prior to the exam,* including on the plane ride to the company physical. Wear ear plugs.
7. *Avoid alcohol for two to three days prior to the exam.*

8. *Follow the company instructions to the letter.* If the airline prescribes a specific diet, follow it.
9. *"Think positive."* If you know what your health is and are doing everything that you can do, approach the exam with a positive, relaxed attitude. Let go and present your best.
10. *Have an extensive advance medical evaluation.* Do this on your own. If at all possible, consult a senior AME. If none is readily available, go to your own physician and say that you want an "executive-type physical," a complete exam with blood tests, EKG, chest X-ray, etc. Explain to him or her that you will be taking a comprehensive pre-placement medical at a company you would like to work for and that it is essential for you to know whether or not you have any condition that might be considered unacceptable. Anything that is found to be even slightly out of limits must be explained by further testing. For example, a murmur may be judged by a physician to be insignificant. However, the doctor needs to do other tests, such as an echocardiogram, a treadmill, etc., to document that this murmur is indeed an insignificant matter.

Be prepared to explain your "abnormals." Bring a copy of all the reports that are pertinent to your company examination. Even more important is a short, concise cover letter by your physician stating the basic medical facts. This doctor should not make judgments about your health in relation to your being hired. That is what a company doctor is retained to do. Your doctor simply should state what the condition is, what tests were done, and the result of those tests, along with his opinion concerning the medical significance of your condition.

Having a medical examination is one

thing; having it reviewed by an aviation physician is another. It is imperative that any testing which you undergo on your own be evaluated and judged by a physician familiar with aviation standards. Many FAA AMEs and most military flight surgeons can do this for you.

Having such a medical evaluation on your own probably is the most important step in preparing yourself for the company physical.

11. *Finally, have realistic expectations.* If you know that a company is popular and has lots of applicants, and you know as well that your vision is 20/200 or that you have a strong family history of diabetes or have an abnormal EKG, you should also accept that your chances of being hired are remote. It is better to concentrate your efforts on companies with less restrictive standards. This strategy can work to your advantage. If you have realistic expectations, you can tell the smaller company that you will not be using it as a stepping stone to the major carrier because you realize your medical condition is non-competitive, although not medically significant. The company then knows that you are willing to remain as a long-term employee, and that's what it is seeking — career employees.

Another source, of course, is friends. If you have a friend who belongs to an ALPA local or who flies for an airline, he or she may be able to pass on the name of a good senior AME.

Most AMEs perform FAA physicals as a supplement to their practice. The majority of AMEs are general or family practitioners; others may be internists, ophthalmologists, or ear, nose and throat specialists.

This advice was prepared with the help of Bruce Jackson, M.D., a Navy Reserve flight surgeon and a senior AME with a practice in Berkeley and Oakland, Calif., and Richard O. Reinhart, M.D., USAF flight surgeon and senior AME practicing in Minneapolis, Minn., who are among a handful of physicians nationwide who limit their practice primarily to aviation medicine.

Dr. Reinhart had advice for pilots who are afraid (or know) that they have medical problems. While understanding the temptation to search for an "easy" examiner, he pointed out that any seeming gains are likely to prove illusory: Major and national airline health standards are stricter than the FAA's, so getting a Class I medical certificate is no guarantee of an airline flying job. Dr. Reinhart counseled against imperiling long-term health for the illusion of career advancement now.

ALPA's Captain Stone pointed out that the FAA knows which doctors give the easiest exams. "They watch those records very closely," he said.

Dr. Reinhart suggested that what worried pilots really need is an AME with a reputation for helping pilots.

Pilots can ask doctors beforehand what they would do if they found evidence of a serious condition, such as a heart murmur. The response should be that the examiner would work with the pilot on his problem.

What Comprises a Class I Medical?

What is checked during a Class I medical, and why? A physical exam includes checks for vision, hearing, blood pressure and pulse. The FAA examiner may look at other indicators, particularly if symptoms are present.

Vision testing checks for visual acuity, color vision, and eye muscle balance. Visual acuity is the ability to see both near and distant objects clearly. FAA Class I medical standards require that pilots have distant vision that is 20/20 in each eye, or that is correctable to 20/20. A pilot whose uncorrected vision is worse than 20/100 also must have an ophthalmologist or an eye doctor check refraction (the eye's ability to focus).

If you encounter a problem with the FAA concerning eye muscle balance, you are unlikely to pass muster with a major airline, the reason being that the FAA will either reject you for Class I certification or issue a waiver. The waiver will tell any potential airline employer that you have a fairly serious problem with eye muscle balance.

Eye muscle problems may not be permanently disqualifying. Many eye muscle weaknesses or imbalances can be corrected through exercise programs. Opthalmologists have a machine specifically designed for eye muscle strengthening. The procedure is painless and completely legal, but is very time-consuming. You may find yourself spending a couple of hours a week for up to a year in the opthalmologist's office and following through with supplemental exercises at home.

While an ophthalmologist may have room for a 20-foot eye lane (generally the most accurate way to test acuity, according to Dr. Reinhart), most FAA examiners use a machine that simulates that distance using a series of mirrors. However it is done, the objective is to learn whether the pilot can see 20/20 with or without glasses.

The color vision test is given to make sure a pilot can detect red and green lights — such as VASI and approach lights — at night. To test color vision, doctors use flip cards with different-colored dots; pilots are asked what numbers the dots form. "They can miss up to four plates" out of 15, Dr. Reinhart states. "Most people pass."

For those with a military background, an option is the Farnsworth Lantern Test (Falant), which the FAA will accept. If you have flown for the military, your records already will contain the fact that you have passed the Farnsworth Lantern Test; simply make sure that you have a copy of your medical records. Unfortunately, the Falant is not widely available outside the military.

To issue a Class I certificate, the examiner also must determine that the applicant does not have glaucoma. To do this, the doctor generally will use a tonometer (to measure interocular pressure). A word of caution: The crude screening for glaucoma that involves simply touching the eyeball with the fingertip, although occasionally used by a physician who does not have ready access to a tonometer, is not adequate to indicate whether or not you have glaucoma. For your protection, you should make certain your vision is properly checked.

The FAA will usually certify a pilot with glaucoma treated with eye drops, but left untreated, glaucoma can deteriorate vision so that a pilot can no longer meet visual acuity standards.

For the hearing test, the FAA again accepts two options. The examiner can administer the whispered voice test. First Class standards dictate that the pilot must be able to hear with either ear what the doctor whispers at a distance of 20 feet. The other FAA-accepted method is to test hearing with an audiometer, which measures actual hearing loss in decibels at various frequencies. "The FAA is only interested in the three communication ranges — the 500-, 1000-, and 2000-cycles-per-second ranges," Dr. Reinhart said. "For a First Class, the FAA will accept a rather significant loss — 40 db in the 500 range, 35 in the 1000 and 2000 ranges." While many pilots prefer to "get by" with the easier whispered voice exam, AMEs stress the importance of learning about high-frequency hearing loss (often caused by exposure to loud noise) in time to prevent loss in the lower communication ranges. Furthermore, as Dr. Reinhart noted, the whispered exam "does you a disservice." Only an audiogram can determine with accuracy whether you have suffered any hearing loss and in what frequency range this may have occurred. Many senior AMEs have audiometers and will perform this test if the applicant requests it.

Blood pressure and pulse are checked to detect such conditions as high blood pressure, coronary artery disease, and heart irregularities. A doctor can glean a variety of useful information from these readings — not only the pressure and pulse rate, but how these change with time and exercise.

A pilot's blood pressure can rise when the examiner takes it simply because of the stress of having so much at stake, Dr. Reinhart pointed out. However, he added, "The FAA has given the applicant every benefit of the doubt." Not only do the standards specify reclining blood pressure, but the acceptable cutoff rates, even for a Class I, Reinhart says, "are higher than most doctors would accept" without treatment.

"A single high reading does not mean you are doomed," according to Dr. Jackson. "The FAA is interested in the overall pattern of blood pressure over time." Most doctors recheck a high reading later in the exam, perhaps after the pilot lies down and relaxes a bit. If blood pressure remains high, the FAA manual recommends rechecking the readings morning and evening for three days.

At age 35, and annually starting at age 40, the FAA requires pilots to undergo a resting electrocardiogram (EKG). While this test yields a variety of information, the intent behind the FAA standards is to make sure a pilot has not had a heart attack. It is possible to have a mild heart attack without being aware of the incident.

The FAA now requires all First Class medical examiners to have the equipment to transmit EKGs directly to its Oklahoma City headquarters via phone lines. FAA personnel usually call the examiner about a questionable EKG within minutes, requesting a repeat EKG or additional tests.

The only laboratory test the FAA requires for all exams is a urine dipstick test. A chemically treated dipstick changes color when certain amounts of sugar (glucose) or protein (albumen) are present. The glucose test is used to screen for diabetes, while protein is checked to screen for kidney disease. "There's not supposed to be any sugar or protein in the urine," Dr. Reinhart said, although their presence does not always indicate disease. Runners, for instance, often show protein.

Urine also is checked for pH (hydrogen-ion concentration) and drugs. A pH above 7 (on the base 10) represents alkalinity; below 7, acidity. Healthy kidneys can produce urine with a wide range of pH (between 4.5 and 8), but the pooled daily specimen is usually acid (pH 6) in the Western world, alkaline in the East and in the tropics. Acidity and alkalinity are affected by the dissolved solids in the urine. Immediately following a meal, the urine becomes less acid (the "alkaline tide"); a few hours later, it becomes more acid again. For best test results, urine specimens should be taken at several different hours of the day. The pH tests allow doctors to assess the ability of the kidneys to maintain fluid balance.

Kidney disorders fall into two main groups: Those produced by generalized disease of the body, such as systemic lupus erythematosis (which involves the kidney), and those in which a local abnormality involves primarily the kidney, such as occurs in spongy kidneys (a congenital abnormality). There are many kidney disorders, and only a doctor is qualified to tell you whether or not you suffer from one. The information derived from urine tests is combined with other data (including other types of testing, a person's dietary habits, and any exercise regimen) to produce a diagnosis.In his book, *The Pilot's Medical Manual for Certification & Health Maintenance* (available through FAPA), Dr. Reinhart writes of the urinalysis: "This is the test that is probably the easiest to mess up and the simplest to protect. Even in a fasting state, you should drink plenty of water; don't go to the exam dehydrated. Playing a hard tennis game the night before can also create an abnormal urinalysis, so go to the exam in a rested state. Some individuals 'spill protein' in their urine, yet this tendency may not be significant. Again, this is a matter you should have learned about before reporting for your company physical; you should have a note from your physician explaining your condition if, indeed, it is a harmless one.

"An individual's urine can tell the evaluating physician a great deal. If it is normal, many health problems can be ruled out. If there is an abnormality, further testing is necessary to determine if there is a risky disorder." Dr. Reinhart said you can "save yourself a lot of grief" by taking along a doctor's explanation of any abnormal readings to either an FAA physician (for your Class I certificate) or an airline physician (for pre-employment screening).

How long the entire Class I medical exam takes depends on the efficiency of the doctor's office and the thoroughness of the doctor. "At a minimum, the whole process would take a half-hour," Dr. Jackson said. If there are complicating factors, or an EKG needs to be done, "it might take an hour."

Pilots generally know at the end of the exam whether they have passed. In some cases, they will need to wait a day or two for further test results.

(Caution: Occasionally a doctor decides an FAA-requested test is not needed and does not include it. The FAA will not issue the First Class ticket until it receives that test, and several months can be wasted this way. So you should check on what tests are requested by the FAA and insist on having them done.)

Certificate Deferral and Denial

If a pilot consistently does poorly on a mandatory test, the FAA requires additional tests upon which to base a decision about whether the pilot is safe to fly. If the FAA then decides to grant a waiver and certify the pilot, the medical certificate is dated from the day of the original exam, not from the day the certification is granted (which may be several months later). To maintain First Class certification, another Class I physical must be taken not more than six months after the previous one.

When certification is questioned, the AME has several options. Dr. Reinhart noted that some AMEs simply send in their findings and let the FAA inform the pilot what additional tests are needed. However, when everything is left up to the FAA, the process takes longer.

"A lot of pilots have been grounded unnecessarily, or it's taken months and months to get them certified," Dr. Reinhart said. When the AME knows what further tests the FAA will require, Dr. Jackson said, "the examiner can send his paperwork to the FAA and tell the pilot to get certain tests done and send them to the FAA. They'll meet up in Oklahoma City. The FAA will review the medical reports. If they decide to issue a ticket, they'll send it in the mail to the applicant."

Suppose test results do not meet First Class standards but do meet those for Second or Third Class. The pilot can ask the AME to issue a lesser certificate immediately, which can be upgraded to First Class if and when further tests prove the applicant is qualified.

"The standards for Second and Third Class are much more generous than the standards for First Class," Dr. Jackson said. "For example, the blood pressure standards for Class II and III are a maximum of 170/100 at all ages."

Dr. Reinhart said the major difference for vision is that "the FAA is going to look at vision more carefully for a First Class."

Audiometric standards for hearing are basically for First Class only; a pilot has to distinguish the doctor's whispered voice at just eight feet, rather than 20, to meet Class II standards.

A Second Class medical certificate is good for one year. A First Class ticket that is not renewed after six months automatically lapses to a Second Class for the following six months.

Probably the most expeditious way to speed First Class certification is for the AME to perform or order the required retesting. In a simple case, such as a positive glucose test, Dr. Jackson said, the doctor can send the pilot to a laboratory that day or the next for a repeat urine test and several blood tests. If these results rule out diabetes, the AME can then issue a First Class certificate right away.

If a specialist is needed to perform tests, such as for a possible heart murmur, Dr. Reinhart suggested, the process can be streamlined if the AME refers the pilot to a colleague, attaches the subsequent results to his report, and perhaps talks directly with an FAA doctor regarding the application. (The doctor may ask the pilot to ground himself during this process if a significant medical problem is suspected.)

For quickest results, Dr. Reinhart recommended that pilots choose the physician most willing to work with the pilot. Dr. Reinhart pointed out that FAA medical regulations are open-ended, with few absolutes. "While the regulations have remained the same, the interpretation of the significance of medical problems, what medications are acceptable, changes every day," he said. "Flexible regulations give the FAA discretion to look at each individual."

Even with vision and blood pressure, where standards have been quantified, he explained, "If we can prove everything is all right, the FAA will accept it."

ALPA's Aeromedical Office

ALPA members with medical or medical certification problems can ask their local aeromedical consultant for help. At the national level, the union's Aeromedical Office employs three knowledgeable, full-time physicians who advise pilots on how to maintan medical certification or get recertified.

Pilots usually are asked to have their AME forward the records from the Class I exam to the Aeromedical Office. An ALPA doctor will then discuss the findings with the pilot in terms of qualification for FAA medical certification.

The ALPA doctors, who (unlike many AMEs) are well-versed in what further tests the FAA will require, may then refer the pilot to other physicians for further evaluation. The office works with some 400 highly qualified specialists, often professors in medical schools or doctors affiliated with large clinics. "You need that kind of medical horsepower to turn the FAA around sometimes," Stone said.

The specialists send their reports back to the Aeromedical Office, which prepares and sends the pilot's application directly to the appropriate FAA personnel in Oklahoma City. In most instances, the FAA discusses the case with the Aeromedical Office and, through the office, recertifies the pilot.

ALPA can be helpful even in very unusual cases. Stone told of one pilot who was grounded for five weeks while his application sat in the FAA mailroom; his FAA doctor had not addressed and stamped his application correctly. ALPA's head physician, Dr. Richard Masters, called Oklahoma City and had the pilot's certification released that afternoon. "We handle about 1,200 cases a year," Stone added. "If pilots get to us quickly enough, they normally will not get grounded needlessly, because our doctors know so well how to work inside the system."

The Aeromedical Office can be invaluable when the FAA changes medical policy. "If the FAA is suddenly approving people on oral hypoglycemic agents for diabetes, for instance, we know about it within hours," Stone said. "We will tell pilots who are on those that we're going to turn the paperwork around and get them certified."

Chapter 18
AIRLINE TESTING

Your job search will bring you into frequent contact with testing programs, although a few companies do prefer not to use aptitude and personality tests. This distinct minority of airlines focuses instead on more practical areas, such as the simulator ride and interviews with management pilots.

Those companies that test have their own examination programs and areas of emphasis in evaluation of applicants, though there are certain factors common to all testing programs. First, on any test there is a wide range of scores that would not attract attention to an applicant or prevent him or her from obtaining a job. A negative factor would be a drastic deviation from the average range. Some companies also include an interview with a psychologist or an employment counselor in the testing and interview process.

The tests indicate only an applicant's ability or personality. The individual will be evaluated on how well he or she does in *all* phases of a company's selection process.

Following is a discussion of the general types of testing you can expect to encounter when interviewing for a flight crew position. The listing is not comprehensive and will not indicate which tests are used by specific airlines or companies. (Such specific information is listed in FAPA's *Airline Testing Study Kit*.)

Intelligence and personality tests most commonly used in the aviation community are those that were developed by the Institute of Behavioral Research (IBR). The IBR, which closed down in 1983, was a division of Texas Christian University (TCU). The IBR developed a testing system that consisted of a battery of 14 tests, 11 of which were intelligence tests and the remaining three, personality inventories. These tests included math, mechanical aptitude, spatial orientation, vocabulary, abstract reasoning, etc. The tests were commonly referred to as the TCU, IBR, Vinsons or Zells. In actuality, these tests have or had no real names per se, but simply went by the names of their creators. One exception is the Minnesota Multiphasic Personality Inventory (MMPI), a personality test still being used today by most of the airlines.

The specific purposes served in the testing of candidates vary greatly among the airlines. Therefore, many airlines work with private consultants — professionals who design and tailor tests according to the airlines' specifications. While a test may be referred to as an "IBR-type" test, it actually will have been uniquely designed for the particular airline.

In addition to the usual series of aptitude tests, such as math, physics and vocabulary,

Avoiding Discouragement

Let us suppose that you have applied at a major airline, passed the physical, appeared to handle your interviews well, gotten through your simulator check without coming unglued, and done your best (well enough, you felt) on the written testing. And yet, despite all of that, you have not been hired; your fine two-day adventure at the airline of your choice has not turned out to be the beginning of your career there.

Just as important as preparing yourself for the job is pursuing it in a persistent and organized way. If the qualifications and experience needed to become an airline pilot could be likened to one leg of your career flight, then a systematic job search is the other. The pilot cannot proceed without both.

Many qualified pilots drop the ball at this point — that is, at the point when they conclude that an attempt to land a major or national airline flying job will encounter obstacles. They feel that the job, while not beyond their piloting abilities, is nearly impossible to obtain, and they assume that there must be thousands of more qualified applicants ahead of them. They are too easily discouraged and think, "I don't have a chance, so why try?"

Unfortunately, such an attitude becomes a self-fulfilling prophecy if you fail to apply yourself.

Keep in mind that many intelligent and determined pilots have an application on file with every major and national airline so as to increase their chances of being hired by one of them. Thus, a report of tens of thousands of applications on file with the airlines does not by any means indicate an equal number of applicants in the field at large. Also, remember that some of the contenders may not be as well-qualified and well-suited, or as persistent, as you.

A word about discouragement: It can be found everywhere, even among people who are close to you and have your best interests at heart.

Ironically, though, the harshest judgments seem to come from people who know the least about the industry or from disappointed pilots who have given up trying themselves. Most of the discouragement and extreme statements you may come across are exaggerated hearsay, uninformed personal opinion, or someone else's defeatist attitude.

You should not be dismayed by such talk. Honest facts about airline hiring situations are one thing, but negativism may be safely disregarded. It never hurts to be a discriminating optimist — and as an aspiring pilot, you may have to keep your hopes up for years.

Attaining this job is neither a pushover nor a mission impossible. If you fill in all the "squares" and apply for the job, you stand as good a chance as the next person of getting hired. If you pursue the job intelligently and persistently, you have an excellent chance.

Handling Rejection

Some airlines hire one of 12 applicants interviewed, with the average being one of six or seven. To ensure success, you must apply with a broad range of airlines. A consistent pressure will produce the best results.

Most important, however, is not to take any unsuccessful interviews too seriously. You need to create as many interviewing opportunities as possible because the more interview practice you have, the better you will become at interviewing.

Do not stop applying when you get the first interview or if you are unsuccessful with your first choice. It is routine to be interviewed by several companies before being offered employment. Above all, to succeed, you cannot take rejection personally. If you do, you will lose your confidence and self-esteem. Your attitude will be reflected in performance during subsequent interviews.

Once turned down by an airline, do not

spend extra effort trying to determine why you were not hired. You probably will never know, and that airline should go to the bottom of the "try" list. Overcome your frustration and channel the energy to complete new applications and resumes. It is always better to pressure the next company on your list than to fret over a missed opportunity. The spurned pilot's job is not to get mad, but to get busy.

the airlines require the applicant to have a knowledge of airplanes. Knowledge of airplanes is tested through interviews, aviation-specific paper-and-pencil tests, and simulator check rides. Of course, you will not take all of the possible tests with any one particular airline. As you interview with more airlines, you will be exposed to a greater variety of tests.

For help on testing, you might resort to such outside advice as the FAPA counseling center or another "job search" organization. (FAPA also can be of help through its *Airline Testing Study Kit*, which consists of sample tests commonly used by the airlines.) Then you should prepare as best you can.

Types of Tests

Written Aptitude Tests. Most airlines give both psychological and aptitude tests. Some preparation is recommended and possible for the aptitude tests, but not for the psychological tests. General aptitude tests cover everything from literature to math, vocabulary, reading ability, hand-eye coordination, physics, chemistry, astronomy, meteorology, logic and aviation knowledge. You may need to know who discovered penicillin, or you may have to select the synonym or antonym of a word from a list of several other words. You could be asked to multiply fractions or add up long columns of numerals. You may have to read a paragraph and answer questions about it, or you may have to know what a nova is or how far the Earth is from the sun.

It is recommended that a pilot job candidate practice for tests of vocabulary, reading comprehension, math, deductive reasoning, number/color stress tests, hand/eye coordination, mechanical aptitude, etc. FAPA's *Airline Testing Study Kit* can be used for practice before the tests. Arco's *Preparation for the SAT* offers good practice for basic vocabulary skills, reading and math. Another very helpful study guide is Arco's *Officer Candidate Tests*. You may be tested also on federal aviation regulations (FAR), basic aerodynamics and instrument flying. *The Federal Aviation Regulations* and *Airman's Information Manual* (AIM) are both excellent sources for help in reviewing these subjects, as is Arco's *Military Flight Aptitude Tests*. At a local library, you can check out books on physics, algebra, meteorology or electronics. You might also review any college books on these subjects that you have not thrown away.

Needless to say, you could spend an extraordinary amount of time attempting to become proficient in all these areas; you cannot be so comprehensive in your preparations if you have only a short time span between being notified and reporting for an interview. But all is not lost because of a short-notice interview. You are not expected to come up with a perfect score, only a reasonable score on any given measure. You are not taking a competitive Civil Service test. Your score will not determine your position on a list.

One of the most sensible things you can do, if you are a full-service FAPA member, is to call the FAPA counseling center as soon as you receive word that you have an interview. Usually, center personnel will have information on what kind of testing, if any, is done by a particular company. Then you can limit to specific areas the amount of studying you must do. (Note: The FAPA counselor will tell you only which areas you can expect to be tested on, not the answers to specific questions.)

In any case, you will need to prepare yourself in aviation fundamentals, meaning that you should study:

- Basic Federal Aviation Regulations (FARs), *Airman's Information Manual* (AIM), weather, aerodynamics, instrument flying.

- Private or commercial pilot certification tests and general aeronautical knowledge texts for good practice on FARs, AIM, weather, etc.

- Arco's *Officer Candidate Tests*.

The following tests seem to be in common use among several companies.

1. *The Vinson's Test.* The Vinson's test is a verbal and mathematical aptitude test. The verbal section has multiple-choice selections of vocabulary, synonyms and word analogies. The math section consists of fractions, decimals, percentages and elementary algebra.

2. *Math Tests.* You can prepare and practice using Arco's *Preparation for the SAT*, Arco's *ASVAB, Practice for the Armed Forces Test*, or FAPA's *Airline Testing Study Kit* (revised regularly; update available for those with first edition).

3. *Company-Derived Tests.* Study FARs (61, 91, 121, 135), AIM, high school physics, turbine engine operations and aerodynamics, and ARCO's Military Flight Aptitude Tests.

Psychological Tests

Most of the tests still in use were written in the late 1930s or early 1940s and originally were designed to identify personality traits of antisocial elements of society (criminals, sociopaths, etc.).

There have been some recent modifications (less than 20 years old) in the types of test that are given. Many companies try to give tests more in tune with the times, covering fairly current subjects. In many cases, the content has been altered to jibe with changes in traditional masculine and feminine roles, and the tests tend to reflect attitudes on equality, sex, racism, and other contemporary social issues.

Today, psychologists have adopted a scoring system for members of society in general, and specifically for airline pilots.

Types of psychological test include:

1. *Minnesota Multiphasic Personality Inventory (MMPI).* The Minnesota Multiphasic Personality Inventory seems to be the most common and widely known of all the personality tests. The usual format has several hundred (560)

statements to which the pilot must answer "true" or "false." The statements cover every conceivable emotion or aspect of one's life. Several examples are as follows:

I like school.

I like to cook.

Someone is trying to poison me.

I like to tease animals.

I would rather win than lose in a game.

I do not like everyone I know.

I am not afraid of mice.

I like repairing a door latch.

I dread the thought of an earthquake.

My parents have often objected to the kind of people I went around with.

The pilot must be honest throughout this type of test. A number of questions are asked in different ways, and if answers are inconsistent, this indicates that the tested individual is lying, and the test results are considered invalid.

2. *The Cleaver Exam.* The Cleaver exam is another of the multitude of personality tests with which airline applicants can be confronted. This particular test is in a self-judgment format. For example, the applicant is given a series of categories; each category has several descriptive words in it, and the applicant must mark or designate the word that is most like him or her.

3. A variation on this format has a list of traits in the left-hand margin; various categories across the top must be indicated in the selection process according to how you perceive yourself or how you perceive that others react to you:

Trait	Your Estimation	Elders' Estimation	Peers' Estimation
Calculating			
Fearful			
Gentle			
Friendly			

Stress Tests

Timed tests are grouped in the category of stress tests. This is because of time constraints associated with completing the test. This type of test is not designed to be finished within the allotted time. The primary emphasis is on accuracy. The purposes of such tests vary, but generally it can be said that the airlines use a selection of tests which they believe will indicate how the pilot applicant may perform in a cockpit environment.

How well do you distinguish colors? How rapidly can you absorb numerically-based instructions? And so on.

There are several types of stress test, including:

1. *Color Stress.* The color card stress test is in three parts.

   In part one, there is a card with 50 random-order repetitions of the words "red," "green," "black," "yellow" and "blue" printed in black ink on a white background. The pilot must read the words aloud as quickly and accurately as possible.

   In part two, there is a card with 50 colored squares in random order. These squares are colored red, green, black, yellow and blue. The applicant must say the colors as quickly and accurately as possible.

   The third part of the test is the most difficult and the most stressful. These cards have the words "red," "green," "black," "yellow" and "blue" printed in an ink color different from the color indicated by the words. For example, the word "red" may be printed in green ink. The applicant must say the color of the ink that the word is printed in — as quickly and accurately as possible.

2. *Numbers Tests.* In one version of such testing, the applicant simply looks at two columns of numbers in a limited amount of time to see if both columns are exactly the same. Sometimes you are penalized for guessing, and sometimes you are penalized for not finishing, so before taking the exam, you must ask how it is going to be graded.

   A second type of numerical stress test has a series of numerals spoken on a tape recording with one number missing. The recording is played quickly, and the applicant will be asked to identify the missing number within a few seconds. For example, if there are 10 numbers in a series, only nine will be spoken. The applicant must quickly identify the number that was omitted and go on to the next sequence.

   The most common type of number stress tests will be sequence tests where the applicant must identify the missing number or determine the next number in the sequence.

3. *Hand-Eye Coordination.* The applicant may be asked to draw a line through a printed maze without touching the sides of the drawing. Beware: Too much coffee before this test can seriously impair your performance.

   Another version of this kind of test will have the numerals 1 through 26 and the letters A through Z on separate lines and out of numerical or alphabetical order. The individual is told to draw a line quickly from 1 to A, 2 to B, 3 to C, and so forth. It's more difficult than it sounds.

4. *Mental Alertness.* There are many variations of mental alertness tests, including number sequence, analogy tests, etc. Some tests are given on a computer.

Sample Question Types

Psychological Tests:

		YES	NO
1.	Do you have difficulty in making decisions?	___	_X_
2.	I often think that someone is out to get me.	___	_X_
3.	I enjoy going to plays more than parties.	___	___
4.	Do you sometimes feel self-conscious?	___	___
5.	Most people are dishonest.	___	___
6.	We had a lot of family trouble when I was young.	___	___
7.	I often have headaches.	___	___

Cleaver Type Exam:

Below are groups of three words. In each case decide which word is most like you, and which word is least like you. Each word group will have two answers.

		Most Like You	Least Like You			Most Like You	Least Like You
1.	Argumentative	___	_X_	2.	Egotistical	___	___
	Gentle	___	___		God Fearing	___	___
	Generous	_X_	___		Outgoing	___	___
3.	Loving	___	___	4.	Aggressive	___	___
	Intellectual	___	___		Sincere	___	___
	Honest	___	___		Religious	___	___
5.	Persuasive	___	___	6.	Humble	___	___
	Mild	___	___		Excitable	___	___
	Friendly	___	___		Jocular	___	___

Vocabulary Tests:

Circle the answer that has most nearly the same meaning as the capitalized word in each question.

1. IMPERATIVE	2. DOGMATIC	3. AUSPICIOUS
A) Possible	A) Canine	A) Mysterious
B) Necessary	B) Funny	B) Favorable
C) Unique	C) Colorful	C) Reliable
D) Feasible	D) Decree	D) Exact

4. RECAPITULATE	5. IRREVOCABLE	6. JOCULAR
A) Capture	A) Unchangeable	A) Jokingly
B) Overdone	B) Foolish	B) Horse
C) Bothersome	C) False	C) Rider
D) Summarize	D) Alter	D) King

Analogy Tests:

In the following questions, determine the relationship between the first two words, then choose the answer that best relates similarly with the third word.

1. Shovel : Dig : : Vice : ___	2. Ear : Hear : : Eye : ___
A) Use C) Chop	A) Head C) See
B) Hold D) Squad	B) Body D) Mouth

3. March : April : : July : ___	4. Water : Drink : : Bread : ___
A) June C) Month	A) Yeast C) Butter
B) Summer D) August	B) Eat D) Crumbs

5. Pretty : Ugly : : Attract : ___	6. Door : Hinge : : Arm : ___
A) Repel C) Nice	A) Hand C) Leg
B) Magnetic D) Beauty	B) Elbow D) Finger

Letter Stress Test:

Connect the letter with its corresponding alphabetical number by drawing a line between the dots. It is recommended for this type of test that you set up an alpha-numeric scale before starting.

A B C D E F G H.....ETC.
1 2 3 4 5 6 7 8.....ETC.

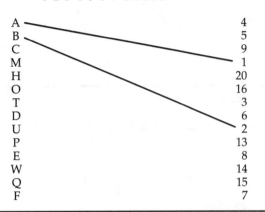

A	4
B	5
C	9
M	1
H	20
O	16
T	3
D	6
U	2
P	13
E	8
W	14
Q	15
F	7

Number Stress Test:

Each question has eight numbers in random order. Determine the ninth number in each question and mark that number in the space provided. You must work as rapidly as possible.

1) 2 4 6 3 1 9 8 7   __5__

2) 3 4 8 5 7 2 1 6   __9__

3) 5 8 1 2 6 9 7 3   _____

4) 9 6 3 8 4 5 1 7   _____

5) 3 6 4 2 1 9 8 7   _____

6) 3 6 4 2 1 9 8 7   _____

7) 5 1 7 4 2 8 3 6   _____

Math Test:

Some of these have been added correctly, others have been intentionally added incorrectly. Circle the answers only if it has been added correctly.

1)	27	2)	43	3)	19
	82		51		17
	15		95		25
	46		4		52
	170		203		113

4)	18	5)	98	6)	49
	46		13		15
	33		2		86

Number Sequence Test:

Determine the next number(s) in the sequence, and circle the correct answer.

1) 1 3 5 7 9 12 ____
A) 13   C) 15
B) 18   D) 9

2) 16 14 12 10 8 6 _____
A) 13   C) 15
B) 18   D) 9

3) 2 4 8 16 32 64 ____
A) 138   C) 116
B) 128   D) 66

4) 9 15 21 27 33 39 ____
A) 40   C) 43
B) 41   D) 45

5) 2 5 9 14 20 27 ____
A) 33   C) 35
B) 29   D) 38

Company derived tests: Questions used by various Part 121 and 135 carriers.

1) When is a transponder required?
   a. By aircraft in controlled airspace above 12,500' MSL.
   b. By all aircraft above 2,500' MSL
   c. By aircraft above 12,500# gross weight

2) To obtain a contact approach
   a. It must be initiated by the pilot
   b. Inflight visibliity must be one mile or greater
   c. Both of the above

3) What is the maximum glide path angle for a VASI?
   a. 3.0°   b. 3.5°   c. 4.5°

Color Stress Tests:

Place the first letter of each word in the corresponding spaces to the right. (Words will be printed in a different color than the word on the test. Example: Red might be printed with yellow ink. Black might be printed in green or red ink.)

1.	RED	YELLOW	GREEN	BLACK	_____	_____	_____	_____
2.	BLACK	GREEN	RED	YELLOW	_____	_____	_____	_____
3.	YELLOW	RED	GREEN	BLACK	_____	_____	_____	_____
4.	BLACK	RED	YELLOW	GREEN	_____	_____	_____	_____
5.	YELLOW	GREEN	RED	BLACK	_____	_____	_____	_____
6.	GREEN	BLACK	RED	YELLOW	_____	_____	_____	_____
7.	RED	BLACK	YELLOW	GREEN	_____	_____	_____	_____

Mechanical Aptitude Tests:

Solve the following and circle the correct answer. Do not use a calculator.

1. Which container will hold more fluid?
    A)   Container A
    B)   Container B
    C)   Both will hold the same

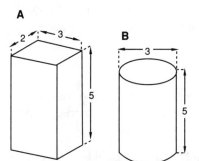

3. Find the volume of the rectangle below:

    A) 30   C) 15
    B) 10   D) 55

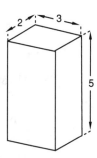

2. Which statement is correct regarding ropes A, B, and C?
    A)   Rope B supports more weight than C
    B)   Rope B supports less weight than A
    C)   Rope A supports less weight than C
    D)   Ropes A, B, and C each support the same amount

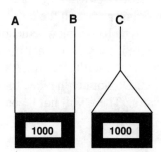

4) Find the volume of the cylinder below:
    A) 18   C) 42.5
    B) 324   D) 56.5

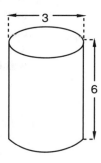

Complete the mazes as rapidly as possible. If your pencil touches a darkened line, your score will be penalized. It is recommended if you are right handed that you start from the center and work outward unless prohibited by the tester.

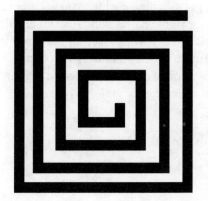

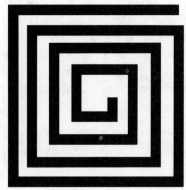

Tips For Good Test Results

- Maintain a good exercise program (which enhances mental ability).

- Practice.

- Be confident but not cocky, and build confidence by preparing for the proper tests.

- Stay calm under fire. Timed tests are designed so that you may not finish them in the allotted time period. You should not be concerned if time seems to be slipping away.

- Listen and read instructions carefully.

- Always do the easy questions first; you get credit for all the answers you are sure of, and some of these questions may lead you to the correct answers of harder questions.

- Know how much time you have to complete a test. You should determine how much time you have for each question and not exceed that limit.

- Use your wristwatch (with a second hand) to help you monitor time.

- Avoid spending a lot of time on one question. If you should get stuck, go on to the next question. If you complete the exam, go back to the questions you did not answer the first time around. On multiple choice tests, you may eliminate several of the choices at once. For those less obvious choices, there usually is a more nearly correct answer. In some cases, no perfect answer will be given; choose the best one. It may also help to find the key word or phrase in the question. This key word or phrase may be underlined or italicized. Knowing whether or not you will be penalized for incorrect answers can help; if there is a penalty attached to wrong answers, keep guessing to a minimum. Don't fret over seemingly ambiguous questions; keep going. (A caution: Do not get the idea that you see a "pattern" in the alphabetical order of answers. There will not be one.)

Scoring

Before taking a test, ask the administrator how the test will be scored. You may or may not be penalized for guessing. If the scoring does not penalize for wrong answers, always guess. You should not guess, however, if you will get more points taken off for a wrong answer than for answering the question correctly.

Another situation calling for a guess is that in which you get more points for the right answer and/or you get points only for right answers and lose an equal number of points for wrong answers. Then you should guess if you can eliminate some wrong answers. If you are unsure of an answer, in many cases the first thing that comes to mind is correct. Also, if you can narrow down the selection of answers to two out of four, then by guessing, you have at least a 50/50 chance of choosing the right answer.

Simulator Check

Basic instruments check. No auto-pilot or flight director.

Stay current any way you can: light aircraft, desktop simulator, National Guard or Reserves. Recent flying experience is desirable (within last 12 months).

Basic Instruments Flying In Large Jets

Traditional scans vs. FAPA's recommendation: Use only two primary instruments; adjust with ADI (horizon) assumes you know "ball park" pitch and power settings.

Why It Works:
Adaptable to any airplane or simulator.
Reduces work load/increases concentration and accuracy.

Particular Instruments: (Control & Periphery)

Explain:
Cockpit from forward panel.

Straight & Level:
Use Altimeter and ADI Bank Index.

Level Turns:
Use Altimeter and ADI Bank Index

Straight Climbing and Descending:
Constant Rate—Vertical Speed Indicator plus ADI
     Bank Index.
Constant Air Speed—Air Speed Indicator plus ADI
     Bank Index.

Steep Turns:
Altimeter plus ADI Bank Index.
IVSI lags and reverses under G Loads.

Takeoffs:
Large movement of the yoke required.
Most pitch to 15. Directional Control.
Limited rudder inputs in the air.

Approaches:
Always be in landing configuration prior to FAF if
     unfamiliar with the equipment.
Precision.
Non-Precision.

Simulator Peculiarities:
Mostly loose in the ailerons.
With no input by pilot, the simulator will not change
     its condition if stabilized.

Typical problems include the following:

- Pilot induced oscillation on approach.
- Over trimming with electric trim.
- Weak cross-check for basic instrument skills.

Remember, the simulator check pilot is acting as an interviewer.

Primary Flight Instrument for Basic Instrument Maneuvers

CONDITION	PITCH	ROLL	REMARKS
Straight and Level	Altimeter	Top of ADI Zero Bank	
Level Turns	Altimeter	Top of ADI Bank Indices for Desired Bank Angle	Lead Rollout by 1/2 to 1/3 Bank Angle
Straight Climbs and Descents at: 1) Constant Speed 2) Constant Rate	1) Airspeed Indicator 2) Rate of Climb	Top of ADI Zero Bank	Lead Level Off by 10% Rate of Climb
Climbing and Descending Turns	1) Airspeed Indicator 2) Rate of Climb	Top of ADI Bank Indices for Desired Bank Angle	Initiate Turn and Pitch Climb/Descent Separately

Notes:

1) Maximum bank angle 30° or flight director command (25° ± 4°). Recommended bank 25°.

2) Constant air speed maneuvers are desirable because airspeed variations will cause large pitch trim changes.

3) For level-offs, the last 1000 feet prior to your desired altitude should be at 500 FPM (FARs), unless your evaluator indicates otherwise (i.e., constant rate climbs and descents, other than 500 FPM).

4) Yaw is compensated for by automatic yaw dampers. Little or no rudder is required with symmetrical thrust.

Flight Maneuvers In Use
(By Airline)

AIRLINE	1	2	3	4	5	6	7	8	9	10	11	12	13	14	15	16	17	18	19	20
Alaska	●	●	●		●	●	●	●	●	●		●								●
American	●	●			●	●		●		●	●		●							
Amer. West	●	●	●	●	●	●				●										
Delta	●	●		●		●				●										
Fed Express				●	●														●	
Metro	●	●	●	●	●	●	●				●			●						
Midway Exp	●	●	●			●				●										
Northwest	●	●		●	●	●		●		●	●									
Pan Am	●	●	●		●	●					●									
TWA	●	●	●		●			●		●	●	●								
United		●				●	●	●			●						●	●	●	
US Air	●	●			●	●				●										
Regionals	●	●	●		●	●	●			●	●				●					

Column key: 1 Take Off; 2 Climb; 3 Steep Turns; 4 Acceleration and Deceleration; 5 Holding; 6 ILS/Raw Data; 7 Missed Approach; 8 Emergencies; 9 RMI Navigation; 10 Landing; 11 VOR Navigation; 12 SID; 13 Strength Test; 14 DME Arc; 15 ADF Navigation; 16 Non-Precision Approach; 17 ILS/Flight Director; 18 Flight Director Available; 19 Auto Throttles; 20 Lost Communications Procedures

Simulator Equipment In Use
By Airline

This is a listing of the airlines known to give simulator evaluations and the equipment they currently use. Some of the compaines listed currently are not conduction simulator evaluations, but the equipment most likely to be used is shown. When more than one airplane type is listed, an X indicates the most commonly used simulators.

AIRLINE	B-707	B-727	B-737	B-747	B-767	DC-8	DC-9	DC-10	L-1011	T-33	AST ATC
Alaska										●	
America West			●								●
American	●										
Delta [1]			●			●		●			
Federal Express								●			
Metro											●
Midway Express				●							
Northwest		X		●							
Pan Am	●	X									
TWA	●	●							●		
United		●						●			
USAir							●				
Regionals											●

Footnotes:

[1] Delta usually gives a simulator checkride only to applicants with no jet time.

Simulator Approach Areas In Use
By Airline

Most companies give simulator check rides in simulators programmed to display their home base.
However, most simulators can be programmed to display a variety of airports.

AIRLINE	Generic	ATL	CVG	DEN	FMN	ILM	IND	IAD	JFK	LAX	MIA	MSP	PIT	SDF	SEA	STL
Airborne						●										
Alaska															●	
American										●						
American Eagle										●						
America West										●						
ASA		●														
Braniff				●												
Comair			●													
Delta		●														
DHL										●						
Eastern											●					
Federal Express	●															
Horizon															●	
Mesa					●											
Midwest Express					●											
Northwest									●			●				
Pan Am									●		●					
Pan Am Express									●		●					
TWA									●							●
United	●															
UPS								●						●		
USAir							●						●			
WestAir										●						
World										●						

The Simulator Check Ride

Companies generally give simulator check rides in simulators programmed to display their home base. However, most simulators can be programmed to display a variety of airports.

Commuters or corporations often will not have simulators but may require a pilot to take a short check ride, either in the equipment they operate or by means of a general desktop simulator. The testing picture is changing in the commuter industry because of the major-commuter relationship: In some cases, the regional/commuter airline has its applicants tested on a simulator operated by its major partner, e.g., Charlotte, N.C.-based CCAIR, Inc. (a USAir feeder), which in mid-1989 was testing pilots on an "as available" basis on an F-27 simulator at USAir's training facilities in Pittsburgh.

Check rides may differ depending on the skill level of the applicant, his or her aviation background, the instructor/evaluator and the progress of the flight. Programmed emergencies may include engine or system failures, fires and/or windshears.

As you approach the simulator check ride phase, you must hone your basic instrument flying skills. If already employed as a pilot, you should use your present situation to help fine-tune basic skills. If you are not flying, you should rent an airplane or a desktop simulator to prepare. If you have never flown a large turbojet airplane or a simulator, your previous experience (or lack of it) will be taken into consideration. The evaluator is not looking for proficiency unless you currently fly the type of airplane in which you are being tested. He will look for basic instrument flying skills. In any case, a pilot should be able to handle basic instrument flight maneuvers: straight and level, level turns, straight climbs and descents, climbing and descending turns, steep turns, acceleration and deceleration. If you are type-rated and current in the airplane, the evaluator may expect you to fly to ATP standards. If you have flown only light single-engine airplanes, the evaluator may look only for the way you make corrections and decisions and make sure you demonstrate normal learning patterns during the evaluation.

In your daily flying, you must strive for perfection. You should concentrate on smoothness, accuracy and precision. If you have an autopilot or flight director, you should not use it except when the technology is absolutely necessary. Hands-on flying will provide the concentrated basic instrument practice essential to success.

If you have access to a jet simulator, you definitely should take advantage of it (consider renting one). You should fly it, sit in it. Even observing others operating the simulator can help you get a good overall view of what you will be doing during your evaluation flight. Observing another crew's pre-simulator briefing is an excellent way of learning jet flying techniques. Desktop simulators also can help improve a pilot's instrument scan.

A practice session in a motion-visual jet simulator is the ultimate preparation for your pre-employment simulator check ride. If you are not sure where you can rent a simulator, you can browse through an issue of *Career Pilot* or *Business/Commercial Aviation*. Many of the flight schools and companies that rent their simulators advertise in these and other aviation magazines.

If you have access to a jumpseat on any airline, you should use it to observe how the airplane is operated by that company. On the trip to the simulator evaluation, the crew may allow you to observe them. You should observe even if you cannot get on the same equipment upon which you will be tested. Flying in the cockpit on any airline or transport jet can help a pilot get an overview of large jet operations and airline crew coordination.

One important fact to remember is that the simulator is part of the hiring and screening process. The pilot should dress and act as if this test were an interview. Several companies ask interview questions during the simulator check ride. You also must pay close attention to personal hygiene. You can be under a lot of stress during the check ride; every precaution should be taken to remain socially acceptable.

Other things to remember about the check ride:

- Study all available information, including FARs and instrument procedures in the AIM.

- Review the aircraft panel the night before your simulator check.

- Review approach and area charts. Military pilots should get a set of Jeppeson charts, since the ones used in the military are very different.* If you are a FAPA member, you should call FAPA's information center for a briefing on the simulator check ride.

You also should:

- Arrive for your evaluation at least 15 minutes early.

- Talk with others who have gone before you, if possible.

- Take notes during your briefing to improve your learning and retention.

- Do your best and remain flexible — and always keep flying.

- Avoid quizzing the instructor pilot about results.

- Have fun. This may be the beginning of your jet flying career.

NOTE: FAPA publishes the *Simulator Training Manual*. This is a comprehensive listing of the airlines' simulator check ride profiles. It covers the equipment flown, approach areas used, and flight maneuvers required; it also includes drawings of the aircraft/simulator panels. It reviews general information concerning cockpit resource management, noise-abatement takeoffs, windshear, wake turbulence, communication failure and emergencies. The cost is $49.95 for members and $69.95 for non-members. Call 1-800 JET JOBS to place your order.

Chapter 19
PROBATION

Even the Air Line Pilots Association (ALPA) cannot help a pilot who runs afoul of management during probation. Grievance procedures cannot be applied until the pilot survives the probationary period.

And probation is an unavoidable fact of life when you are just starting your tenure with a carrier. Whether you have had 10,000 hours of military or commercial flying, or only a few thousand hours of corporate or private flight time, probation is part of the first year with any new employer.

Probation is a trial period. It affords both the pilot and the employer an opportunity to spend time together on a day-to-day basis, to test whether they have a joint future. And because grievance procedures do not apply during this period, the employer has an opportunity to terminate the relationship without having to worry about union-negotiated contractual agreements, which often mandate lengthy grievance procedures that must be carried out before a separation can occur.

Not that airline management is so self-defeating as to be looking for a way to find fault with a pilot. Airlines hire pilots because they need them. The odds favor your being able to survive probation, even though you are being closely watched.

Following are some airline profiles sketched to highlight the probation policies and practices that a new-hire pilot can expect to encounter. Airlines profiled include a large passenger airline and an overnight package carrier.

United Airlines

For pilots at United, probation begins the first day after graduation from the airline's flight training center at Denver-Stapleton International Airport. The probationary period subjects a pilot to management scrutiny of his/her technical skills and attitudinal performance.

A paramount evaluation tool is the line check, survived only by those pilots who are able to keep their binders up to date at all times. The binder, which you must have with you when you fly, contains required FAA documentation as well as the latest revisions to your Jeppesen charts. You also must keep your company aircraft and operations manuals current.

The first line check is done shortly after you take your first trip in revenue service (i.e., your first flight carrying passengers or freight); the second is done at three months;

B-727 / 100 Pitch and Power Chart

Phase of Flight	Flaps (Degrees)	Pitch Attitude (Degrees)	Power (EPR/# N_1)	Air Speed (Knots)
Enroute Climb	UP	7° UP	Max Climb	250/280
Level Flight	UP	2°—3° UP	1.75/82	(1) 280
Descent from Cruise	UP	0°—2° DN	Idle	280
Maneuvering or	UP	3° UP	1.30/69	(1) 250
Holding	UP	5°—6° UP	1.23/65	(2) 200
Final Approach (3° Glide Slope)	15°	6°—7° UP	1.42/72	(3) 150
Final Approach	30°	1° UP	1.25/66	REF +05

(1) Clean at 250 knots is equal to 2500# fuel flow/engine. Clean at 300 knots is equal to 3000# fuel/engine. Usually fuel flow — airspeed 250 knots — 2500# fuel flow clean

(2) Clean at 200 knots is equal to 2000# fuel flow/engine. If an engine is lost, continue at same total fuel flow for aircraft.

If 2000#/engine was required for 200 knots. 6000#/hr. is total. On two engines you still need 6000#/hr.; this means the remaining engines be operated at 3000# fuel flow/engine.

(3) Slightly more power (as well as more pitch) is required with flaps 15°. Add 500#/engine after slowing to desired speed.

and the third is done at six months. You can tell which trip will involve a line check by observing which dates on your schedule indicate a "freeze." The freeze locks you into the trip for which you are scheduled for a given date and assures that you will be available for a line check.

The third line check is passed by those pilots who demonstrate an ability to fly the plane well and work effectively with fellow crew members, as well as keep all paperwork up to date.

A pilot's first proficiency check comes at about nine months. The proficiency check involves a line-oriented flight training (LOFT) scenario, conducted in a simulator and representing a flight between two points on the United route system.

In this check, you will no longer be the center of attention, for you will be working with a first officer and a captain in a test of each cockpit member's performance as an integral part of a team. United Airlines subscribes to the command leadership resource management theory of flying, which stresses the team approach to the flight deck. However, you will need excellent mnemonic powers to memorize such hard data as the specific flap extensions of the B-727 at various speeds, the amount of hydraulic fluid that must be on board prior to takeoff, the aircraft's fuel capacity, and more than 100 other facts of this kind. You will have to answer questions on these matters during a 30-minute oral exam.

Your probation comes to a close with a home study course covering flight safety, aircraft performance, weather, and the use of the Jeppesen charts. You receive the course, along with a booklet and a questionnaire, after you complete initial training. You have to complete the course on your own time, and the questionnaire has to be filled out and returned to the company by the end of the ninth month of employment.

You might possibly also have to undergo a random spot check during this probationary period; about 10 percent of United's flight engineers experience this kind of professional "pop quiz."

United looks very favorably upon the pilot who asks questions during the line checks because they show that the pilot is making an effort to learn.

United does not permit its pilots to fly for a competitor, but working for Part 135 carriers is allowed as long as the amount of time put in with that kind of airline does not take away from the time the pilot can fly at United. The FAA mandates a 100-hour monthly maximum flying time for Part 121 operation. For Part 135 operation, the FAA mandates a 120-hour maximum flying time.

According to a United management official, fewer than one percent of the new-hire pilots fail to survive probation, while as many as three percent wash out during initial training.

Termination of a pilot at United is rare, but when it happens, it usually involves both poor technical performance and attitudinal problems.

Airborne Express

An equally stringent probation period for pilots is in effect at Airborne Express, the Wilmington, Ohio-based overnight package carrier. At Airborne, pilot probation commences on the day the pilot is hired and lasts one year. "Probation is considered to be an integral part of an extensive selection and training process," said Bob Fischer, vice president-flight operations. "During that time, we get to know the pilot, not only as an employee but as a person. We see how he does his job, how conscientious he is toward improving his skills."

At Airborne, all new-hire line pilots begin as first officers. Depending on the aircraft operated (Airborne's fleet consists of DC-9, DC-8 and YS-11 aircraft), the new-hire pilot at Airborne goes through a $1\frac{1}{2}$- to $2\frac{1}{2}$-month training period consisting of ground school, cockpit procedures training, simulator training, and initial operating experience.

If you are an Airborne new-hire, the initial operations exposure, which includes about 25 hours of flight time, takes you to various points on the system in revenue service. During that time, you are supervised carefully by the check airman with whom you are flying.

After initial training, you then are subject to what Fischer calls "an extensive period of evaluation that lasts throughout the pilot's first year." This includes regular and ongoing performance monitoring by line captains. You will get as many as three to four evaluations per month. In addition, every four months, the chief pilot or one of his assistants will fly with you.

After the first six months, you will get an evaluation ride from a flight standards pilot. The purpose of the ride is to see how well you support the captain in the first officer role; to determine your proficiency in carrying out pre-flight duties (including weight and balance calculations); and to note how efficiently you communicate routine checklist information to the captain. The evaluation also examines the pilot's performance throughout the flight regimen.

At the end of your first year, you must pass a proficiency check, which includes an oral exam and a simulator ride. An actual flight is used in place of the simulator for YS-11 first officers because there are no simulators for that aircraft. Successful completion of the year-end check ride is required in order to complete the probation year.

Fischer said that Airborne's intensive evaluation and high standards account for high attrition rates of about 10 percent in the training phase and five percent before the probation period fully runs its course. But Airborne is not deliberately trying to discourage pilot applicants.

"Surviving probation at Airborne means being more than just a good pilot," Fischer said. "We are very concerned with how our new pilots work with and learn from other people, including fellow crew members and the scheduling office."

As Fischer pointed out, Airborne considers attitude to be on an equal level with the pilot's ability to fly the aircraft.

Along with the arduousness of probation is the fact that Airborne, like all of the overnight package operators, is a nighttime airliner.

Airborne has no objection to Reserve or Air National Guard flying, but will not permit its pilots to work for other commercial carriers. Training center positions, which are restricted to flight management personnel, are not open to probation pilots, since the company insists on more experienced pilots for that kind of work.

Fischer summed up Airborne's attitude about probation. "We expect people to ask questions, to seek counsel from the captains with whom they fly. We expect our pilots to learn a great deal simply by observing how the other pilots operate. Enthusiasm and attitude are probably the most important things necessary to be successful at Airborne."

Other Carriers

The authors discussed probation with several carriers, including Piedmont, United, Airborne and CCAIR. All of the carriers pointed out that they value the experience that each new pilot brings into the company. While none of the carriers wants to see that experience cast aside, each said it is essential that, as a new-hire pilot, you adhere to your new employer's standard operating procedures.

Also, as Charlotte, N.C.-based CCAIR's Emmett Merricks stated, pilots who come from a non-airline background, such as corporate aviation, must learn to observe the FAA regulations pertaining to commercial flying. Merricks said they should not attempt to transfer the regulations for the type of flying they did with their last employer.

Another important point about getting through probation, brought out by all of the airlines contacted, pertains to those pilots who held captain's positions at their last carrier.

In most cases, moving to a new employer means starting in a non-command situation in your new job. During probation, it is especially important to realize you are no longer in command. This has caused some former airline captains to fail probation because they have demonstrated that they can no longer work in a subordinate position on the flight deck.

What must be kept in mind about probation is that it is as much a test of attitude as of flying skills. The pilot who cooperates with his co-workers, asks questions, and shows the company he is willing to learn and to grow will not only get through probation but probably will have a long and prosperous career at the airline with which he has chosen to fly.

Note: This chapter is based on a *Piloting Careers* article by Paul Seidenman and David Spanovich, free-lance writers living in San Francisco.

Chapter 20
MAINTAINING YOUR HEALTH

Consider yourself lucky. Your profession demands that you take care of your health. Many people do not have this incentive.

You are on a career path that will lead you, with any luck at all, to a well-heeled bourgeois lifestyle. In *Buddenbrooks*, the novelist Thomas Mann brilliantly used gluttony and its attendant ills as a metaphor of what was wrong with the bourgeoisie of his day. In an age of painless dentistry, you do not have to worry about some of the ills that beset the Buddenbrooks clan, but the human constitution remains the same, and it will not tolerate excessive abuse. It behooves the well-heeled pilot, then, to recognize the value of a spartan lifestyle even in the midst of plenty.

Smoking is bad for you. Booze is bad for you. Narcotics are bad for you. Too much food, especially fatty food, is bad for you. Sloth is bad for you.

Conversely, a steady exercise regimen is good for you. Sobriety is good for you. A lean, moderate diet is good for you. A bloodstream uncontaminated by nicotine, lungs not burdened by tobacco tars — these are good for you.

The first group of habits would be bad and the second good even if you were not a pilot. But you are one, so smoking, boozing and overeating are triply bad for you. These habits can make you ill; they can make you a less skilled pilot; and they can cause you to fail a physical and lose your license.

Smoke Gets in Your Eyes

The full-page ad in the *New York Times* showed Roscoe Turner, celebrated aviator, emerging from an open-cockpit aircraft with a cigarette in his mouth and doing his spiel for Camels.

"Like most pilots I smoke a lot," Turner was saying. "But I watch my nerves as carefully as I do my plane. I smoke Camels for the sake of healthy nerves."

This ad appeared in 1933, in an era when a whole generation of Americans regarded the pilot as the epitome of physical perfection. Testimonial by Turner was telling since he belonged to a group possessing "no flaw of body, nerve or character" (to cite a description of the professional pilot taken from the *Literary Digest*, p. 22, Nov. 14, 1936).

How wrong was Turner?

Recent research indicates that the "calming" effect of smoking is at best simply an easing of the jitters caused by NOT having a cigarette; at worst, it is in part a drug-induced dulling of the mind.

A psychogenic addiction, smoking is a "closed system" that creates and satisfies its own craving. It not only calms the jitters that it causes, but it produces the illusion of helping a smoker think and of keeping him or her alert.

The illusion is created by an injection of adrenalin into the bloodstream. The adrenalin, however, raises the blood sugar level, thus increasing fatigue until the next dose of nicotine. Even the scientific community once concluded reluctantly that smoking can help job performance. Not so, according to recent research.

George Spilich, of Washington College in Chestertown, Md., has reported to the American Psychological Association that the earlier belief of the scientific community in the performance-improving power of cigarette smoking depended on studies "based on tasks which demand little or nothing from high-order mental processes."

Spilich set smokers and non-smokers to such complex tasks as reading and recalling a short story, driving (using a computerized simulator), and remembering a series of letters on a short-term basis. He divided people into three groups: non-smokers; smokers allowed, in testing, to smoke freely; and smokers who were not allowed to smoke for an hour before the experiment.

All groups abstained from coffee and soft drinks for two hours before the experiment. To equalize the effects on performance involved in the physical routine of smoking (generally negative and time-killing), those who did not smoke during the tests were asked to "sham smoke."

Spilich found that while both smoking and abstaining smokers performed slightly better than non-smokers on simple repetitive tasks, the results reversed as tasks increased in complexity.

Notably, in the simulated driving test, smoking smokers got involved in almost three times as many rear-end collisions as non-smokers did, and in nearly twice as many as did abstaining smokers.

Especially significant is the fact that merely spurning cigarettes for one hour (and then not smoking during the test) resulted in an emergency-conditions driving record nearly twice as good as that of the "smoking smokers." Thus, the smoker puffing away on a cigarette would seem to be a sort of "ticking bomb" for complex activities in which safety is involved.

Spilich concluded that to smoke is to err. Smoking may help with simple repetitive tasks, but "it exerts a negative effect upon more complex tasks which require access to working memory, [to] long-term memory, and [to] one's extensive knowledge base." He also suggests that the smoker's handicap is by far more pronounced when the situation demands the most complex thinking — as when "a pilot is taking off or landing, or a machine operator is faced with a serious malfunction."

If Spilich's research is correct, smoking makes you just a little bit dumb before it makes you dead. It could cause you to make a piloting mistake.

As for the "dead" part: About 1,000 people a day die from tobacco-related disease in the United States of America. Practiced by only a third of the adult U.S. populace, smoking causes 85 percent of this country's lung cancers, 80 to 90 percent of long-term severe lung diseases (emphysema, chronic bronchitis), and 30 percent of the deaths from coronary heart disease.

The Prudent Lifestyle

The rules for a healthful life are not new. Overall, what you should be hoping to achieve is a prudent lifestyle (the Romans called this "the Golden Mean") resulting in health, fitness and inner stability (according to the Romans, "a sound mind in a sound body"). If you achieve these goals, you will not fail your flight physical. Unless you are a rare physical type, you also will not have to resort to drug treatments to control your cholesterol level.

The rules of good diet apply whether an individual already has a high blood cholesterol level or is trying to avoid such problems by keeping fit. The foods to avoid or eat in extreme moderation are red meat, such as beef and pork; processed meats; eggs, especially if you already have a cholesterol problem; whole milk and most other dairy products, including ice cream and yogurt made with whole milk; and anything fried. Foods containing saturated fatty acids are bad for you; those containing polyunsaturated fatty acids are good; in between are the monounsaturated fatty acids, which can be consumed without harm as long as total fat in the diet is moderate.

The key is moderation, as in the Golden Mean. Even the strictest of non-fat diets for confirmed heart patients should include at least one tablespoon of a polyunsaturated oil each day. The reason is that polyunsaturated fats are a source of the essential fatty acid, linoleic acid, without which the body cannot make fats properly. As noted earlier, polyunsaturated fats also help lower the blood cholesterol level. In addition, without some fat in your diet, you would not absorb vitamins A, D, E and K. A diet utterly devoid of fats would be a disaster.

But saturated fatty acids are not needed in the diet at all. And diets rich in saturated fats raise the level of blood cholesterol.

Stay away from oils or fats that are solid at room temperature. Even though some solid shortening products say they contain no cholesterol, it pays to read the fine print. Any label that reads, "Contains partially hydrogenated fat" is a tipoff that the product can increase cholesterol levels. Studies have shown that the process of hydrogenation (to turn a liquid vegetable oil into a solid) saturates an unsaturated oil.

One egg yolk contains practically the entire recommended adult daily allowance of cholesterol consumption. Three ounces of beef kidney or beef liver exceed it. Such organ meats as brains, sweetbreads and heart also are very high in cholesterol, as are sardines, anchovies, caviar and fish roe.

No cholesterol is naturally present in any vegetable foods, although some (coconut and palm oil, for instance) contain saturated fats. Vegetable fats do contain sterols, but unlike cholesterol, vegetable sterols are not absorbed by the human digestive tract. Therefore, vegetables, fruits and nuts should be high on your list of preferred foods. Broccoli is the single most complete food of any kind. A combination of oatmeal and grapefruit for breakfast has been found highly effective in lowering blood cholesterol.

As indicated above, there are two dietary keys to controlling blood cholesterol levels: one, rationing the amount of cholesterol we consume; two, limiting the total amount of fat consumed, especially saturated fats. For this reason, chicken is a more healthful food than beef or pork because it contains less total fat and less saturated fat, even though three ounces of dark chicken and three ounces of lean beef contain the same amount of cholesterol (77 milligrams). White meat of chicken and white turkey meat are even better, and such fish as halibut, haddock and flounder are low in cholesterol and in both saturated and total fat. Even beef of the right kind is okay: Broiled lean top round, dark-meat chicken with the skin removed, and salmon cooked with dry heat all have about the same amount of saturated fat.

Two natural means of controlling cholesterol levels besides diet are exercise and meditation or relaxation techniques.

The best exercise, according to Senior AMEs Dr. Robert P. Tucker and Dr. Richard O. Reinhart, is fast walking because such "endurance aerobics" raises the level of HDLs relative to LDLs and reduces lipids without the damage to the joints involved in jogging or some other forms of exercise. The purpose of the fast walking, Dr. Tucker said, "is to get your heart rate up to about 60 to 75 percent of maximum. The formula for this is 220 [beats per minute] minus your age times point-six (0.6) — get it up somewhere around there." For a 40-year-old pilot, that would be about 108 beats per minute. (For most adults, from 60 to 80 beats per minute is a typical range of heart rate at rest, according to Dr. Jerry Hordinsky, who heads the Aeromedical Research Division of the Civil Aeromedical Institute of the Federal Aviation Administration in Oklahoma City.) After a session of fast walking or any other exercise that raises the heart rate, you should "cool off" slowly, continuing your walk at a slower pace or engaging in three or four minutes of slow-down exercises, in order to allow your heart and pulse rate to return gradually toward resting rate. This regimen will help you avoid damage to your heart.

Convenient for the person who wants to follow a total program and reduce stress, fat intake and the buildup of harmful LDLs produced by inactivity is the fact that aerobic endurance exercise not only raises "good cholesterol" and helps burn fat, but also triggers the release of endorphins. An endorphin is described as "a morphine-like chemical in the brain that acts as a natural tranquilizer." So an exercise program becomes the first part of a "tranquility" program.

Relaxation techniques, supportive relationships and reduced stress all can contribute to psychological and physical well-being. By contrast, studies have shown that cholesterol levels rise and lipids are knocked out of balance during various types of emotional stress. In other words, fighting with your spouse could mess up your arteries. A confrontational lifestyle is not prudent.

Rather, the prudent lifestyle calls for a mode of life that will promote tranquility, fitness and health. You became a professional pilot partly in order to enjoy the good life. Perhaps the time has come to redefine that good life.

If you do not, your heart, your lungs, or your blood pressure could end up doing the redefining.

If you smoke and manage to avoid dying of any cause that is clearly smoking-related, you still do not come out ahead, medical studies show.

According to the U.S. Department of Health and Human Services, smoking costs $26 billion in lost productivity each year in this country, while another $16 billion is spent annually on smoking-related medical costs.

Again, smokers arrive at old age with 20 to 30 percent less bone mass than do nonsmokers. The results of this deficiency are a more fragile skeleton and a greater risk of fractures. That is a hard landing for anybody's life.

Mind dulled, health impaired, body debilitated: If you like this picture, then smoking is the habit for you and yours.

Or maybe this fact will make you think twice before lighting up. According to Captain Dick Stone, ALPA Executive Chairman for Aeromedical Resources, some airlines do not even hire smokers. "They don't want to make problems for themselves down the road."

The Cholesterol Story

Your cholesterol level is not acceptable unless it's somewhere below the threshold of 200 milligrams of cholesterol per deciliter of tested blood.

A cholesterol level above that threshold is dangerous and can put a pilot's livelihood and life in jeopardy.

What is cholesterol and why is it dangerous?

Dr. Kenneth H. Cooper, a well-known aerobics guru, describes cholesterol as "an odorless, white, powdery, fatty substance that is both manufactured by your body and introduced through your diet, mostly from animal fats. Among other things, you need cholesterol for membrane synthesis in your cells. Without it, your cells could not function; indeed, you could not even stay alive."

Cholesterol is produced by the liver, the small intestine, and some of the body's other cells. The cells use cholesterol to make strong cell membranes, to mold the sheaths that protect nerve fibers, and to produce vitamin D and certain hormones, including the sex hormones. The liver uses cholesterol to make bile acids needed for digesting fats. In one day, the liver typically produces 1,000 milligrams of cholesterol to meet the body's needs.

So far, cholesterol does not sound like a "bad guy." But this crystalline kind of alcohol that is not soluble in water, this odorless, white, powdery, fatty substance, this necessary ingredient of life is also a buzzword on the tongues of Americans because it can be a deadly contributor to atherosclerosis and heart failure. While the situation has improved in recent years, the American public is one of the unhealthiest in the world in terms of blood cholesterol levels. The main reason is diet. Not surprisingly, since high cholesterol levels have been linked to heart disease, the greatest single killer of Americans is heart trouble.

According to Dr. Robert P. Tucker Sr., an AME (aviation medical examiner) in Atlanta, 22 percent of deaths in the United States in 1986 were caused by cancer. By contrast, he said, 48 percent were accounted for by atherosclerosis, which Jane Brody, health columnist for the *New York Times*, calls "the accumulation of 'crud' in arteries until the arteries become so clogged that blood cannot flow through them properly." The disease is "similar to what happens in an old water main: Eventually the opening gets blocked up with accumulated minerals."

Dr. Tucker said the 1986 breakdown of U.S. deaths through atherosclerosis was 36 percent from coronary artery disease; seven percent from thrombosis of blood vessels in the brain; and five percent from "atherosclerotic process in the rest of the body," yielding the total of 48 percent.

Dr. Cooper said that atherosclerosis "and its consequence," coronary heart disease, are responsible for 550,000 deaths each year in the United States. The American Heart Association's figure was slightly lower: 1.5 million Americans would suffer heart attacks in 1989, the association said, and 540,000 would die.

Three of the facts that pilots need to know can be stated very simply: First, the FAA calls coronary artery disease "coronary heart disease" and attaches mandatory certificate denial to the condition. Second, coronary artery disease, which involves the two arteries branching from the aorta (the main artery of the body) and supplying blood directly to the heart tissues, is the most frequently fatal form of atherosclerosis. Third, high cholesterol is the single worst culprit identified in the onset of atherosclerosis.

Dr. Tucker said ongoing research has continued to place the "safe level" of overall blood cholesterol at a lower and lower figure. He said an "almost zero" risk of heart attack "carries on up to about 180.

At 180 milligrams per deciliter (or mg/dl), "you begin to get a significant number of heart attacks. Beginning at about 200 . . . the curve for heart attacks starts getting mighty steep and ever steeper. The American Heart Association says 200 is borderline high; it's high, period. Anything above 200 is elevated; above 240 is dangerously elevated." (The Heart Association does not label a person's cholesterol level as "high" until it reaches 240.)

Above 200 mg/dl, he said, "for every one percent the cholesterol level goes up, the heart attack rate goes up two percent." Conversely, for every one percent an individual with elevated cholesterol lowers his cholesterol level, his/her chances of having a heart attack go down two percent.

In almost everyone, exercise can reduce the risk of atherosclerosis by raising the amount of HDLs (high-density lipoproteins, or "good cholesterol") in the bloodstream relative to LDLs (low-density lipoproteins, or "bad cholesterol").

"Good" cholesterol is good only because it moves on through the body's ejection system; "bad" cholesterol is bad because it stays in the blood vessels and clogs things up.

Being a fatty substance, cholesterol does not travel in the blood by itself but is carried in an envelope of lipoprotein. Like cholesterol, lipoprotein, which literally means "fatty protein," is produced in the liver. HDLs are referred to as the "good" kind of cholesterol package because they seem to protect against atherosclerosis. In *Jane Brody's Nutrition Book* (W.W. Norton & Co., Inc., © 1981 by Jane Brody), Ms. Brody states that HDLs perform their useful function "apparently by removing cholesterol from artery walls and returning it to the liver and by helping the liver excrete unneeded cholesterol as bile through the intestinal tract."

On the other hand, she says, "two other types of cholesterol carriers, the *low-density lipoproteins (LDLs)* and the *very-low-density lipoproteins (VLDLs)*, have the opposite effect. They keep cholesterol in circulation and depend on scavenger cells to clear out excess cholesterol from the blood. Some of these scavenger cells are found in the muscle layers of the artery walls, and this is believed to be how the arteries become clogged with cholesterol-laden deposits."

An exception to this rule, however, is the kind of HDL that is found in eggs. Eating a lot of eggs can be very bad for your cardiovascular system. Here is why:

A study sponsored by the American Egg Board (an industry group that promotes eggs as a safe food) and conducted by the National Heart, Lung and Blood Institute in Bethesda, Md., came up with a finding that bore immediately on the impact of eggs on cholesterol levels but reflected more broadly on the question of "good" and "bad" cholesterol. The finding could be regarded by the Egg Board only as a terrible piece of bad news. The study showed that even if the total level of cholesterol in the blood did not rise in response to a lot of eggs in the diet, the balance between the various cholesterol-carrying lipoproteins was adversely affected.

According to Ms. Brody, the researchers found that eating eggs led to a dramatic increase in a type of HDL cholesterol that behaves in the body like harmful LDL cholesterol. Although most HDL cholesterol appears to protect against heart disease, this particular type, called HDL-c, "is even more damaging to blood vessels than LDL cholesterol."

If the cholesterol story is not a simple one, its lessons are plain and unvarnished. If you eat like a glutton, you probably will learn soon enough why gluttony is placed among the Seven Deadly Sins.

To control cholesterol levels, you can do three things naturally and one "unnaturally." The natural controls are diet, exercise and a tranquil mind; the "unnatural" one (if ingestion of drugs is unnatural) is to swallow cholesterol-inhibiting chemicals. AMEs counsel that you try diet and exercise first.

By itself, a high cholesterol level will not ground you, "but high cholesterol leads to high blood pressure and coronary artery disease, either of which will ground the pilot," Dr. Tucker said.

According to Dr. Richard O. Reinhart, Air Force Flight Surgeon and senior AME, in his book, *The Pilot's Medical Manual of Certification & Health Maintenance* (available through FAPA), "Coronary artery disease (CAD) is one of the major causes of both permanent and temporary medical certificate denials. FARs use the term coronary *heart* disease. . . . The current FAR Part 67 states that even a *history* of coronary artery disease requires *mandatory* certificate denial by your Aviation Medical Examiner."

The reason for this ruling is that a person with coronary artery disease has a greater risk of heart attack or "other disabling conditions leading to sudden incapacitation." Moreover, coronary artery disease is progressive: It gets worse. The disease, Dr. Reinhart explains, "is either a plugging up of coronary arteries or a stiffening of the walls of the arteries, greatly compromising the ability of the arteries to bring blood to the heart muscle.

If there is too little blood and therefore inadequate oxygen and nutrients, either chest pain (angina pectoris) develops or a myocardial infarction (heart attack) occurs."

Recognized risk factors for developing coronary artery disease, he says, are "age, increased weight or obesity, increased blood pressure (or hypertension), cigarette smoking, family history of coronary artery disease, poor cardiovascular (heart) conditioning, [and] high cholesterol, triglycerides, and other fats in the blood." Another risk factor is stress.

Only age and one's family history of heart disease are beyond an individual's control. The others are an interrelated complex of manageable "risk factors."

Triglycerides, for instance, are fatty molecules in the blood that have been implicated in the destructive process of atherosclerosis. Proper diet can reduce triglycerides to healthy levels. Similarly, diet can reduce blood pressure, weight, cholesterol and blood fats.

Smoking affects the heart picture in several ways: It lowers blood levels of HDLs, deprives the blood of needed oxygen, contributes to atherosclerosis, pushes up the blood pressure, probably affects clotting mechanisms, and often negates the beneficial effects of jogging or other exercise by eliminating any rise in HDLs. According to the American Heart Association, the incidence of both heart attack and stroke are considerably higher in smokers than in non-smokers.

The truth about cholesterol is that after six months of age, the human body does not need it as a nutrient; the body produces, by itself, all the cholesterol that it needs for cellular synthesis, manufacturing cholesterol from fats and carbohydrates. A second truth about cholesterol is that the American way of life (the so-called "good life") provides far too much of it — and far too little physical exertion.

Diets rich in saturated fats tend to raise the level of blood cholesterol by stimulating the liver to make more of it, whereas polyunsaturated fats help to lower blood cholesterol. A physically lazy, sedentary lifestyle lowers the level of HDLs in the bloodstream, thus contributing to heart disease; a good exercise regimen raises the level of HDLs and contributes to sound heart conditioning.

A frequent misconception is that vitamins can reduce cholesterol. As Dr. Tucker pointed out, "Vitamins as such do not reduce cholesterol levels; massive doses of niacin, which is one of the vitamin B complex group, are used in treatment of high cholesterol, but just plain use of vitamins, no."

A wide variety of drugs can be used in the treatment of high blood cholesterol, but Dr. Tucker counsels that such an approach be avoided in favor of diet and exercise unless natural controls have failed for an individual. "The drugs are expensive and aren't good for you: They produce liver damage and other undesirable side effects," he said.

A pilot using drugs to control cholesterol will be allowed to fly, however, so the drug approach to the problem can be used as a "last resort."

The FAA has no standard for cholesterol levels. In airline screening examinations, however, a high cholesterol level would be one factor in deciding whether or not to hire a pilot.

Hypertension and Suspensions

Heart disease *will* ground you; high blood pressure *can* ground you.

You have a wild card working for you, however, if you are grounded for high blood pressure: Your exile from the cockpit may turn out to be only a suspension, not a loss of license and career.

The FAA has standards for high blood pressure that vary with the age of the pilot. In order to renew certification of a pilot found to exceed the blood pressure limits for his age, the FAA requires that the individual go on a program of successful treatment for hypertension (high blood pressure) and that an AME issue "a fairly satisfying report that there's no underlying heart condition," according to a medical technician with the FAA's Southern Region. The FAA also requires, of course, an annual followup (semiannual for a captain). Pilots on drug treatment for hypertension are allowed to fly as long as they have not developed heart disease and can show that their treatment is keeping blood pressure within proper limits.

Dr. Jerry Hordinsky, who heads the Aeromedical Research Division of the Civil Aeromedical Institute of the Federal Aviation Administration in Oklahoma City, said the report referred to by the FAA technician is "an expanded health check," the purpose of which is to learn whether or not the pilot's hypertension is related to some more serious disease, such as a damaged kidney or a thyroid problem, as well as whether a heart condition exists.

Applied stringently by the FAA to the First Class Certificate are the following maximum reclining blood pressure readings: For ages 20-29, the reading cannot exceed

140 over 88; for ages 30-39, the limit is 145 over 92; for ages 40-49, it's 155 over 96; and 50 and beyond, 160 over 98.

Airlines, like the FAA, weigh the overall blood and heart profile of the pilot in deciding whether he or she can be allowed to fly. But Dr. Reinhart points out that high blood pressure "requires exercise cardiac stress testing for certification by the FAA, and the stress test is often the first indication that CAD [coronary artery (or "heart") disease] is present." Dr. Reinhart's advice: Don't wait until hypertension or CAD develops to take the common-sense measures needed to maintain health.

"Consider this," Dr. Reinhart writes in *The Pilot's Medical Manual of Certification & Health Maintenance*. "If the treatment for a person with high blood pressure or coronary artery disease is weight control; the avoidance of cigarettes, alcohol, caffeine and high-fat foods; and the development of a good exercise program — why not begin such therapy *before* developing the disease that could take away your certificate?"

Chapter 21
BEING READY FOR A FURLOUGH

You have taken care of your health, kept yourself current in instrument flying, done everything possible to make yourself an excellent pilot and good crew member. Is there anything you have forgotten?

Perhaps. If you have not remembered that no one is guaranteed anything on the planet Earth; that Fortune is fickle; that companies, like nations, are sometimes subject to decline; — if you have not borne in mind that security is five parts illusion for every one part reality, then you may have neglected one of your cardinal duties to yourself and your family: Plan B.

There was a time when pilots frowned on a Plan B for their career planning. Sure, a Plan B is necessary for flying, but life is a different kind of thing, it's — it's — well, it's not the same as taking off in a jet for a faraway city knowing that you might possibly have to put the machine down somewhere else, is it? Mmmmmm.

Well, maybe it is.

Let's posit a scene: You have just finished probation with a major airline. These are the great days, the halcyon days. A pilot flying for a major: This is Cloud 9, the goal you have cherished.

And now along comes the first waggle of the Fickle Finger of Fate. Senior management, the group that has guided this airline into the ranks of the majors so quickly, has been watching the bottom line write itself in red as the economy struggles, reservations fall off, planes take off more than half-empty. The ugly word "stagflation" is on the lips of TV newscasters again, and the word "furlough" is rife at Pan Global Airways.

Low in seniority, you watch as fellow pilots with even less seniority are given their furlough notices. Through subsequent weeks, as the furloughs continue, you throw mental darts at the calendar for the day when your own number will come up, and you wait numbly, hoping the furloughs will end before then.

And one more thing: You wish you had a Plan B.

Whether you have or have not considered the possibility of a furlough and prepared for it, being furloughed creates stress, can cause severe financial hardship, and may generate a loss of self-esteem and sustaining routine in your life.

In 1981, The Company Doctor, management consultants, compiled a study from a questionnaire answered by 155 first-time furloughed Continental Air Line (CAL) pilots. The study found that the pilots had difficulties finding other flying jobs and even non-flying ones, had trouble meeting their financial responsibilities, and began questioning

The Flying Career Needs a Backup

Until 1978, the major airline pilot with ten years of seniority could begin to believe that he was home free: Economic fears, even for his old age, need not trouble him.

But the world of the career pilot has changed. As an airline pilot, you should be considering what you will do if the bottom suddenly drops out of your career. You should have alternatives in mind. This reality has led many pilots to develop sidelines to their aviation careers.

The turmoil at United, Northwest and Eastern at the end of the 1980s perhaps best exemplifies the new instability. NWA, Inc., the parent company of Northwest Airlines, was purchased by financier Alfred A. Checchi for $3.6 billion. United went through a series of buyout attempts in 1989, the most nearly successful one being a labor-management bid that fell short of the financing needed. Eastern Airlines was struck by its unions; then it filed for Chapter 11 reorganization.

The unpredictability of the post-deregulation airline industry can be daunting if looked at in isolation. When looked at in the context of the national economy and that of the world, it takes on an aspect that can be summarized in an epigram: If a Japanese *kacho* can deal with instability, surely a Yankee pilot can.

The *kacho*, until recently, lived in an even more secure-seeming world than did the pilot. The *kacho* was industrial gentry in the land of lifetime employment. He was rewarded with his title not for effective performance, but for longevity on the job. He was assured that his company would take care of him. So certain was it that a well-behaved employee would make *kacho* that many workers were promoted to positions that had no duties and became what the Japanese call *madogiwa zoku,* or "window-side sitters," so-named because they had nothing to do but gaze out the window.

Goaded by international competition, by a glut of tenured workers between the ages of 35 and 50, and by a shortage of young blood, Japanese business has had to change the way it functions. In companies that have switched to the new regimen, middle-management salaries are based on performance, not tenure. Gone is the *kacho* who can be a window-side sitter. In some firms, gone is the *kacho*: Companies like Toyota and Nissan have eliminated whole layers of middle management, reassigning many workers to lower-level jobs.

In the United States, the airline industry, in becoming unpredictable, has simply followed on the heels of newspaper publishing, high technology, many kinds of manufacturing, the motion picture industry, mining and oil exploration, farming and the food business (from processing to retail distribution), and other industries. It has been followed in this regard by telecommunications, banking, trucking, maritime shipping and the railroad industry. The turbulence imparted by intense competition has been increased by corporate raids, leveraged buyouts and Wall Street manipulations.

In the world of private enterprise, there are no sinecures. The modern emphasis on speed of reaction to changes in the competitive climate assures that only the fit can survive.

The point: As a professional pilot, you are in the same world with which the rest of humanity (except perhaps a few million government workers) has to deal. The message this world has for you is that no matter how smoothly things are going or how secure the future may appear, you may find yourself in need of a cat's ability to land on its feet when dropped.

The airline pilot has always had an excellent reason, the medical checkup, to be thinking beyond his or her flying days. Without a Class I medical certificate, the airline pilot is grounded, suffering permanent loss of license — a potentially disastrous scenario. Now there is a second, equally compelling reason to secure a future independent of actions taken by the company.

One of the best ways to assure that you can land on your feet after a fall is by developing a sideline to your aviation career. With liberal time off from your major or national airline flying job, you have every opportunity to develop one.

Many Americans (not just pilots) pursue investments as a sideline. For those who are good at investing their money in properties with a high yield (whether stocks, bonds, real estate, entrepreneurial ventures or whatever), the pursuit of investments is a great avocation that can guarantee a well-endowed future. Not everyone has the knack of knowing a good investment from a bad one, however, so for many individuals the key to security lies in a business on the side. It can keep you from having to sell or mortgage your house if your airline ever begins furloughing people in a time of financial distress or if you lose your license for medical reasons.

There are some "dos" and "don'ts" to know if you decide to start a sideline.

The riskiest kind of business to begin is the one based on a technological innovation. The second-riskiest is the business built on a perceived consumer "need" rather than on perceived consumer "wants." The best advice that you could follow would be to avoid high-risk ventures.

Related to the high risk-avoidance caveat is, first, the need to avoid putting your home on the line and, secondly, the need to set definite limits, not to be trespassed under any circumstances, on the amount of your airline income you will commit to your own business. The reason is obvious: No one functions well under chronic financial stress, and raiding your airline flying income or mortgaging your home for operating capital can be the start of such stress. Your sideline then could become your main line, distracting you from your airline career and from the safe performance of your flying duties.

Another important caution: Do not go into a sideline business without considerable preparation for it. After all, you put a tremendous amount of your time, energy and money into becoming a good airline pilot. You prepared for the job of major airline pilot by getting a college degree, taking lots of aviation schooling, and building many hundreds of hours of flying time. You were able to become a successful major airline pilot because you had prepared well to do so. The same front loading is necessary before you commit financial resources and your ego and time to a sideline business.

• Know the fundamentals of running a business.

• Do not enter a business for which you lack sufficient financial resources.

• Once up and operating, don't let the business run out of cash. The business must be able to meet its obligations.

• Avoid having negative leverage applied to your business by those to whom the business owes money (e.g., a bank may apply heavy pressure for you to pay its note even ahead of paying for the absolute necessities — goods, services — of running the business).

• Do not make yourself too dependent on one or two clients. Be careful where you locate your business (are you in a place which, either demographically or distributionally, is a liability for you?).

• Because credibility is important, never compromise quality for price.

• For the same reason, make only those promises that you can keep.

• Do not stake too much on computers as a competitive edge.

• Make sure you know what the competition is doing; stay on top of this kind of "snooping" as long as you are in the business.

• Learn fast and keep learning.

• And know when to get out — e.g., if your business has succeeded beyond your ability to manage it or to devote sufficient time to it, sell it.

These are simply the rock-bottom essentials of running a reasonably safe sideline business.

Know them; know the business you are entering; know as much as possible about how to compete in such a business and about how to run such a business.

You will then be ready to add a bit of needed financial cushioning in the event your airline career should go sour.

their career choice. Among some of the pilots, the financial effects of furlough included the strain of giving up an elegant home for a less expensive one (even, in the case of those who re-enlisted, for military base housing); relocation to another area of the country where there was a job offer; renegotiation of previous divorce agreements; establishment of special agreements with creditors; and loss of self-esteem.

One pilot pointed out that lopping $10,000 to $30,000 from a senior pilot's salary would be uncomfortable but that such a loss from a junior pilot's salary is devastating since he has put little money into savings and is completely losing his salary.

The classic furlough consists of 10 percent of a company's most junior pilots; this industry track record enables a pilot to plot his place in an approaching furlough. The bottom 10 percent of the seniority list will be the top 10 percent of the furlough list. A furlough still is possible, however, for up to 25 percent of the bottom of the seniority list.

If an airline furloughs more than 25 percent of its pilot force, this deep cut can be an indication of financial instability, and all of the pilots should evaluate their company's financial status and prepare for the possibility of an operational shutdown.

Some pilots view airline furloughs with distaste and choose to fly only corporate aircraft to avoid such an occurrence. What they may not realize is that corporate pilots also get furloughed. Little is heard about corporate furloughs because of the small size of most company flight departments and the small number of pilots being let go. But if a company begins to see red ink in its ledgers, the first "luxury" to be eliminated may be the flight department. XYZ Ball Bearing Company's flight department is helpful, but is it essential to keeping XYZ in the ball bearing business?

Airline pilots, because of union contracts, usually have recall rights for as long as seven to 10 years after a furlough. Corporate pilots may not be so lucky since the company may not feel obligated to recall laid-off employees.

Anticipate Furlough; Plan Accordingly

Although the psychological effects of furlough are probably the most important, the financial effects, being more visible, get the most attention. But everything is connected; as the wallet shrinks, the psychological wound deepens; a continuous downward spiral can await you if you are unprepared to combat it. Furloughs are a fact of airline life, and knowing this, you should plan ahead for the protection of yourself, your family, your home.

The sidebar "The Flying Career Needs a Backup," suggests a Plan B option called Plan C.

If you foresee weeks or months in advance that you face a possibility of being furloughed, you should begin immediately to organize your finances. Bills should be consolidated and paid if possible; credit sources should be requested and/or amplified cash should be collected; you may purchase a smaller house, with correspondingly smaller payments.

What you should be doing is preparing for an extended lean period. The minimum furlough period tends to be four to six months long; most are longer: up to five, seven, even 12 years. Financial advisors have stated in numerous publications that every employee — every paycheck-earning worker — should keep at least three months' salary tucked away in a bank account for emergencies. This advice holds true for a pilot and his family.

It takes time to collect such a large amount. Substantial savings are not easily amassed; the savings effort should be started when you land your first job.

This money serves as a cushion to keep the panic away when the paycheck disappears. It should be kept in a high-interest account that allows day-to-day liquidity, possibly a money market account or a checking-with-interest account. Opening a line of credit also may be a good idea. Getting a bank loan prior to the furlough may be wise since there will be little chance of doing so once the furlough begins. Extending credit card limits also is a step to take ahead of time. These cards can allow for the purchase of necessities or be used for cash advances during the furlough.

You also may find that, though furloughed, you retain some employee benefits from your company, at least for a time. Some companies extend pass privileges for their furloughed pilots for two or three months; federal law requires that companies permit you to keep your medical benefits by paying an additional amount; and a few companies have purchased FAPA memberships for their furloughed pilots in order to help them get a new job. Whatever help is offered, you should accept it unhesitatingly.

When notification of the furlough is given, there are additional measures that the clear-thinking pilot can take to slow the approaching financial drain. The first step should be a budgeting session involving the entire family so that everyone understands the reasons behind the coming lean months. Examine the household assets, develop a budget, and cut out anything that is not necessary. You and your family may have to do without new clothes, junk food, cable television, even children's allowances, until jobs and salaries return to normal. Forget about keeping up with the Joneses; you have a more challenging task.

Remember, too, that there are sources of quick cash that may not normally be considered assets. You may be able to borrow money against your life insurance policy. You may be able to collect debts owed to you. You may be able to sell a car, boat, vacation home, or other luxury in order to keep creditors happy. If cash is still scarce, you may be able to work out a special arrangement with your creditors, paying monthly only the amount you can afford.

It is important not to avoid creditors. Fewer than three months of missed payments can cause repossession actions to begin. Most pilots do not let the financial situation get this close to the brink of credit ruination, though, even if they have to serve burgers part time in order to pay the bills.

All of these measures are an attempt to keep body, soul and family together until you can begin drawing regular paychecks again, either from a new employer or from your old airline. You and your creditors must know that your situation is a temporary emergency; the debts will be paid because, one way or another, you will return to the line of work that is "still the best job going," as one furloughed pilot remarked.

Throwing Off the Limitations

Probably the worst aspect of a furlough is the psychological strain it places on you, strain which could prevent preparation for the furlough and depress your activity level at the time when you need to be most active. The furloughed pilot is apt to suffer a loss of self-confidence and feelings of frustration and humiliation during a job search. It is important, though, not to allow natural depression to immobilize your plans for the future.

Furloughed pilots tend to limit themselves psychologically in their efforts to get another job. They have preconceptions about what they can and cannot do. Those who have been furloughed from a major airline at first do not consider applying to a corporate flight department or a regional carrier, and those who have been flying for a corporation or small carrier do not consider applying to a major airline, even if they may be qualified.

Pilots need constantly to evaluate their qualifications against those required by potential employers in order not to corner themselves into one quadrant of the job market.

Furloughed pilots also tend to rely too much on going back to their airline. Optimism is fine, but it should not obscure your vision of the future and hinder your job search. "Your" airline could go out of business or announce a recall that entails an unacceptable 50 percent pay cut. If you are in a position to be furloughed, you need to market yourself before and during the furlough — and not look back. As Satchel Paige used to say, "Something may be gaining on you."

Signs of a possible furlough in the future include the cessation of hiring, downward turns in the economy, slow or deferred equipment orders, low load factors, operating losses, and furloughs among other employee groups, such as flight attendants and mechanics.

Those who are facing a furlough need to begin examining their training, experience and qualifications, and they should be updating their resumes. Remember that while previous airline training is a valuable asset, it also is a perishable one. The value of your training with an airline diminishes slightly by the sixth month of the furlough, greatly by the twelfth month. It may become negligible after two years if you do not continue flying. These facts underline the importance of re-entering the job market as soon as possible following a furlough.

You should get records of your training before a furlough occurs so you will have proof of all training when you try to sell your skills to another company. If your company were to cease operations, training records could become unavailable, and you would be unable to document your training.

By the time a furlough begins, you should be well into your job search. "The important thing is to stay in an airplane," according to Kit Darby, a former furloughed pilot now flying for another major airline.

If you are furloughed, you need to be wary about allowing yourself to become unqualified, an event that could happen quickly if your new job is in a non-flight field. It is tempting to take non-flying jobs after the furlough situation sinks in: Job searches are not easy. You may find that you become more depressed during your job search because of the small return you seem to be getting from your initial effort of sending out resumes and requesting applications. Remember, though, that in any job search, results generally take four to six months to see.

Any pilot who anticipates the furlough can cut down on his or her dry spell by beginning the job search before the furlough begins.

Initially, you may get applications but no calls for interviews. Keep trying, update your file every two or three months at the companies to which you have applied, and reapply every six to 12 months, the same as in any pilot job search.

Maintain your network of pilot friends, make telephone calls and personal visits, and get recommendations. If another furloughee gets a job, he or she may be able to help friends get jobs with the same company.

Poor Attitude Can Lose the Job

The mental attitude of the furloughed job seeker can be the key that bolts the door against re-employment. If highly experienced, the furloughed pilot often refuses to believe that another carrier will not snap up an aviator of such quality immediately.

The experienced pilot has difficulty acting eager for a job because looking for a second airline job is not as exciting as going after the first one. The veteran is likely to be competing against less experienced but more enthusiastic pilots, and the interviewers may hire the more eager applicants because of their obvious interest in the job.

Experienced pilots often are the worst job applicants. They don't keep up their logbooks; they don't re-write their resumes; they don't apply for many of the available jobs; they don't want to have to prove themselves again.

Some of the experienced pilots take their furloughs personally, and this attitude may project into job interviews, making the interviewers unlikely to hire the pilot because of a chip-on-the-shoulder attitude. Furloughed pilots have to build themselves up mentally for the job search, generate enthusiasm for the task, and remember what it was like to get their first piloting jobs.

Enthusiasm during unemployment is difficult to achieve when the pilot is feeling intense pressure to get another job. Atlanta job search consultants Virginia Hall and Joyce Wessel have drawn up recommendations for relieving the stress of unemployment that apply quite well to the furloughed pilot seeking a new job. Hall and Wessel urge that you establish a routine to prevent feelings of disorientation and loss of control over your life. They suggest choosing a quiet place at home, near a telephone, as a base from which you can conduct your job search. You also should establish a definite period of time each day to search for a job, then put the search away after that daily period, just as if you had a job. Your job at this time is to find another job.

You should plan an exercise program to keep physically fit, to reinforce the daily routine and, most importantly, to relieve the stress of being on furlough. There is nothing like exercise to release pent-up frustrations. A physical routine also can be important if your job search turns toward other airlines. Interviews with other carriers often include medical examinations by company physicians, and the results of such exams will be enhanced by a long-term, regular schedule of exercise and diet begun two or three months prior to the interview.

Hall and Wessel caution against falling into the soap opera syndrome (physical and mental isolation) and suggest fighting the practice by getting out of the house every day to be with other people, even if only to the library or to the park. You could go to the airport and talk to people who may have information about job openings.

They also recommend taking time for recreation with the family or friends, a practice that will allow you to return home refreshed, ready for the job search.

Also suggested is the buddy system: connecting regularly with another person who can help you vent your frustrations over being furloughed. Family members often do not make good "buddies" during a furlough because they may be hurting from their own furlough-related worries and loss of self-esteem. The best help may come from another furloughed pilot, someone who knows the pressures of the furlough and the ensuing job search, someone who can empathize. Keeping in touch with other furloughees also is important because of its networking aspect. If one pilot gets a job offer, he may be able to recommend his friends for other piloting positions, or at least notify his friends that the company is hiring.

You may also wish to upgrade your FAPA membership if you are not a full-service member already, in order to take advantage of the JET JOBS Referral System, pilot counseling, and other services.

In the search for another job, you naturally should try to get employment with a company good enough that you will not hesitate about giving up your seniority number to work there. If such a company is hiring and you are accepted, your furlough is over. You start from the beginning with another carrier.

However, such a fairy tale ending is rare, and in most cases you should try to hold on to your seniority number for as long as possible. Some companies may be willing to use you for a short time, expecting to let you go when you are recalled by the airline that furloughed you. They may not require the number to be resigned until after your probation. Other companies may say that a pilot must give up any previous seniority number, but in the real world may be willing to negotiate this requirement at the time of hire because they need your experience. Still other companies, sitting in the catbird seat, may not budge at all in their demand that you relinquish your number. At this point, you must decide if this company is where you want to continue your career.

Some furloughees may find non-flight jobs with a carrier, using other professional skills they have developed. Ex-military pilots may wish to re-establish themselves in the Reserves, National Guard, or even active duty, retaining both their seniority number and their flying skills. Some pilots find they can make a reasonable living this way.

Other pilots may find positions with the FAA or with airport management, or they may be able to go back to whatever work they did before they became pilots. The 1981 CAL furloughees who took non-flight jobs found themselves in fields as varied as stock brokering, computer services consulting, marketing, and carpentry. Pilots who take this route, however, should find some way to continue flying regularly.

If there is a section of the industry that is booming, that may be the best job source. For instance, in 1982 and 1983, deregulation allowed for tremendous growth in "upstart" carriers, accompanied by the hiring of large numbers of pilots.

Your mobility is your biggest advantage at an interview. You should be willing to move nearly anywhere there is an acceptable job offer. The one exception to this, though, is in taking jobs outside the United States. Overseas pilots risk losing touch with the U.S. job market. Be aware that many foreign countries are not allowing U.S. pilots to upgrade or build toward a pension and that they may not allow you to maintain employment there beyond the duration of the contract being offered.

A Body in Motion Tends To Stay in Motion

Nothing that has been said in this chapter is meant to imply that piloting is any more insecure than any other line of human endeavor. It is not. In fact, it is one of the greatest opportunities in the United States and in the world for an individual with significant technical ability to have a lucrative career and retire very well off. Moreover, most people go into piloting because they love to fly. So the pilot is doubly blessed: He gets to do what he loves and get wealthy doing it.

The pilot is in a dynamic industry that draws its participants into contact with a great many people, ideas, and opportunities. Of course, the road to a flying job with a major airline is arduous and demands a great deal of your time and effort. Until you land a position that you are able to regard as a career objective, you may have little time left over for other kinds of endeavor. But once there, you need not wear blinders. Opportunity is all around you.

You have accomplished Plan A, landing a seat with a major airline. You should definitely take care of Plan B, which is making sure a furlough or a loss of license does not catch you unprepared. And you can even be looking into a Plan C — some other form of endeavor that may add fun and profit to your life when you are not flying.

Chapter 22
THE HORIZON

If you are contemplating or have begun an aviation career, you are in the midst of, or are about to begin, a rigorous journey to one of the most exciting "career destinations" offered in the modern world. In days of old, the career of the warrior probably held that sheen; somewhat later, the sea was a powerful claimant; but today, there is no career with more "kick" in it than flying. If a pilot so chooses and proves acceptable to the airline, he can even take a flying job with special challenges, e.g., the climatic and weather conditions of Alaska or Canada; and many pilots, in fact, prefer this type of highly demanding flying to uneventful autopilot flights in more tranquil zones.

You are embarked on a career that carries with it responsibility, financial rewards, prestige, and a few drawbacks; the average surgeon would most likely debate with you, however, whether the perils you run are worse than his. Like you, he holds people's lives in his hand; unlike you, he runs a risk of career-threatening lawsuits, and he often works a grueling long week that leaves him precious little time for non-medical pursuits or even, in many instances, for his family. By contrast, pilots with major airlines often are able to do their flying jobs and run other businesses simultaneously while putting in fewer total hours per month than the average physician puts into his medical practice alone.

No matter what profession you decide to compare yours with, piloting will come out quite well. Your career choice is excellent. The worst drawbacks that your career can face will come from you, not from the nature of the game. To play the game fully, you must do the "extras": Go the extra mile in making your skills and flight record airline-ready; take the extra trouble to be completely prepared for a crucial job interview; make sure you shine during probation; do everything possible to enhance your instrument skills constantly, rather than letting them erode from too frequent reliance on the autopilot; take care of your health and fitness; put together a "survival" plan in case of a furlough; and be developing other interests and skills, even a full-blown business, in case the unthinkable should happen and you should wind up without a flying job.

If you do not do all of these things, you are falling short of the full game plan in the same way that a baseball player does when he fails to "run out" an infield grounder. If the ball player is still standing at home plate when the shortstop commits an error, either the shortstop or another infielder will have time to recover and throw the ball player out before he reaches first base. But if the baseball player had "run out" the play, he would have been safe at first.

"Run out" all of your grounders; the maximum safety resides in optimum hustle, and only there.

The authors hope the information in *Airline Pilot* has been helpful to you in molding your career plans. If it has, we have accomplished our goal with this book, just as you undoubtedly will achieve your goals if you give them a total effort. Happy flying.

GLOSSARY

A&P (Airframe and Powerplant) mechanic's license — An FAA-regulated and issued license for aircraft mechanics. It involves formal training in aircraft systems and theory.

ALPA — Air Line Pilots Association. This is a national pilot's union that represents the bulk of all airline pilots in the United States.

AME — Aviation Medical Examiner. A doctor designated by the FAA to examine pilots and pilot candidates.

APA — Allied Pilots Association. Union representing American Airlines pilots.

ATP (Airline Transport Pilot) license — An FAA-regulated and issued license that is a necessity today for a pilot aspiring to an airline flying career. For an ATP, a pilot has to have 1,500 hours of logged flight time, with necessary minimums of cross-country, night and weather flying. First Class Medical Certificate required.

Ab initio **training** — In this book, *ab initio* (Latin for "from the beginning") refers to pilot training programs that take pilot candidates from zero flight time to an Air Transport Pilot license and a type rating on an airliner. Generally, the "airliner" is not a big jet but is instead a turboprop of the kind used by regional/commuter airlines. Some programs, however, also type-rate their pilots in large jets.

Captain — The flight officer in command.

Certified Flight Instructor rating — An FAA-regulated and issued certificate permitting a pilot to instruct others in flying. It requires a Second Class Medical Certificate. Commercial Pilot License and Instrument Rating required.

Note: A candidate must take two written tests for the basic CFI-aircraft instructor's rating: the Fundamentals of Instruction and Flight Instructor Airplane exams. A third test is required to earn the CFI-instruments rating.

Commercial Pilot Certificate — An FAA-regulated and issued license to do commercial flying, i.e., carry passengers for hire. Second Class Medical Certificate required (the more restrictive medical requirements arise from the fact that the pilot now is certified to carry paying passengers).

Designated Flight Examiner — An FAA-designated individual who checks out a pilot's flying skills for whatever level of flying he is attempting to qualify for or to continue to qualify for.

Domicile — The town at which an airline pilot is based for scheduling and flight purposes. This town may or may not be the community in which the pilot lives. Some pilots commute to domicile from another city, often one several states away from domicile.

FARs — Federal Aviation Regulations. These are the FAA rules for the piloting, operation and maintenance of aircraft of all kinds in the United States.

FBO — Fixed-Base Operator. This is a facility that provides a variety of services, including aircraft maintenance, fueling, charter flights, aircraft for hire, small-package cargo service, etc.

Note: Some FBOs have either charter and/or cargo airline subsidiaries or activities. The cargo operations are worth discussion. The advent of large overnight express cargo carriers (Federal Express, United Parcel Service, DHL, Airborne, etc.) gave an opportunity for FBOs to establish feed services to the hubs of these large carriers, and quite a number of these services have grown into substantial turboprop operations.

FE (Flight Engineer) certificate — FAA-regulated and issued certificate to control the complex systems found on many commercial aircraft. The student pilot must go quite deeply into aircraft systems and principles of operation in order to acquire an FE.

FEPA — Federal Express Pilots Association. Union representing Federal Express pilots.

FEX — Flight Engineer/Turbojet combined test. See "Flight Engineer Basic (FE) and Turbojet (FEJ) tests," below.

Feed traffic — Passengers brought to a major airline by a regional/commuter airline. Major carriers maintain hubs at large airports. Many small airlines have contracts with the major carriers to supply these hubs with "feed" from small towns in exchange for various benefits, often including joint marketing, use of the major's CRS (computer reservations system), some ground handling, the display of certain insignia of the major airline, ticketing at some stations, and a pro rata share of through-fare revenues.

First Class Medical Certificate — Also called Class I Medical Certificate. This is the certificate that a pilot must have in order to fly for an airline. It signifies that the pilot is in top physical condition with no serious health problems.

First officer — The copilot.

Flight engineer — The third crew member in a three-person crew. He/she controls the complex systems found in some aircraft.

Flight Engineer Basic (FE) and Turbojet (FEJ) tests — The written and flight tests, respectively, that a pilot must take to qualify as an FAA-certified flight engineer.

Hub airport — An airport at which one or more major airlines have established service hubs, i.e., clearing sites for traffic. The airlines' routes branch out in "spokes" from the "hub" to form a service "wheel." This kind of operation, a product largely of airline deregulation, has proven to be the most efficient method of moving both people and cargo by air.

Instrument rating — Written and flight tests are taken to get the FAA-regulated instrument rating. An instrument flight test determines a pilot's ability to control the airplane safely under instrument meteorological conditions and under the control of Air Traffic Control (ATC). Third Class Medical Certificate required.

Line check — An in-flight, in-revenue-service check of an airline pilot's flying skills.

LOFT — Line Oriented Flight Training. This is a type of training for pilots that is keyed to actual routes and route airports flown by the airline for which the pilot works. Simulators that can replicate these flying conditions are used for such training.

Major airline — A commercial airline with more than $1 billion in annual revenue (U.S. Department of Transportation's definition).

Multi-engine aircraft — Aircraft with two or more engines.

Multi-engine rating — An FAA-regulated and issued certificate to fly aircraft that have more than one engine. The medical certificate is keyed to the pilot's license held.

Myopia — Near-sightedness.

National airline — A commercial airline with revenue from $100 million to $1 billion (U.S. Department of Transportation's definition).

Pilot Logbook — The pilot's log is a legal document that is inspected thoroughly by prospective employers and the FAA to verify flight training and experience. In it, the pilot records each flight he/she makes, the type of aircraft, tail number, date, point of takeoff and landing, duration of flight, flight conditions, and training received.

Piston-engine aircraft — Also called "reciprocating engine" aircraft. These are propeller-driven aircraft that are powered by piston engines.

PFE — Professional Flight Engineer. This is a profession separate from piloting; a PFE is not allowed to advance to a pilot seat, and PFEs have their own unions, seniority systems, etc. A PFE at a major airline is required to have both a full FE Turbojet rating and an A&P (see above for A&P).

Regional/commuter airline — An airline with less than $100 million in revenue (U.S. Department of Transportation definition).

Note 1: Future Aviation Professionals of America (FAPA) defines a regional airline as one flying turboprop or other propeller-driven aircraft and having less than $100 million in revenue. Such industry listings as FAPA's do not exclude the $100 million-plus turboprop carriers from the group of turbo-prop/regional airlines.

Note 2: There is some FAA sanction for the view (held by many airline operators) that regional and commuter airlines are separate types of entity. The "regional" airline, in this view, is larger, with more traffic, more expensive aircraft, and a core traffic basis in hub feed (see "feed" and "hub," above). It often, but not always, operates under a FAR Part 121 certificate. The smaller "commuter" airline tries to find a niche in O&D (origin-and-destination) traffic, i.e., it does not feed a major or national carrier as its main business, but instead seeks to satisfy the needs of pairs of rather small towns for connecting air service. Such airlines operate under a FAR Part 135 certificate. Atlantic Southeast Airlines (ASA), which feeds Delta Air Lines in Atlanta and Dallas, is an example of a sizeable "regional" airline under this definition. Iowa Airways, which handles a small amount of feed traffic for Midway Airlines but has the bulk of its business in O&D routes between small Midwest communities, is an example of a "commuter" airline.

Second officer — The flight engineer in a three-person airplane crew.

Seniority — Pilot pay, work assignments, promotions, benefits, etc., are pegged to seniority, based on date of hire. The more senior pilots not only make more money but get the aircraft, route and scheduling assignments of their choice.

Simulator — An aircraft-specific computerized training device that simulates actual flight in the aircraft. Simulators are used for training in preference to utilizing actual aircraft because (1) planes thus are not taken off the flight line for training duty and (2) simulators really are more effective for many aspects of training (e.g., the devices can simulate emergency situations that would be extremely dangerous to induce in an aircraft with a student pilot at the controls).

SWAPA (Southwest Airlines Pilots Association) — Union representing Southwest Airlines pilots.

Student Pilot Certificate — See "Third Class Medical and Student License," below.

Teamsters Union, Airline Division. Union organization representing pilots and PFEs of several airlines.

Third Class Medical and Student License — This serves as one's Student Pilot license; it is a medical certificate and must be endorsed by a flight instructor when one has met the flight time and skill requirements specified for solo flight.

Turbojet aircraft — Jet airplanes. The turbojet or turbofan engine propels the aircraft with a jet of forced air. The engine continuously generates tremendous compression and heat in its compressors; this is the energy that drives the aircraft.

Turbojet airline — A jet carrier with less than $100 million in revenue (a distinction made by some in the airline industry, including Future Aviation Professionals of America).

Turboprop aircraft — Aircraft powered by turbine engines that circulate hot, compressed air through a series of ducts, generating the force necessary to turn the propeller or propellers of the aircraft. Like the turbofan engine, the turboprop engine runs on a fuel akin to kerosene.

Type ratings — FAA-issued pilot ratings by aircraft type. The rating means that the pilot is qualified to fly this make and model of airplane.

VTA/CTT (Vision Testing Apparatus/Color Threshold Test) — This examination shows a series of varying colors of different intensities in order to learn whether a pilot who has shown some problems with color testing has sufficient color perception for flying demands.